The Hogan Edge

HOW THE BEN HOGAN GOLF COMPANY FOUND AND LOST THEIR EDGE

JEROME AUSTRY

Copyright © 2022 Jerome Austry
All rights reserved
First Edition

Fulton Books
Meadville, PA

Published by Fulton Books 2022

ISBN 979-8-88505-056-2 (paperback)
ISBN 979-8-88505-058-6 (hardcover)
ISBN 979-8-88505-057-9 (digital)

Printed in the United States of America

To my son Brian who encouraged me to write this book. To my wife, Sharon, and my son Michael who encouraged me to finish this book, and to the memory of our beloved son, Mark Stanley Austry, whose love of golf inspires me every day.

Acknowledgement

Many people helped me with this book. First of all, I would like to thank J. W. Wilson and Jeff McInnis because, without their advice and continued support, this book would not have been possible.

Many thanks to the former Hogan employees, Doug Hendershot, Randy Kelch, Don Rahig, Henry Felipe, Buzzy Jones, Mike Taylor, Ronnie Mcgraw, Michael Finn, Dick Lyons, and Doug McGrath, who with their many stories and recollections of their years at Hogan contributed enormously to this book.

Also, a special thank you to Steve Dreyer for all the wonderful background information he allowed me to review from the Hogan archives.

I'm enormously grateful to James Dalthorp, Galen Greenwood, and Blair Franklin who were an intricate part of the creative team that helped save the Hogan Company and for providing the award-winning advertising campaign and photos of the Hogan commercial that were instrumental in repositioning the company in the market place.

I also appreciate the information provided by Lanny Wadkins, Mark O'Meara, Ed Sneed, Ben Crenshaw, Tom Kite, and Marty Leonard and for sharing their insights and memories of their relationship with Ben Hogan over the years.

I am especially grateful to Nick Raffaele for all the information he provided in regards to the relationship Ben Hogan maintained after the sale to his company to AMF and finally to Cosmo World. That background certainly enhanced the credibility of the story.

I owe an enormous debt of gratitude to my dear friend and longtime executive secretary at Ben Hogan, Fanny Meyers, and honor her memory.

A special thank you to Susan Terry a bright tech-savvy young woman who showed me how to navigate my computer, for without her help, I am afraid I might still be on page 9 of the manuscript.

Finally, A very special thank you to Joe Kelley who was instrumental in providing the guidance and marketing insights that guided me through those critical years and for making the centennial of golf one of the greatest celebrations of all time.

I thank you all for the help you provided.

Introduction

What is there left to say about a man, often considered the greatest to ever play the game of golf? Five decades of competition left him with sixty-three professional victories, nine of which were majors. A feat so lofty that its only other honorees can be easily identified by their first names. Only Jack and Tiger and Arnie can boast such accomplishments. The man in question here defied all odds, twice, to sit atop this pyramid of greats. Ben Hogan was born dirt-poor in Dublin, Texas, on August 13, 1912, four months after the world was handed its most famous maritime tragedy with the sinking of the RMS *Titanic*. Ben Hogan was born into the more unlikely of circumstances, with a father who labored hard as a blacksmith. Hogan might never have found the game of golf had it not been out of sheer determination to help support himself and his mother. His father's self-inflicted gunshot to the chest left nine-year-old Hogan fatherless and forced his mother to move what was left of their family to Fort Worth, Texas, for a restart.

Ben Hogan never finished high school as the need for food outweighed the need for education. Selling newspapers at the train station earned little, but working as a caddy at east Fort Worth's Glen Garden Country Club offered the chance for more, a whole 65¢ around more. Legend shares that Hogan would utilize extra newspapers as bedding in the eighteenth hole bunker so he could be first in the next morning's caddie line. Golf magically offered Hogan an opportunity to learn and play the game. He would soon learn to dominate—a man who would pioneer the art of practicing, a relatively unexplored notion at the time, to becoming better at one's craft. His explosion onto the golf scene was undeniable and consistent. He would grace the covers of magazines and publications regularly, creating a celebrity environment around him that he never felt comfortable around.

His revered mastery of this game nearly ended in 1949 on his way back to Fort Worth from a Phoenix tournament. On a foggy road, as his face still adorned *Time* magazine, his Cadillac was hit head-on by a Greyhound bus that easily should have taken his life. His selfless action of throwing his body on top of his wife, Valerie, in the passenger seat not only saved him from the crushing force of the Cadillac's steering wheel but the life of his wife. The accident snapped his collarbone, two fractures of his pelvis, crushed his left ankle, and chipped off a piece of his rib. His recovery was questionable until a blood clot moved toward his lung, which required doctors to tie off the main vein in his leg in emergency surgery to save him. Doctors felt sure Hogan would likely never walk again, let alone return to the golf course. The planet mourned its loss.

Sixteen months later, the golfing world would witness an exhausted Ben Hogan line up on the seventeenth fairway as the huge crowd lined each side of the fairway up to the green. Here, he would pull out his one iron and swing, unknowingly creating one of the most iconic sports photographs in history, at the US Open at Merion, where he would ultimately triumph in a playoff and win Player of the Year. His career would become one of legend and, as such, received more media coverage than any other athlete of that time. Those trying to dissect his perfect swing and make sense of his unimaginable journey have spent countless hours attempting to give us insight into the man. Numerous books, articles, legends, statues, plaques, movies, and documentaries have captured everything Hogan ever accomplished in golf. His career has been discussed ad nauseum, and his stories have become grander with each retelling. Until now, there has not been a book that delves into the business side of Ben Hogan.

The company he formed in 1953 had one purpose, to create the best golf clubs ever made. Hogan would design and build a quality product once referred to as fine jewelry. He would see his company grow to the pinnacle of the sport, emulating his own career. The introduction of the first cavity-backed forged iron called the Edge would shoot the Hogan Company into the golfing stratosphere. The man most responsible for its existence, aside from Ben Hogan, has finally detailed the historical rise of the company he ran during its peak years and its subsequent decline. Jerry Austry's poor upbringing mirrored Hogan's and landed him a front-row seat during the most prosperous years at the Hogan Company. Jerry knew Ben as most never did. He arrived on the scene at a pivotal time for the company and engaged with its founder to save the golf brand from destruction. Jerry found himself face-to-face with golf's greatest and what most would consider a dream job. The time together would change the face of the Hogan Company forever. This is a story never told before about the business side of Ben Hogan.

Jerry Austry

My journey started March 10, 1941, the day I was born in Chicago on the south side in a poor working-class neighborhood. My upbringing would take me through high school and college, playing sports as a way of following my dream. Growing up, I was not aware I was poor because all the kids in the neighborhood were the same. I walked to the elementary school, which was two blocks away from our house. I was the third of four children, and my father worked in a factory as a tool and diemaker all his life. My mother was the stay-at-home mom. We lived above a bar that was permanently closed but once owned by my grandfather. That storefront was empty for all the years I lived at home. In our front upstairs apartment, there were two bedrooms, a living room, a kitchen, and a single bathroom with one shared closet. My brother and I slept in one bedroom with my parents. My two sisters slept in the back bedroom. There was no central heat but rather an oil-burning stove in the living room. The bathroom did not have a shower but an old tub where the family bathed. In the back, upstairs apartment, my father's sister lived with her two children, and after my older sister got married, she moved downstairs into a two-room apartment behind the bar.

No one in my family attended college, because education was never emphasized to any of us. Sports, in my mind, was the only way out of the slums of Chicago. Playing baseball offered me a ticket to something bigger, whatever that may be. I had played well enough in high school to pique some interest from a few colleges. So after a false start at Upper Iowa University due to grades, I was given the opportunity to play at Western Michigan University. I recognized that I needed to keep up with my schoolwork if I wanted to continue playing. The university was in Kalamazoo, Michigan, about 150 miles from Chicago, about a two-and-a-half-hour drive. So for the first time in my life, I got to meet a lot of different people with different backgrounds, which showed me how poor I never knew I was.

The Western Michigan baseball program was one of the top programs in the country, and I believed it could be my ticket to professional baseball, as many of the graduating seniors were signing baseball contracts. In my three years, I played well during the 1961, 1962, and 1963 seasons, where we never lost a conference game, going undefeated with a record of 33 and 0 over that period. We also won two of three district championships and qualified for the college world series in 1961 and 1963 in Omaha, Nebraska. The year we lost the district in 1962 was to Michigan after they defeated us in a doubleheader and went to the college world series and won the national title that year. We won the district again in 1963 and qualified to go to the college world series in Omaha. We competed with the best in college baseball and held our own. I was a catcher on the team and voted the team captain my senior year. I loved playing catcher because at that position, you were involved in every pitch and every play all game long. I loved the action and the control that position had on the game. You were considered the field general and responsible for directing the pace of the game and calling all the signals.

While I still believed professional baseball was all that mattered, I graduated with a college degree in business administration in 1964. So after graduation, I now faced the hardest decision ever about my baseball career. Should I sign a contract and continue chasing my dream, or was it time to give it up and move on to a business career utilizing my degree?

Back then, there was no draft, so turning pro and the subsequent contract was something a scout had to offer you if they saw promise in your abilities. The signing bonus typically helped with the decision. If the amount was large enough, then the scouts and the minor leagues were the next steps. If the signing bonus was too small or absent, the player would have to make the tough financial decision that usually meant finding a real job to earn a living. So I had to make one of the hardest decisions of my life that meant ending a dream I had been chasing since I was eight years old. I was not considered a well-rounded player, one who oozed speed, power, great arm, so in order for me to excel, I had to grow on people. The Chicago White Sox offered me a $5,000 signing bonus when most other prospects I would be competing with were signing for ten times that amount. The reality of that situation was hard to ignore. Playing ball in college taught me a lot about politics and seizing opportunities. My chances of making a big-league roster were almost impossible, and getting any meaningful playing time made things tougher. Without the luxury of a parental backer, I needed money to live, so as hard as it was, the decision to walk away from baseball was made. I had to think about my future and the beautiful Sharon I had met and gotten engaged to at college. So now more was at stake than just my dreams.

    I met Sharon my sophomore year in college, and as they say, it was love at first sight. This complicated my baseball decision as bringing a wife with you in the minors would have been very difficult with the money I would be making. So we changed our plan, and we would get married after graduation, and I would go to grad school, and Sharon would go to work. We did not have any money, but we also did not have any debt due in part to my baseball scholarship money and summer jobs. In the sixties, manufacturing was everywhere in the United States, and every small town had a manufacturing plant that was the economic engine of the town's economy. They were recruiting at all the universities, and the promise for the future seemed unlimited. This opportunity seemed to make much more sense as we both were ready to start our life together and be on our own.

    So after many long discussions and a lot of reservations, that is what we decided to do. I entered graduate school, and my wife became a schoolteacher, and we moved into married housing on campus at Western Michigan University. I started my classes, and Sharon started teaching school in Plainwell, Michigan, a small city about 20 miles from Kalamazoo, Michigan, which is where the university was located. Many of our friends from college had also stayed in Kalamazoo, so we all went to the same church and Sunday school. Most of my friends were working and making much more money than we were, as Sharon was the sole breadwinner with a salary of $4,800 per year. Our friends had double incomes as they were both working and making more than double what Sharon and I had. This started to wear on me because I felt I was letting Sharon down by not providing for her like my father had done for our family when I was growing up. This lasted for about six months, and without the release of baseball, I felt immense pressure to do something. So we decided I would drop out of full-time school, get a job, and pursue my master's degree part-time.

I found a job almost immediately as an advertising trainee for a small printing company in town that did catalogs and advertising printing. I was the assistant to the VP of advertising and was learning all about the printing business. So for the next six months, we were riding high. I was now making $6,000 per year. Coupled with Sharon's income, things were looking much better for us. And now we were pretty competitive with all our friends. Things were going good for us, as we settled into a small two-bedroom rental house, which we decorated and began enjoying married life. Six months later, Sharon became pregnant with our first child and could only work for the fall term and would take pregnancy leave in January. So our newfound riches would be dented with a new mouth to feed. I had to do something about that to make sure we could afford our new circumstances. The company I was with was a very small firm, so there was no possibility of advancing fast enough to fill that void. I was still connected to the university, so I could take advantage of the university placement program, which provided interview opportunities with all the companies that were recruiting from the university.

So I put my name into placement service, and to my surprise, within a couple of weeks, I was interviewing with the Parker Hannifin Corporation out of Cleveland, Ohio. They were looking for a manufacturing trainee that they could groom to become a plant manager for one of their manufacturing plants. Their offer was a starting salary of $11,000 per year, and they wanted me to start in January, just as Sharon would be going on maternity leave. The plant I would be assigned was in Otsego, Michigan, a sister city to Plainwell, Michigan, and only 25 miles from Kalamazoo, Michigan. It was a small plant of about two hundred people that made brass fittings for the automotive companies. The yearlong trainee program provided the opportunity for me to learn every operation by working in the factory to understand each aspect of the operation that I would eventually manage. The current plant manager was an incredible manager, and everybody looked up to him, so that was my role model to follow. So as I was settling into my new job, Sharon and I decided we needed to upgrade our living quarters, so we decided to buy our first home, a three-bedroom ranch-style out in the country. I had to borrow $500 from my sister to make the down payment on the house. I was only making $11,000 a year, so we were both worried the bank would find out and come take the house back. This was my first experience with a yard and grass, which I loved. The only furniture we had was Sharon's bedroom set and a kitchen table that her family gave us to get started. Our weekends entailed going to the antique malls to see what we could buy to decorate our new house. Our first son Michael was born in the spring of 1966, and we never looked back.

  I was really missing playing sports, so I got involved with our church baseball and basketball leagues to satisfy my competitive juices. Finally, I was asked to join the company golf league. My lack of golf knowledge left me at a disadvantage. My first order of business was to get some background information on the game and procure some equipment so I could play. I was starting from scratch, so I bought a few golf magazines to read up on the sport and familiarize myself with the game and the required equipment. I had never been to a country club, so I visited a few sporting goods stores to check out what was available to buy. My research of golf clubs led me to many different brands they were offering for sale. I found companies like Browning, Daiwa, Dunlop, MacGregor, Wilson, Ram, and

Spalding. I was not aware of the other brands such as Ben Hogan, Walter Hagen, Titleist, Tommy Armour, Taylor Made as they were only sold at country clubs, where I wasn't familiar. Northwestern Golf was the biggest of all the brands and made a very inexpensive model. I was familiar with the name Wilson as they made all the equipment I used when I grew up playing football, basketball, and baseball. So I felt comfortable with their brands.

The Sam Snead Blue Ridge clubs were my first set of clubs. You could also buy half the set at a time with club irons 3, 5, 7, 9, and PW and then fill in later with the numbers 4, 6, 8, and SW. You also could buy a driver, three-wood, and a five-wood and a much-needed putter, and you were ready to go. In addition, I was now getting some golf magazines to read about the game, which introduced me to the advertisements that were in each magazine.

It did not take long before I realized these magazines did not advertise certain club brands. In fact, none of the brands that were featured in the magazine were in any of the sporting good's stores that I would frequent, even the Sam Snead Blue Ridge clubs I now owned. The brands that were advertised were all considered professional models by Ben Hogan, Walter Hagen, Wilson, Macgregor, Ping, Acushnet Mizuno, Ram TaylorMade, and Tommy Armour.

These were all forged clubs and only available at pro shops at the local country clubs. This did not sit well with me. I was beginning to understand the business side of a game. Golf, though, and its great unknown, was now becoming a major focus in my life.

After the training program ended, I was offered the position of quality control manager at Parker of all the products that they produced for the automotive industry. There was a big push in the industry to increase the quality of American cars, so each parts supplier created an approved quality control program by the various car manufacturers in order to become an improved supplier. The longer I worked at Parker, the more I felt myself slipping away from the manufacturing side of the business. I was getting a little concerned about this as I felt I was now out of the loop for promotions into manufacturing positions. I was only twenty-seven years old, and I am sure my inexperience and impatience were getting the best of me.

Then out of the blue, I got a call from Snelling and Snelling, which was a prominent placement firm in the early sixties. They had a position open up at Clark Equipment Company in Battle Creek, Michigan, for a quality control engineer. I was not particularly interested in this position as, again, this would take me in a different direction from my plant manager goal. Clark was a much bigger operation than Parker, with more money than what I was making at Parker Hannifin. In the interviewing process, I outlined my goals to be plant manager, and the quality control manager affirmed that this position would give me the visibility in the company to eventually achieve my goal. Sharon and I decided to make the switch. Clark, as it turns out, had a much bigger golf league which allowed me to get to know the management and staff quicker due to the weekly golf games, which were typically followed by a few drinks as the scores of the teams were figured out.

Our second son Brian was born, which now filled our three-bedroom house. Each of the boys had their own bedroom, along with a kitchen, dining room, living room, and I finished the basement, which served as a big family room for everyone to enjoy. Our little family enjoyed much more than I had ever imagined growing up in Chicago. I also now had some extra money, so it was time to upgrade my original set of Sam Snead Blue Ridge Golf Clubs. This would be a little harder to do as all the pro models were sold through a country club, and I still had no access. I was playing all my golf at public golf courses, and their selection of clubs was very limited.

Then one day, as I was looking for my new set, I saw this beautiful set of Gary Player Black Night graphite shafted golf clubs. I was very familiar with the name Gary Player, and the company that was offering this brand was not one of the traditional companies but a well-respected local firm in Kalamazoo, Michigan, that was one of the leading manufacturers of fishing's rods called Shakespeare. Reading the product literature made a lot of sense as the graphite was promoted as being lighter, so you could swing it faster, therefore, hit the ball much farther. As I would watch golf tournaments, there was Gary Player playing with those clubs with the graphite shafts. As I remember, he was the only tour player playing with a graphite shafted product that made the most sense to me, so I purchased both the Gary Player woods and irons. I was now playing golf at least once a week and, on many occasions, would play a morning round on Saturday before any of my boys' activities would get started.

My golf game was quickly improving, and my scores were coming down from when I first started playing. The first year I could not break a hundred on a consistent basis. As I progressed, I started to break one hundred every time out, and now I could play a full round of golf without swinging and missing the ball completely with a single shot. My shots became more consistent, and my scores kept dropping. Now I was breaking ninety on a regular basis and looking to break into the seventies as I continued to practice. My job was going well. My homelife was excellent. What more could you ask for out of life? Occasionally, I would sometimes look up and thank God for all the blessings I was privileged to have. As I continued to work for Clark, my boss, the quality control manager decided to leave for another opportunity, leaving his position open. I interviewed and was promoted to quality control manager for the lift truck division. The department had around one hundred employees, so this was like managing a small plant. In my new role, I was on the plant manager staff and on the same level in the organization as the superintendents, one step from plant manager.

Then one night, as I was playing in league with my new set of Gary Player "Black Knight" graphite shafted woods and irons, I made a beautiful swing, and the club felt like a feather. Something felt different. I looked down at the face of the three wood, and the face insert was gone. It flew out of the club and somewhere down the fairway, never to be found. So over the next couple of weeks, I was short one club from my set. Then as I was hitting one of my irons, the club broke, and the head flew farther than the ball did. I have never had that happen to me playing golf, and so I went back to the store where I bought the clubs and asked them about the problem and if there was any warranty to replace that club. Unfortunately, his answer was no, so I was out of luck. Then shortly after that, a reporter was checking golf clubs in the bags of the touring pros, and they discovered that the irons that Gary Player was playing with were painted black and really were not graphite shafts at all. That pretty much did for me; it was time to look for a new set of clubs.

Then my brother called me and asked me if I would place his résumé with Snelling and Snelling, as he was looking for a new position and wanted to move away from Chicago to a smaller town like Kalamazoo or Battle Creek, Michigan. I was happy to do that, but as I was giving them my brother's résumé, they asked me if I was looking, and I said, "No, I am not."

They replied, "It would not hurt anything if you put your résumé in just to see if there was any interest," so I decided to do that. I did not give a second thought to interviewing as my job was going well, and the company was getting ready to open a new lift truck division, and they would need a plant manager to operate that facility. I was waiting anxiously to hear who would be selected as the new plant manager for the electric division. To my disappointment, I was not chosen even though I thought I was more qualified than the guy they gave the opportunity to.

Then out of nowhere, I got a call from Snelling and Snelling, saying they had a corporate staff position with a major sporting goods company that was looking to implement a new quality control system in all their sporting goods manufacturing facilities. This sounded really interesting, so I decided I would accept the interview and gave them the okay to set up the meeting. To my amazement, the company was Wilson Sporting Goods in River Grove, Illinois. I grew up playing all my sports with Wilson equipment and now having the opportunity to go to work for them sounded amazing. I went to the interview with the corporate quality control manager, and he explained that Wilson was looking to become the first billion-dollar sporting goods company, and they wanted to make sure that the quality of their products kept pace with that growth. My background at Parker Hannifin, setting up their quality control program, was very interesting to them as this would be my main function as a corporate quality staff guy working with the plant managers in each of their facilities and bridging the gap between the factory, engineering the customer to assure Wilson products were of the highest standards.

I was very excited about this opportunity because this was a company I had grown up with. I was given the choice of products I wanted to work with as I would be their first hire—golf, team sports, tennis, and hockey. So, of course, my first choice would be golf. That responsibility would include the River Grove Plant, where the corporate headquarters would be and my home base. I would be responsible for setting up the quality standards for the three golf manufacturing plants in America, along with a plant in Berwick, Scotland. My main responsibility would be to assure that every golf product manufactured would be of the highest quality standards, regardless of where it was produced. Sharon and I were vacationing with our family in the Boyne Mountain area of upper Michigan, and we went to dinner at a very nice restaurant outside of Traverse City, Michigan, where we discussed this opportunity much of the night. It was a great opportunity with the number one company in the sporting goods business. They were into every sport. This decision would require us to move to Chicago and sell our house, and the kids would have to start school and make new friends. That was hard because I had a good job, and we had a beautiful house and a lot of friends in Kalamazoo, Michigan, but this would be a very big move and possibly a career-altering change. I would not have anyone working for me as this would be a staff position. I have always been the hands-on type of manager with direct responsibility and authority for the function I was managing. I would have the responsibility for the quality of the golf products Wilson would be producing, but my role would be to develop those standards with manufacturing and engineering that would be implemented in each of the plants.

So I accepted the offer, and my start date was going to be July of 1974. My wife, as always, was very supportive of my business career, even if she was not crazy about the move. My family lived in Chicago, and Sharon's family lived in Detroit, so Kalamazoo was right in the middle, about 150 miles in each direction to visit our families. I would travel to Chicago for the first couple of months and stay in a hotel as I worked at the corporate headquarters in River Grove, Illinois. I also was able to spend a part of my week at home as one of the plants I was responsible for was in Grand Rapids, Michigan, which was only a forty-five-minute drive from our house in Kalamazoo, Michigan. Shortly after I started and I was walking from the golf plant in River Grove through the warehouse up to the corporate office, I passed baseball gloves, golf gloves, basketballs, footballs, tennis rackets, and baseball bats, which transformed me into a little boy in a candy shop. I now had access to all this equipment, and I was usually dancing as I approached the corporate office. The approach that would be taken was to bring research and development, manufacturing, and our customers together to make sure we were all on the same page in regard to producing the highest quality products for our customers' satisfaction.

So my main role as an independent arbiter was to interpret the engineering standards that are being used in the factory, measure the actual results of the products being produced on a daily basis, and finally audit the products in the field and gather data on our competitors and how they compared to Wilson and Walter Hagen products. Once all this data was collected, then the quality standards could be developed into a standard manual that each one of the golf facilities would implement. My responsibility would cover the River Grove Pro club plant, the Walter Hagen Pro club and ball plants. The Tullahoma commercial golf club plant and the Berwick Scotland Pro Wilson and Walter Hagen golf club plant—each of these plants operated independently from each other, and Walter Hagen had their own engineering department and sales force for their products.

One of my first visits to the River Grove Plant was to the golf club research and development department to introduce myself to the Wilson golf club designers, Mr. Art Lazette and Bob Mendrella. These two men had been with the company when it first started, and I was not sure they had a formal engineering background, but they learned their trade working in the factory and the model shop and knew everything there was to making golf clubs. The main product Wilson was producing at the time in the River Grove Plant was the Wilson Staff Blade, which at the time was viewed as the number one club in the marketplace. They looked at me with disgust in their eyes of who the hell is this guy to come in here and tell us if our products meet the quality standards for the industry when he has no background whatsoever in the club-making business. They were not happy with the decision that the corporation had made to bring someone in that would have a voice on the quality standards and direction the company would be headed in the future. That was their job, and it was clear I had a lot of work to do to win them over to let them know I was not a threat to them or their power. The next move was to introduce myself to the manufacturing department and let them know what my role would be, and low and behold, I got the same reaction from them as I did from the engineering department. The same thing happened when I would visit the Walter Hagen facility in Grand Rapids, Michigan. Three weeks with the company and it was clear, I was not looked at favorably.

As I was adjusting to my new position, Sharon and I decided to build a house instead of buying an existing one. We decided we would move to Downers Grove, Illinois, about twenty minutes southwest of the River Grove Plant, which is where my office would be. The home was considerably bigger than the home in Kalamazoo and about doubled the price. This would also be about twenty minutes from all my family. So this was the first time since I left for college that I returned to my hometown and family. Sharon would handle the move like a trooper as I worked in River Grove part of every week, but I would go home on the weekend too. Kalamazoo, Michigan, was only about a two-and-a-half-hour drive from Chicago. I also would spend a couple of days a week working from home as I traveled to Grand Rapids, Michigan, which, as I said, was only about forty-five minutes from Kalamazoo.

As work progressed, I would meet with the engineers and ask them what measurements we needed to control when building a golf club. Once these parameters were established, we could go to the factory floor and measure them to see how well we are maintaining these parameters. So we started with loft, lie, swing weight, overall length, and overall weight of each club and then measured the completed sets to determine the overall variation within a set.

It's fairly common knowledge to even the most casual of golfers what is meant by loft, lie, length, and weight. However, swing weight is a specification that most casual golfers don't give much thought to and have just come to assume it's the same with every club, but serious golfers and club fitters will pay close attention to. It is all about balance and how weight is distributed through a golf club.

Swing weight, simply put, is how heavy a golf club feels when you swing it. It is not a finite measurement and is not something measured in grams like the weight of a golf club shaft or grip. The measurement was invented in the 1920s to describe the dynamic feel of a golf club as a player swings it. Breaking it down further, swing weight aims to measure the distribution of weight across the golf club by accounting for four factors, (1) weight of the clubhead, (2) weight of the grip, (3) weight of the shaft, and (4) weight of the golf club. If each club in the set feels the same to the player, ideally, they will swing each club with the same level of confidence and play their best golf.

The swing weight of a golf club is measured on a fourteen-inch fulcrum that assesses the balance point of a club, which is displayed on an alphanumeric scale. The heavier a club "feels," the more the club will tilt toward the clubhead side when balanced on that fulcrum. The scale ranges anywhere from A0 (the lightest) to G10 (the heaviest), but most men's golf clubs fall in the range of C7 to D7, and ladies' clubs are usually between C4 and D0. One point on the scale is equivalent to a weight difference of .07 ounces at the clubhead, about the weight of a penny. Few players would even notice such a small change.

It's important to remember that swing weight and overall weight are mutually exclusive. A heavy club can have a light swing weight and vice versa. That's because swing weight is merely addressing the balance point of the club, not the actual weight of the club overall.

One of the benefits I had was I had access to two different plants, making essentially the same product to the same standards. So with the plant manager's blessing, I was provided the manpower to start auditing the product in the factories. I would also ask the engineering department, sales department, and manufacturing what the standards should be, for instance, what the swing weight of a pro-grade set of clubs should be and what the tolerance should be for that set. Everybody pretty much stated the same objective, a set of pro-grade irons or woods should be D1. Okay, I then asked the manufacturing organization what the tolerance is now. No one could answer my question because they did not measure the completed sets and had no records to indicate what the process was producing. This was a major step to establish what the standards should be and how we were performing to these standards.

In the mid-seventies, a set of irons consisting of nine clubs would all have the same swing weight. A set of woods would be three clubs at the same swing weight. So we started to collect data to determine the standard range of swing weights within the set of irons and woods. The data we collected would provide the necessary information to set the tolerance range of swing weights within the set of woods or irons. I was also one of the only people that would go to the shop floor to observe the operation that was performing the swing weight function to see what controls were in place to assure the clubs met this standard. I was also the only one that had the data, and I had to be very careful with sharing this data until a determination could be made in regard to what the stranded should be because engineering, marketing, sales, and manufacturing all had different agendas, and if this data would be used to embarrass a specific function, my ability to get the cooperation I needed would be lost.

In addition, this data would be shared with the sales force at the annual sales meeting to help reinforce how good the quality of the Wilson and Hagen products are in regard to our completion. So the factory data by itself needed to be compared to the field audit information that would be gathered from the country club's new club inventory at the local pro shops in Chicago and Michigan.

In addition to that exercise, I would also spend a portion of my day on returned goods to see what our customers were returning and what problems were being reported from the field in regard to the quality of our products. I also got to know all the players and their respective attitudes and opinions about what they felt about the quality of each other's products. The Walter Hagen factory had the feeling that they were making a higher quality product than the Wilson factory and vice versa. Also, the marketing and sales departments felt the same about Wilson but felt Walter Hagen a grade higher. Also, our sales force felt the Ben Hogan Company out of Texas was the highest in quality products in the pro shop.

It was amazing how strong each of these people felt because no one had any data to reinforce any opinion about the standards because no one collected any data to determine compliance to any kind of standard. Once we had the data, it would eliminate a lot of the opinion of what some thought was being produced. In addition, we would also have the benefit of during a field audit to compare our products to our competition. The job was going very well, and I was learning a lot about golf clubs and how they were made. In addition, my family moved into our new house in Downers Grove, and my boys Michael and Brian were now in their new school and making new friends and participating in all kinds of sports.

The second responsibility I was given was handling customer complaints and reporting back to my boss about the problem, the corrective action taken, and what needed to be changed to prevent the problem. The first major problem reported to me was the grips on Wilson clubs were melting. I immediately went into the warehouse to check to see if I could find the problem. I brought an inspector with me, and we opened up all the boxes of finish clubs and could not find the problem. We then went into the factory to check all the clubs on trucks getting ready to be cleaned, packed into set boxes, and moved into the warehouse to be shipped to our customers. Again, our inspection found no clubs with the problem. I reported to my boss my initial findings, and he reported back to marketing to get more information. When he came back, he informed me that we have this complaint at a large customer distribution center in North Dakota that all their clubs have this grip problem. So I was to get on a plane and sort through their warehouse for all the sets that had this problem. This issue took me to the middle of North Dakota in the middle of winter. This was one of Wilson's biggest accounts, and they had about at least a thousand sets of Wilson clubs in their warehouse.

When I got there, the manager took me into the warehouse and showed me where the clubs were stored where I went to work, checking the inventory to see if I could find the problem. As I started to open up the boxes, I could see the grips looked a little gummy, and if you touched them, they would rub off on your hand, and they would become black, just like the grip. I called my boss and informed him I found the problem but did not yet know what caused the grips to melt. The next step was to get a hold of research and development to let them know what I found and request some technical engineering help to determine the cause. That is when I met Mike Malatesta, who I would work with to determine how to correct the problem. Mike worked for the vice president of research and development and provided technical guidance in resolving quality problems. Once Mike was on board, it did not take long to find out that the grips we had were painted metallic gold, which was attacking the rubber grip, causing the deterioration of grip. Now we understand what caused the problem and how to fix the problem. In order to use gold metallic paint, the grip had to be protected from the paint fill. The golf engineering department blamed the grip manufacturer, and the grip manufacturer blamed our engineering department for not including that in the specifications that were sent to purchase the grip. We had all the clubs re-gripped at the North Dakota distribution center and re-gripped all the finish clubs in our warehouse with the new grips, and everybody was very happy with the end result. This also would highlight why we needed standards to make sure these problems could be prevented. This problem also highlighted that we do not do any durability testing using heat, cold, and other weather conditions that golf clubs have to endure. So in addition to the corrective action that was taken, I was asked to develop a performance test for a new golf club design to assure our products would stand up under extreme playing conditions.

The Water Hagen factory was feeling overly confident about their quality as early problems seemed clearly on the Wilson quality side. Then out of nowhere, we got a call that the Ultra Dyne 11 Male Hozel clubs were breaking in the field on impact. So now we had our first major issue with the Water Hagen factory. I again got in touch with my engineering counterpart, Mike Malatesta, and we developed a plan to address the problem of a warehouse full of products that could be defective. We pulled some clubs from inventory to see how we could determine the problem. We both determined the problem must be with the metallurgy of the iron heads as the clubs were breaking upon the impact of the clubhead to the ball or the ground. With the testing we did in the lab, we discovered the heat-treating process left some of the heads brittle and, therefore, would break on impact. We did not know how many of these heads were defective and how we handled the finished product would have to determine the problem without destroying the club. All the raw heads could be sent back to the vendor to correct by heat treating all the clubs, and that would solve the problem. This, however, was not possible with assembled clubs. So Mike developed a torque test that we could use to sort finished clubs by bending them a couple of degrees in both directions, and if they did not break, we could validate the heat treating of that club to engineering standards.

So we went into the warehouse in River Grove and pulled all the finished clubs and started to torque test each set. Once the test was completed, we could certify the clubs would perform well in the field. After the test, the sets would have to have the loft and lie reset cleaned up and repackaged and returned to the warehouse. Once we completed the sorting, we drove to Grand Rapids to perform the same test on all assembled products and clubs that had been in the warehouse in Grand Rapids. The percentage of clubs that were determined to be defective was very small, which luckily didn't require a field recall of the entire finished product in the field. Grand Rapids and Walter Hagen now realized they were not immune to quality problems in the field.

The overall reception to the way I handled this problem was appreciated by all concerned, engineering, manufacturing, and marketing, as we corrected the problem to the customers' satisfaction without damaging the quality reputation, and both manufacturing and engineering were not blamed for this problem. This problem further enhanced the need to have a strong quality representation in the company. My boss was very pleased with how I handled the problem and received a lot of positive feedback about how effective the corrective action had been. This one experience would open the doors for more cooperation from both engineering and manufacturing to implement the quality standards in each of the plants. In particular, marketing and sales now felt they had an ally that would help to solve any problems that we would encounter without worrying about who caused the problem. This also allowed me to build my reputation as a problem solver within the company. Who would have known this visit to a cold warehouse in North Dakota in the middle of winter would help cement my reputation within the company and would open up all the doors with manufacturing and engineering to establish the overall quality standards for the corporation? Wilson then hired two other quality engineers for their tennis and team sports.

Once I got back to the factory, we had completed the gathering of all the data in regard to club specifications, loft, lie, length, swing weight, and total weight. The next step of the project was to conduct a field audit at local country clubs in Chicago and Michigan to assemble the same data points. I was to present this report to the VP of manufacturing, VP of marketing, VP of sales, and the VP of club design. This meeting would set the direction the company would follow in regard to our quality standards and could also serve to highlight problems within the company between the department heads. I reviewed the report first with my boss, where we decided to omit the names of the brands such as Hogan, Ping, MacGregor, etc., and instead, each company would be assigned a number one through twenty to eliminate any potential bias. This was a brilliant move on the part of my boss as no one would be able to reach any conclusions until all the data had been presented and the final results displayed. It was believed that the Ben Hogan company, along with Walter Hagen, would be on top, and Wilson would be on the bottom. The final results showed Wilson and Walter Hagen were tied at number one, and the Ben Hogan Company was in the middle of the pack. Now you understand the differences between all the companies was not very much, for instance, one parameter was tightness of control, and another was swing weight. A set marked as D1. How many clubs were actually D1, and how many were not? In addition, what was the overall range of the swing weights within the set? It was not uncommon to find a swing weight spread one point in each set of nine clubs.

For instance, a set of D1 clubs would have seven clubs at D1, two clubs at C9. The overall spread of the set was one point. If a set had more than one-point spread, it was considered poor quality. If the swing weight range was more than one point, it meant the clubs within the set would not feel the same to the player when performing a shot. As the length of each club changes, the head weight needs to be heavier to provide the same balance point for the three iron as you would feel with a nine iron. Every golfer has played with golf clubs that just felt right. You were able to make your best swings consistently, the clubs felt good in your hands, and they made you a more confident golfer. But have you ever wondered what it is that gives golf clubs the right feel when you swing? This is where swing weight comes into play.

Everyone was pleased with the report, and almost everyone came away with the feeling that Wilson was going in the right direction. In addition, Walter Hagen and Wilson were the number one and two brands preferred by the touring pros at that time. Wilson clubs won a total of sixty-one major golf tournaments, with many of the greatest golfers having played with the Wilson Staff Blade at one time in the past, names like Arnold Palmer, Billy Casper, Sam Snead, Ben Hogan Hale Irwin, John Daly, and even the famous Gene Sarazen. Wilson

Staff golf balls were the brand all the pros seemed to prefer and were considered one of the best performing golf balls in the market. The Wilson company had been purchased by PepsiCo, and that was the reason the quality position was created that gave me the opportunity to join the company. PepsiCo would use Wilson as a training ground for up-and-coming marketing and sales executives in the mid to late seventies.

And my boss, the VP of manufacturing, was very satisfied, and I was invited to the Wilson and Walter Hagen annual sales meeting at Pebble Beach to make the same presentation. I was prepped on what items to be careful of within the presentation as the salesmen all had their ideas on what the most significant feature of a golf club was and how Wilson and Walter Hagen controlled that feature. Again, Walter Hagen felt they were much better than Wilson with the quality of their products even though they were both produced with the same process but in different plants. So I decided to bring a club at my presentation with a swing weight scale, a Walter Hagen Haig Ultra 5 Iron, joined with a Wilson Staff 5 Iron as I was making my presentation. The Wilson, I would have in my hand, and the Walter Hagen, I would have on the swing weight scale. They were both D1 clubs, the preferred swing weight at the time for a pro-grade set of irons. As I conducted the meeting, they all came to the agreement that swing weight was the most critical feature of a pro-grade golf club. The club on the swing weight scale showed it was a D1, the same as the Wilson Staff I was holding in my hands. As I concluded the presentation, everyone was in agreement that controlling swing weight is the most important thing we had to do. So I invited a salesman up front from the audience, where I handed him the Wilson Staff club and asked him to swing the club and tell me what he thinks of the feel of the product. His comment was "This is a great feeling club." Now no one knew the Hagen club on the swing weight scale had lead inside from the head to the top of the grip, so even though it measured at D1 on the scale, as soon as someone would pick it up, they would know something was wrong with the club.

I called another salesman up from the audience, and I went to the scale. I grabbed the Walter Hagen Haig club and gave it to him to swing. The minute I gave it to him, he dropped it because it was so heavy even though the swing weight was the preferred D1. So as I looked up, the point was made without control of overall weight. Swing weight is not the most critical feature of a golf club. The example and point of my presentation were well received, and my boss and the VP of manufacturing and marketing and sales were all very pleased. They shared the information we had collected to build confidence in the sales force that Walter Hagen and Wilson products are of the highest quality compared to our competition. After my presentation, I got to play golf at Pebble Beach in the golf tournament that everyone in attendance was invited to play.

After the sales meeting was over and I returned to River Grove, the implementation of the standards in both River Grove and Grand Rapids was well on its way, which allowed me to take those quality standards to Tullahoma Plant. There they changed their tolerance for their product which was commercial grade and sold in sporting goods stores, not country clubs. I also had some free time so I could concentrate on the durability testing that was requested to assure our pro clubs would stand up during play in the field without shafts breaking or heads flying off or face inserts coming out of the clubs. I worked closely with my technical engineer Mike Malatesta. He would provide the technical parameters, and I would develop the durability cycle in order to pass the durability standards.

My job was going really well, and we were very comfortable with our new home in Downers Grove. I was now very aware of all the personnel in both River Grove and Grand Rapids. There was a plant manager of River Grove Club, one for Grand Rapids Club, and one for Grand Rapids Golf Ball. Everyone knew that I wanted the opportunity to run a plant someday. Then one day, to everyone's surprise, the general manager of the Grand Rapids facility decided to resign. That created an opening for a new position in Grand Rapids, Michigan. The first move they made was promoting the general manager of River Grove to the general manager job in Grand Rapids.

The first move the new GM made was to promote the plant manager from River Grove Club to that position. I knew all the players, and they knew me as the department's heads were all in the meeting that I was conducting about field audits and quality, so I threw my hat in the mix. I got an interview and was promoted to plant manager of River Grove Clubs. All I had to do was move into the factory office vacated by the plant manager that was moving to Grand Rapids, Michigan. I also received a nice increase in salary. The promotion required no change to the social circles that we were involved in. My drive in the morning would be the same; I would not have to travel as much anymore as I did not have responsibilities for the other plants. What a great feeling to have accomplished my goal. I would wake up every morning and could not wait to get to work and start my job. I loved the factory floor and being able to walk through the plant and see the operation being performed to complete a professional set of golf clubs. Things were going well on all fronts. I was playing more golf and getting better, and I had new clubs anytime I wanted to play test new designs before they would be introduced into the line. My boys were into sports, and any equipment they needed, Wilson had in their product lines at cost. My boys had all the latest equipment you could buy for hockey, baseball, football, basketball, and tennis. I had to pinch myself as things were going so well.

Then one day, the general manager, Don Levault, for Grand Rapids and River Grove plants, invited Sharon and me to dinner, along with the plant manager, John Cagny, of Grand Rapids plant. We went to a very expensive restaurant in the west Chicago suburbs. We had a wonderful meal with light conversation when suddenly, the GM dropped the bomb. The corporation has decided to consolidate the two plants. They were not sure yet which one would be closed, but he stated if River Grove is the plant, then the plant manager of River Grove will move to Grand Rapids as the superintendent of manufacturing. If the Grand Rapids plant is closed, then the plant manager of Grand Rapids will become superintendent of the River Grove Plant. Talk about bursting your bubble. I had only been a plant manager for about six months when overnight, that opportunity would disappear.

John Cagny was a friend of mine, and if they closed his plant, he would come back to River Grove as the superintendent. How would that work? Also, I did not see myself going back one step after it took me so long to achieve my dream job. I clearly did not know what to do, so I quickly started looking for another job. It was at this time that I found out Sharon was pregnant with our third son. She was due in October of 1977. So we were up in the air about what to do. Grand Rapids was a beautiful city and a lot smaller than Chicago, and the quality of life would be much better for my three sons. The decision to close the plant would take some time, so I continued to be the plant manager of the River Grove Plant.

As fall approached, the decision was made to close River Grove. So I would have to take the superintendent's position or find a new job. Wilson had a very attractive relocation package back then, so the move to Grand Rapids would be seamless from a financial standpoint. So as Sharon and I discussed this opportunity, I got a call from the general manager for the Grand Rapids Golf Ball operation. The Grand Rapids ball facility also had a general manager. It did not take long to jump at that offer, and so I decided to take the plant manager of golf ball operation and move to Grand Rapids. I informed my boss, Don LeVault, of my decision. Grand Rapids was going back home but just a little farther north than Kalamazoo, Michigan. My wife was very pregnant, so we made a trip to Grand Rapids immediately to look for a house. We could not find anything we really liked, so we decided we would build our new house away from town in a new development in the country. They were anxious for me to start in Grand Rapids as other management staffers were also transferring from River Grove, so we rented a two-bedroom apartment. The relocation of the product line and management from River Grove to Grand Rapids was a nightmare with the production schedule in the club plant. The employees of the Water Hagan plant did not feel that Wilson was a part of the same company even though Wilson Sporting Goods' name was on their checks. My adjustment to the ball manufacturing was going much smoother, and the operation was humming in no time.

A lot of attention and pressure was being put on the Grand Rapids Club plant manager, blaming him for the schedule problems. Then a decision was made, and the general manager of River Grove decided to relocate to Grand Rapids to concentrate on fixing production problems. Now we had two general managers at the same facility, one for club and one for ball. This seemed like a lot of overhead for one plant, and the longer it lasted, the more the corporation pressure increased to eliminate overhead. My background was in club and quality control, so I had to really learn about golf balls and the manufacturing process. The general manager was brought in from Titleist and was supposed to be an expert on balls, so I would be able to rely on him for technical support. In very short order, it became obvious he was not that close to the process and was not adding a lot to the process, so about three months after I transferred, he was terminated, and my previous general manager was now over both ball and club.

As the new year approached, my wife and I found out our house would not be ready until May, and I was not going to be traveling back and forth from Grand Rapids to Downers Grove, so we decided we would put some of our furniture in storage and move into a three-bedroom apartment so the boys could start day care and school and make new friends. Michael was ten, Brian was eight, and Mark was six months old. The apartment was only about five miles from where our new house was being built, so the boys would enroll in their new school, and when the house was complete, no other adjustments had to be made. Shortly after I moved to Grand Rapids, the general manager that promoted me resigned, and a new GM was installed from PepsiCo. In addition, the general manager that I worked for in River Grove also lost his ally with this resignation, and the new general manager was not easy to work for and had no manufacturing experience to draw upon. This also created another problem for everyone in the golf division as the new GM was not a part of making the decision for consolidating the two pro plants and would criticize how stupid this move was and how it has disrupted the flow of both Wilson and Walter Hagen pro golf plants. When he would visit Grand Rapids to review our performance, his disdain for our performance was obvious. Our ball was performing well, but the consolidation of the club was a major problem, and the hostility between the GM of the Grand Rapids facility and the general manager of the golf division was on full display.

As the year went on, it became obvious that the GM of Grand Rapids was blaming the club plant manager for all the problems. He was the plant manager of River Grove, working for the GM at that time, and he promoted him to the Grand Rapids position, and they were very good friends. So this became a major problem within the plant. As more and more pressure was being applied to the GM of the Grand Rapids facility, he decided to terminate the club plant manager and have me take over both plants reporting to him. When he presented his plan to the GM of the golf division, he said, "No, you cannot replace the plant manager until the problems are fixed." Everyone thought this was a way for the new GM of golf to get rid of the GM of the Grand Rapids facility. Sure enough, that is exactly what happened about eight months later. They called me in on one of the visits the GM made to Grand Rapids and informed me that they had released the GM and wanted me to assume the position. The GM was a close friend as I had worked for him now for about three years, and prior to that, I worked with him when I installed the quality systems in the golf club plants. That phone call I made to him did not go very well.

So I am now in charge, and if I do not fix the problem, I am surely next. My greatest strength is being able to work with people and get everybody on the same team. I would be considered a people person, and that strength has gotten me to this position, so let's continue with that approach. The biggest problem the club plant was having was producing clubs to the schedule that was given to us by River Grove, so the first meeting I had was with the production control from River Grove, and we were able to bang out a new schedule and a recovery plan so we would get credit for making our schedule and also reduce the backlog. In the early days of the consolidation, they missed the schedule by about 50 percent, and each and every month, they would add them onto the schedule, so no matter what manufacturing did, they would never make the production schedule. The first thing we did was establish a running rate for the schedule, and then we would also have a recovery schedule to reduce the backlog. So after a couple of months, the factory was making our schedule and also reducing the backlog. With the cooperation of the material manager, we were now getting some positive reports of how the club faculty was performing against schedule. The next moves were designed to improve morale both with the hourly employees and the salary employees. We introduced a summer hour working schedule which the union agreed to by working one hour more each day so we could work a half day on Friday. That would become our summer work schedule to take advantage of long weekends and play more golf. We also set up a baseball match between the supervisors and the hourly personnel so people would get to know each other a little better. I was having the time of my life and could not wait to come to work. The corporate visits, were a pain in the ass, were much more pleasant as the division was receiving a lot of positive feedback from corporate staff that would work with the various departments on a regular basis.

Things could not be better, but they were still cutting the club schedule, which meant that we were losing market share, and there was a concern another consolidation would come to close the Grand Rapids facility and move everything to Tullahoma, Tennessee. The major brands that marketing thought we were competing with were Spaulding, MacGregor, Ram, Ben Hogan, Cleveland, Lynx, Dunlop, Mizuno, and Tommy Armour. Three new companies were also emerging that eventually would have a major impact on golf in the future, Taylor Made, Cobra, and Ping. Everybody was making a good player's blade, along with wood woods, either strata block or persimmon. No major company was offering metal wood, graphite shafts, or game-improvement clubs to the marketplace. No one on tour was playing any of these products, and the mood on tour was very negative toward anyone who would suggest that a particular product would improve the professional game.

A new technology in the midseventies and the early eighties was frowned on by the touring professional. They would refuse to even hit the product. So the new companies like Taylor Made with their metalwood, Cobra with graphite shafted clubs, and Ping with game-improvement technologies were struggling to get footing. The worst part of my job was when I had to go to River Grove to present my budget to the president of Wilson Sporting Goods. We would spend months preparing each line item with detailed backup and explanation to justify every dollar in the budget. There was no specific time we had to meet with him as he would be meeting with all the other divisions during this time frame. We would sit for hours until it was our time in the barrel. When we finally got the call, we would head into the conference room, just the two of us, my comptroller and myself, waiting for the king.

As he would walk into the room, followed by a large entourage, his suit jacket would be draped over his shoulders, and as he was going to sit down, he would flip his jacket off, and one of his staff would catch it before it hit the floor. This was the first time I had met the president and my first budget presentation to him and his staff. We had already gone through a presentation to my boss, the general manager of golf, and he was very pleased with the numbers. So we were not expecting any problems presenting these numbers to the president. The meeting took about one hour and a half to get through all the material, and not one word or question was raised by anyone in the room. As we finished, there was a silence in the room, and then he commented, "Thank you for the presentation," and stated, "I do not like your numbers. I want you to cut it by 10 percent," and he got up and walked out. We were stunned, and no one made a comment about what to do next. My boss got up and left the room without saying a word, and we got back into the company van and drove back to Grand Rapids. Nothing else was said, and no other action was taken, so we made no changes to the budget that was presented. In reality, it would change many times throughout the year as running rates would change, and we would go up or down based on the number of clubs and balls our schedule demanded.

Luckily, I would not see the president again until next year's budget presentation.

The tension with my boss was increasing even as the division was performing above expectations. He would challenge everything I would do, and we would disagree on the approach to take to run the plants. I knew this would not last forever, but I was having too much fun overall to leave. It finally came to a head when he confronted me on some decisions I made without his approval. I thought they were meaningless, but he made a big deal about them, and we agreed it was time for me to move along. Just like that, it was over. I guess I was fortunate to quickly find a new position in town for the leading furniture hardware manufacturing in the country. They had a general manager position for the furniture division that had the responsibility for the five furniture hardware manufacturing plants in and around Grand Rapids.

The fun times of making golf clubs were now over, but I was able to bring the same enthusiasm to my new position as I did at Walter Hagen. The product was not as much fun, but the people were great. We were able to stay in our home, and our boys were growing up and doing well in sports. Life could not be much better. I was really missing the folks I worked with at Walter Hagen, but I was able to maintain a relationship with a lot of them through playing golf and hunting on the weekends. I also kept up with the changes that were being made at the old Wilson plant and the rumors that plans were being developed to move the Grand Rapids operation to Tullahoma, Tennessee. Talk about a drastic change in culture.

Several years went by, and then one day, early in 1984, I got a telephone call from someone at the Hogan Company asking me if I would be interested in the vice president of manufacturing position, which they had open in Fort Worth, Texas. I had been out of golf for about two years, and I had fallen in love with golf, so getting back into the business was a great opportunity for me. I also knew the vice president of research and development at Hogan, as I had worked with this guy when he was an engineer in R&D at Wilson Sporting Goods in River Grove, Illinois. In my conversations with this executive, he explained why Hogan was looking. They were having trouble with producing their clubs and balls, resulting in the sales force complaints about delays and quality issues in the field.

During the interview process for the Hogan position, no one ever mentioned Ben Hogan himself or what, if any, relationship I would have with him as the vice president of manufacturing. I had been playing golf now for about fifteen years, and while at Wilson working on club quality specifications and testing, my golf intellect had become sizable. Wilson also had many tour players that I had a chance to meet at golf tournaments, so I was surprised to hear the reverence that all the staff had for Mr. Hogan because this was 1984, and he hadn't played on tour for close to thirty years. The entirety of the interviews went well, and they expressed a sincere interest in me. Ultimately, the allure of the Hogan company was too much, and I accepted the job.

The first couple of weeks after I started, I attended meetings and got to know all the top management and listened to their concerns about the quality of the product and the delivery problems they were having on filling the orders they had placed for clubs. Then about the third week of July of 1984, the president of the Hogan Company let me know he was going to introduce me to Mr. Hogan. The only warning he gave me was never to call him Ben, always refer to him as Mr. Hogan. So midmorning, the call came to report to the president's office as we were going to meet Mr. Hogan.

Now I had been at the Hogan Company for just a couple of weeks, but every place I would go, someone had a Mr. Hogan story they would relate to me. Now remember, I was not yet a Hogan disciple because I got into golf long after Mr. Hogan's career had ended. So I did not know what to expect, but I sure was expecting to see this incredible personality from all the stories that I had been told. I was expecting to meet someone bigger than life. When I walked into the room, I could not believe my eyes. Here was this little guy smaller than me, and I was only about 5'9", so you can imagine he was about 5'7". My first thought was *How this guy could be that good of a golfer?* Boy, would I learn quickly!

While working at Wilson Sporting Goods, I met a lot of professional players, and they all were much bigger and more athletic-looking than Mr. Hogan, so when he shook my hand, I was surprised how small his hand was, but it felt like I had just put my hand in a steel vice. At the time, I was not aware that this gentleman had won thirty professional golf tournaments in three years after a major car accident that almost took his life. I probably should have done some research on his life before the meeting to appreciate that experience. He was very polite, and you could tell he was from the old school where a handshake and his word were his bonds. The meeting lasted about ten minutes, and he wished me luck with my new responsibilities and to let him know if I needed any help, he would be happy to help.

After that meeting, I went to work the next couple of months, getting to know the people and the operation I was responsible for. It was like a honeymoon. Everyone was very nice and pleasant. I met with the VP of human resources, who reported directly to me so I could understand the background of all the people that were my direct reports, so I could understand how best to manage each department. I would also spend a lot of time meeting with other department heads, such as sales, marketing, finance, warehousing, customer service, sportswear, and engineering. One of the first things that I got into the habit of doing was first thing in the morning at about seven o'clock when I arrived at work, I would go into my office, take off my suit coat, roll up my sleeves, check my messages, and take a tour of the factory operations. This habit came very early in my career when I was a management trainee at Parker Hannifin, and their main emphasis was that if you were going to manage a plant, you needed to understand the operations you managed. This became very important to me as I walked through the plant and each department, starting with woods, irons, the ball factory, warehousing, and finally back to my office. This made the plant managers very uncomfortable as I walked through their operations without any escort. I would stop to inspect the products and talk to the operators to get a feel for how things were going for them and, more often than not, how they felt about their job and the company.

To my surprise, I would learn no one in management had ever walked through the plant on their own, so this was viewed as remarkable to the hourly employees. After the tour, I would go to meet with the various department heads and ask for their input into what problems they felt I should be concentrating on, so I had somewhat of a road map as to what people perceived the manufacturing problems were and what they thought needed my immediate attention. Almost everyone stated that delivery was the biggest problem. I would also meet with the VP of R&D and manufacturing engineering to see if I could figure out their working relationship and how they contribute to the delivery problems. So for the next month, this would be my routine learning about the operation and the people that manage the process. Through this process, I also became aware that manufacturing was everybody's whipping boy. Research and development had a very close relationship with marketing and sales, but manufacturing was the odd man out. The VP I replaced was from the south and came up through the ranks, and all the department heads were college graduates and from the north, and the staff had convinced the president that he was the problem.

I had been with the company only a month, and the national sales meeting was coming up in August, I was invited to speak and explain to the sales force what changes have been made to improve delivery. So that gave me my first opportunity to get the parties together to determine what the problems are and how we could fix them. We started weekly meetings with R&D, manufacturing, engineering, and quality control to determine what steps needed to be taken to improve our delivery performance. It did not take long to figure out. Everyone had a hand in the problem. It was not just manufacturing. In the very first meeting, I learned marketing, and R&D decided they needed a persimmon wood to introduce at the national sales meeting, so R&D made the samples for the sales force without setting up the manufacturing process to actually produce the product. During my morning tours, I could see the operations that were struggling to build the parts as the tooling to produce the design was not completed as yet. The salesmen samples were made by hand by the engineering department, so no production tooling was used and was in the development stages. The workers were struggling to make the parts by hand because the tooling fixtures had not been completed. So everything had to be done with a loose piece. This was a very difficult process, like trying to drill into a pipe molding by hand without the use of a vise to keep it steady.

During these meetings, it became apparent to me, manufacturing, engineering, and manufacturing did not talk to each other, along with any communications with R&D. Being the new guy on the block, I was the only one without skeletons in my closet, so I could bring everyone together to produce the product that was introduced to the sales force. After the meeting, I met with the VP of R&D, and we both agreed we needed a design review meeting process like we were both familiar with at Wilson Sporting Goods that included manufacturing, manufacturing engineering, research and development, quality control, and marketing. These meetings would be conducted weekly to follow rigorous procedures with each department given assignments to complete before the next meeting. Each department now had a stake in the group being successful with the introduction of the design. I was surprised that a company like Hogan, which had such a high-quality reputation in the field, would be so lacking in the disciplines needed to deliver a design to the marketplace. Each department operated independently of the other, and there was no coordination between the parties. In fact, they all took pride in how well they did their job, and the lowly people that made the product always failed. I was embarrassed at how long it took me to discover that flaw in our design systems. So for the next several weeks, I spent time building these relationships with the help of the VP of R&D and setting up the meetings with all the departments to assure the tooling, materials, and processes were completed to successfully manufacture and ship the product to the market.

These meetings were a tremendous success, and everybody involved felt good about a successful design introduction. With these meetings working very well, it allowed me to concentrate on production schedules to make up for the lost time we caused by the delay in tooling and components to make the design. The sales meeting was scheduled for the end of August, and all the salesman and their wives were invited to Fort Worth to enjoy the party. This also would be an opportunity to bring my wife down and spend the weekend with her. Since my start date, I spent most of my time in Fort Worth in an apartment and would go home on the weekends every other week, as the home we purchased in Fort Worth would not be completed until mid-September. So I was missing my family as my wife stayed home in Michigan while our two older boys finished school. Those were very hard times being away from my family and friends and all alone in a strange city. The sales meeting was first class, and the Hogan Company provided gifts for all the invitees, along with their wives and all the executives. We received cowboy boots from Fort Worth-based Justin Boots, along with a Stetson cowboy hat for the men and women. They had dinners planned for the week and a golf outing for all the salesmen, along with top management at one of the exclusive country clubs in town. It was a gala event. They also had a program conference with all the sales programs that the salesmen had to attend, and they invited many of the customer service personnel to join that presentation. It did surprise me that they did not include any foreman or plant personnel in any of the festivities. I thought, what a great company to be working for and how welcoming they were to the families of the employees.

 One of the great highlights of the meeting was a dinner meeting at Shady Oaks Country Club, which is the club Mr. Hogan is a member of, and he was scheduled to give a speech to the sales force, along with all the touring professionals that were invited to attend. The room was electric with anticipation of the man making an appearance. This would be the second time I would have the chance to see Mr. Hogan. It was evident how he was worshipped by all in attendance waiting for him to speak. All the executives were on hand, and I got the feeling they were not as excited as the salesman and the pros for his speech. This was one of the few times that the management of the company with his name would have him participate in a company affair other than the annual employee Christmas party.

As he walked to the podium, a hush came over the room as everyone was waiting for him to speak. You could literally hear a pin drop in the room. He was not a polished public speaker, but it became obvious he was speaking from his heart. His speech covered the starting of his company as Mr. Hogan started to talk about the formation of his company and many of his golfing experiences, but not much about the company of today or the product lines the sales force was being asked to sell. Then the tone changed as Mr. Hogan started to rip the present management of the company, saying they had no idea of what a player's blade was or how to make one. I gasped at the remarks as he ripped into the president and the products that were being introduced. It became apparent to me that present management did not involve Mr. Hogan in the daily operation of his former company. This went on for a while. After he concluded, he left the podium and moved to the side of the stage where everyone that wanted a picture with him or to shake his hand, he would be available. He was very gracious and stayed to accommodate anyone who wanted a picture or to shake his hand.

As I talked to a few of the VPs as to how shocked I was at his comments, I was equally shocked to learn that he pretty much does that all the time, and this is nothing new. Everyone is used to it by now as he doesn't agree with making anything other than a good player's blade, and everyone knows if that is all we made, our sales would be so small. We would never have a meeting like this again.

It was apparent that Ben and present-day management were not on the same page with the products they were producing as Ben was from the old school, feeling that a forged player blade was the only club that a golfer should ever buy. This was the early stages of consumers being introduced to a couple of new terms in golf club manufacturing—game improvement and cavity back along with a move away from forgings. Many of the pros also felt the same way that the club should not improve the players, believing the skill of the players should provide the improvement. I felt comfortable with the explanation one of the VP gave me about Hogan and how important that he was or was not as Hogan Company owner, AMF approved of the direction of the company, and they were all content to have him in the background but not involved in any day-to-day decisions, only a figurehead. I did, however, pursue this discussion with the individual VP of finance to see what interaction any of them had with Mr. Hogan on a daily basis. To my amazement, no one, not even the president, had much interaction with Mr. Hogan, and his office was right next door. It became apparent to me that Mr. Hogan was a recluse even in the company that he had his name on the door. The only meetings that Mr. Hogan was included with were when some dignitary would come down and they would want to meet him, so that person would be accompanied to his office for a social visit and sent on his way. So now it made sense to me; I was now with the company for three months and saw Mr. Hogan once in his office and then at the salesmen dinner at Shady Oaks. This would be something for me to fix.

This sales meeting was my first exposure to the friction that existed between Mr. Hogan and the president and marketing executives. After the meeting was over and everyone was back at work, I was able to discuss this friction with the VP of finance and the VP of human resources. In my discussion with the VP of finance, I was particularly interested in knowing if any of the division finances were reviewed with Mr. Hogan, and the answer was none. I followed up with the VP of human resources, who reported to me, to find out if any sharing of employee information was being shared with Mr. Hogan, and again, the answer was none. So now I know what to expect in the future. So I was back to my routine of the factory tour every morning before going to my office.

Since 1960, the Ben Hogan Company had been run by one of the largest recreational sports companies there was, American Machine and Foundry or AMF. AMF was founded in Brooklyn in 1900 by Rufus Patterson. Rufus first found success when he invented the very first automated cigarette manufacturing machine at a time when smoking was very fashionable. His company, AMF, would quickly grow and move into the automated bowling equipment space, followed by bicycle production. Success seemed to follow AMF at every turn. Their vice chairman during the late 1950s was a man named Walter Bedell Smith, who had been Eisenhower's chief of staff during the war. Smith would years later become the director of the CIA. As head of AMF, Smith parlayed the company into a major player in President Eisenhower's "military-industrial complex" after World War II. The AMF conglomerate expanded into consumer goods like scuba gear, mopeds, Nimble bicycles, Alcort sailboats, Hatteras Yachts, Harley Davidson motorcycles, bowling equipment, snow skis, and the acquisition of the Ben Hogan Company from Mr. Hogan in 1960.

Mr. Hogan started his company in 1953 with the thought in mind of making the best player's blades you could buy. He struggled in the early years and almost went bankrupt. Ben was very adamant the clubs had to be of the highest quality. He would refuse to ship some of the clubs that hadn't met his standards, and it's rumored to be in the tens, if not hundreds, of thousands of dollars' worth of equipment would go to the junkpile. These high standards and refusal to ship subpar production runs caused a split with his partner at that time. Ben was in dire need of funds to buy his partner out and operate his company the way he envisioned. In talking with the late Marvin Leonard's daughter, Marty Leonard, she shared that her father, Marvin Leonard, and Ben started a strong relationship in Ben's younger years when he caddied for Mr. Leonard. Mr. Leonard took a liking to Ben and treated him like his own son. Ben would later give Mr. Leonard a copy of his first instructional book on how to play golf, addressing it to "Leonard, the best friend I will ever have." This relationship proved to be fruitful for Ben in his earlier years when Mr. Leonard funded Ben's golfing career, but also during his time with the Ben Hogan Company. Mr. Leonard agreed to loan him the money not only to buy out his partners, but he wanted him to also make sure and take enough to buy out his partner and have enough money to operate the company until he could make a profit. Ben used this opportunity to operate the company to his own high standards and continue to develop his product line, scrap the inferior products, and keep paying the bills. As the company grew and he established its reputation as the leading club maker, the revenue grew, and Hogan became profitable. Ben later sold the company to AMF, and Marvin was rewarded for his support of Ben.

Mr. Hogan was kept on and consulted in the early years on designs, but very few decisions came from his desk over the last twenty years. I struggled mightily to understand how such a man could go underutilized in a company he founded and an industry he dominated for so long. Mr. Hogan had more to offer the Hogan Company than he had been granted by AMF.

The first week after the sales meeting, after I completed my tour and returned to my office, my secretary informed me, "Mr. Hogan would like you to come to his office." I asked her if she knew what it was about, and she said no. I had no idea what this could be about. Now you can imagine, I was being told of the many stories about the early days when he owed the company and how he ran it, and many, if not all, of the hourly employees, were with the company at the beginning. This was even true for all the office staff in customer service, finance, quality control, warehousing, and data processing.

So off to his office I went as I walked through the door. I said, "Good morning, Mr. Hogan. How can I help you today?" As he looked up, I saw those steely eyes looking straight at me, and I felt he was looking right through me. At that moment, I knew this was not going to be as pleasant as our first meeting. He was not happy about something, but what could it be? It did not take long to get the answer. On his desk was a pan of iron heads that weighed fifty pounds.

He said to me, "This is garbage. You need to fix them right now." He commented, "I thought they hired you because you knew how to make a quality golf product. If this is the best you can do, we will be out of business before the end of the year." He did not say what was bad about the heads, and I did not ask. I took a couple of heads with me and let him know I would have someone come back for the rest of the heads, and I would let him know how we fixed the problem. So off I went. Holy cow! I was embarrassed and worried about what my boss would think about being dressed down by Mr. Hogan, but I wanted to get to the bottom of the problem before I would let my boss know about the situation.

So the first thing I did was go to the club plant manager's office to show him the parts. I was hoping he would see what was wrong and fill me in, but that did not work. So the next place I went was to the work station where the irons were being made to see if they might know what the problem was. They did not know. So finally, I called the VP of R&D as he had the responsibility for quality control and asked him to come to my office to see if we could figure out the problem. The VP came to my office, and he brought with him Gene Sheeley, his iron master model maker. Gene was a World War II Navy veteran and Korean War Marine. Gene came to Fort Worth in 1964 and was handpicked and trained by Ben to become the master model maker for the Hogan Company and worked with Ben on all club designs. Gene's job was to craft by hand the iron heads that eventually would be sent as masters to make the tooling to order the raw iron heads. He was also one of the original employees with the company and was not happy with the new management of the company. It became apparent he thought manufacturing did not know how to make a good iron head. As we discussed the problem, the master model maker pointed out the problems with the top line, sole, and shape of the iron. This was somewhat of a surprise as I wondered why we would let the operator produce these clubs if none of them were acceptable. I asked again, "How do we let the worker grind clubs that get rejected and end up in Mr. Hogan's office and then Mr. Hogan points out the problem to me?"

No one answered that question.

The answer that I got was a lot of excuses. No one wanted to get anybody in trouble, so it was hard to get to the bottom of why this happened. We did identify the problem, and I called the foreman and the club plant manager into my office and instructed them to work with the master model maker to make sure the iron grinder knows how to grind these irons. I also asked them to bring a couple of heads back to me that the master model maker thinks are ground correctly so I could show them to Mr. Hogan and let him know how we corrected the problem.

So I have been on the job for three months and finally had a quality crisis. These would happen almost every day at Wilson Sporting Goods. The honeymoon at Hogan was now over. One big difference between the two was culpability. As general manager, my responsibility included quality control and manufacturing. Here at Hogan, the structure allowed for much finger-pointing when mistakes were made. A couple of hours later, they brought me a couple of new club heads that I reviewed with the master model maker. That is what Mr. Hogan was talking about, so I could show him what corrective action was taken to correct the problem. As I headed to Mr. Hogan's office, I felt pretty satisfied with my solution. This meeting went a little smoother for me. I showed him the heads, and he gave a nod followed by silence. No good job, thanks, approval, questions, or any other words until I left the room. I was relieved that the meeting went so well.

It was time to inform my boss, the president of the company, of the outcome. I was a little nervous about the meeting, wondering what his reaction would be, but to my surprise, he let out a laugh and remarked, "I wondered when you would have your turn in the barrel." He seemed unconcerned about the actual problem or the confusion between departments. He did offer up, "You know, the sentiment in the factory is not in favor with the direction AMF is taking this company. All the top management, with the exception of the VP of human resources, are not from Texas. You also replaced a local Texan when you came aboard." That conversation shed some light on the problem.

So the loyalty of the employees was a big factor for me in getting the manufacturing departments moving in the right direction. The first order of business was working on getting the employees to accept the direction we needed to go and be on the same team. This little fiasco was one example of us not working together in the factory to produce a quality product. The failure lay with quality control, manufacturing, engineering, and manufacturing to communicate and make sure each department did its job. When I first started, Hogan had no formal manufacturing, engineering, and quality control review to implement the necessary steps to produce a quality product. So back to work I went and set up meetings with the plant managers for club, ball, and grip plants to review their budgets, to identify the necessary reporting, to track the operations before problems popped up. This also gave me a chance to get to know each foreman a little better and be able to understand what help he needed to accomplish our goals. I was feeling pretty good about the progress we were making and how everything was working.

So another couple of months went by, and all seemed to be going well when one morning after my tour, my secretary informed me that Mr. Hogan wanted to see me as soon as I was available. This didn't feel like a simple update meeting. As I walked into his office, the stern looks on his face let me know we had a problem. This time, he had about ten wood heads sitting on his desk, to which I knew the drill. I kept my mouth shut. He proceeded to dress me down again for the lousy quality I was producing in his plant. I picked up several heads and retreated to my office. This one should be a little easier, as all the same players would be involved. But before that, I started to consider how the hell these heads are getting to Mr. Hogan's office, outside of the regular flow of product through the plant. Someone had to be taking these out of production and performing a show-and-tell with Mr. Hogan at my expense. So I decided to walk out to the factory floor to the operation that the heads had been taken from to see what if anything that I could learn. The first employee I encountered was friendly upon my arrival. I asked him if he was having any problems, to which he answered no. Before I could ask another question, he responded, "I am sure the master model marker is going to get somebody in trouble today."

I responded, "What do you mean?"

He replied, "The master model maker likes to rub quality control's face when he disagrees about the quality standards they are setting. So he will go to Mr. Hogan's office to get his support."

I asked if the master model maker spoke to the employees. The answer was no. "How about the foreman?" I asked again. The answer was no. "How about quality control?" And again, the answer was no.

He finally added, "He doesn't get along with the quality control inspector either."

I did not expect to get all this information from one visit to the factory floor. I went back to my office and started to formulate a plan to fix this problem once and for all. Once again, we had a breakdown in communication between manufacturing, engineering, and quality control. I called the VP of R&D to inform him of what I found and requested a meeting with him and the master model maker. Both the model maker and the quality control inspector reported to R&D. I addressed the pair that I have had enough of this behavior. I am tired of being called to Mr. Hogan's office and dressed down on a regular basis. The VP of R&D and I had known each other for years. He worked at Wilson Sporting Goods at the same time I did. We both were aware of how the departments communicate with each other, and what was happening here was not normal.

The master model maker, foreman, and quality control inspector were called to my office to review the problem. It became apparent to me everyone knew what happened, but no one wanted to tell me, so I concluded the meeting by outlining the procedure on how to handle these cases in the future. Everyone agreed, and as the meeting ended, I asked Gene Sheeley, the master model maker, to stay behind.

After the room cleared, I started by saying, "I know you are the one that got Mr. Hogan involved. Now it's happened again if you remember the last time with the iron heads. Let me be very clear on what is going to happen if you ever do this again. If you see a problem, go to the foreman and let him know. If he does not correct the problem, inform the quality control inspector. If there is no response, go to the plant manager, and if all else fails, come to my office and let me know. Do you understand what I am saying?"

He replied, "Yes."

"In summary, if I ever get a call to come to Mr. Hogan's office again and this new procedure is not followed, my first move will be to fire you. I want us all to work together by rowing the boat in the same direction. Do you agree that is the best way to proceed?"

He answered yes, and the meeting ended. This was a very constructive meeting, and I felt we made a lot of progress. It was apparent the model maker was very loyal to Mr. Hogan, and I needed him to see that his behavior was very destructive to the company and a detriment in achieving the quality goals of the company. I also needed him to develop the same loyalty with me for the benefit of the company. I am happy to say that was the last time I was called to Mr. Hogan's office about a quality problem in the factory. The biggest problem everyone wanted to be fixed was improving delivery times for new products. This was a real hard time for me personally as anyone knows taking a new job in a new environment, without friends or family, is tough living. My family was back in Grand Rapids, and all the friends I knew were at Wilson Sporting Goods or Keeler Brass.

Many times, I considered forgetting all this and returning to Keeler Brass and my old job. My old boss even called me and asked me if I would like to return. We were having problems selling our house, and I knew my wife would rather stay instead of moving to Texas. After a lot of thought, my wife and I decided I would go back, but I needed to come back as the VP of operations, not the general manager of the Brass Division. He agreed to everything, except the new title, which turned out to be the deal breaker. With that door now closed, I had to put my head down and make Hogan work for my family and me. I decided to embrace my new responsibilities at Hogan. My goal was to change the atmosphere within my operation. My office was up front with all the other executives, and I felt I needed to be closer to the manufacturing operations. I needed the manufacturing team behind me now more than ever. This way, I could keep a much better watch over my department. My staff generally would answer any questions I would ask, but they rarely would volunteer any solutions to correct the problems. I wanted them to know I had their backs when problems occurred.

During my morning tours, I had discovered a large office area near the manufacturing floor that I could move to and change the perception of my loyalties and hopefully garner some more support from the manufacturing staff. This turned out to be the right move as it did exactly what I had hoped it would do. Even though I was an outsider, I became one of the manufacturing team, and everyone felt more comfortable opening up to me. I was determined to remove the manufacturing department as the scapegoat for the company's troubles. I also needed to get each department working together and stop playing the blame game.

October of 1984 arrived, and our house was ready, so my family moved down, and that was a great relief to the empty apartment I had been surviving in. The staff was finally comfortable with me, and the flow of timely information eased the tensions across the company. My list to fix in manufacturing though was lengthy, but everyone company-wide felt the number one Hogan problem was club deliveries. Trying to convince anyone that the ball plant, which was run by R&D, was a bigger problem was wasting my breath. The Hogan ball plant was a messy situation. The relationship between R&D, manufacturing, engineering, and quality control was in dire straits, and I knew once the club problems were fixed, the ball factory would be next. As long as no one would be screaming about the ball factory, I had time to concentrate my efforts on the club operation.

During my tours of the plants one day, I discovered a separate building off by itself in the back of the facility and wondered its purpose. I was told it was our grip operation. The Hogan Company actually molded their own grips. No golf manufacturer I knew of made their own grips. This building was a terrible mess. I had visited the major grip company factories, and our operation was archaic. We could not expect to compete with a large grip manufacturer. We did not have the equipment or capital with the volume we were producing to be competitive. Were grips one of Hogan's original ideas? I needed to do some research before I mentioned the possibility of eliminating this operation completely. No one had ever mentioned to me we were making our own grips, and the building location away from everything else was odd. I started asking questions about the grips and why we were making our own, and no one seemed to know or care why we were doing it.

So I paid the VP of finance a visit to get a cost breakdown of the grip operation. I also asked my purchasing manager to get some quotes for comparison. What he found was unbelievable. Our manufactured grips were quadruple the price of a top-quality purchased grip. With this information, I contacted the R&D department to ask them if there was any reason we were making our grips versus buying them. The answer I got was they did not know of one. I asked them to include that in their discussions with marketing to see if they objected. Once all the parties were on board, the last step was to make sure the employees that worked in the grip operation could be absorbed into other production operations. I now had this in my pocket any time we decided to make the change. I decided for R&D to introduce this idea at the monthly staff meetings and gauge their reception. Everyone agreed, and the grip department was dissolved without dissent.

Our grip molding equipment was old and in need of a lot of maintenance. The tooling cost to make the tools was also extremely high. By purchasing the grips from a more cost-effective modern-day grip manufacturer, we freed up a lot of time, space in the production plant, and costs. We eliminated the molding presses, the maintenance and tool cost, and all the labor and overhead cost to produce the grips in-house.

By purchasing a grip instead of manufacturing a grip, we were able to eliminate the maintenance cost to maintain the presses. We eliminated all the tooling cost that was needed to make the tooling produced. Finally, the labor cost and all the overhead to support the grip operation were also eliminated. This change would lower our grip cost by 75 percent. This change, coupled with other manufacturing efficiency gains, I was able to add two positions into the 1985 budget and still lower the manufacturing cost of the products forecasted. The R&D VP was instrumental in selling this idea to the marketing VP. That would make a big difference in regard to completing the project by the end of 1984 and just in time for the January 1985 PGA merchandising show and sales meeting. Without this backing and the marketing blessing, the project would have probably failed.

Next up, the wood department implemented regularly scheduled product design review meetings to get everyone on the same page to reduce problems. Prior, there were no such design review meetings as the Hogan Company introduced our popular Apex woods earlier in the year. Our new protocol meeting highlighted a major problem that the club had with its brass back weight and the fact that manufacturing did not have any process or tooling to perform the operation. At one of the meetings, it was disclosed the salesman samples were all produced by R&D. The back weight was added after the model was presented to manufacturing to produce. No one had to say anything as it was apparent that the VP of marketing asked the VP of R&D to add this without any other persons involved in that decision. It was not important at this time who to blame. What was important was to find a solution to the problem and to start producing the product. I did not know at the time, but the manufacturing operation was very pleased that they finally got the help they needed and left only late delivery as their major pain. We got the tooling project completed, which greatly improved our deliveries. This was a small step to have manufacturing gain confidence within the company that people knew they could count on our performance to support the sales effort.

By December of 1984, things were starting to come together. The recovery had made up quite a bit of the schedule, getting Hogan to about 85 percent of the original delivery schedule. That meant we had about five thousand of our Apex woods on back order at the end of the year. I was hoping for more as I was invited again to speak at the national sales meeting at the 1985 PGA show in Orlando, Florida. I was expecting to get hammered by the salesmen with all the late deliveries. I was welcomed to the meeting as the salesmen were pleased with the improved performance. They were getting in their orders being shipped. We were still behind on our schedule, but the improvement in delivery was impacting the delivery of orders on a daily basis. The product shipments improved, and back orders were minimal, and customer complaints and late deliveries were down. The year ended on a good note. We were having increasing success with production, and the Hogan Company people had more confidence that manufacturing could produce what was expected. Things were also looking better on the home front. My family was settled in Texas, and my two older boys were into school, and my wife was in our new house. So the family life was back to normal.

In 1953, after Ben decided it was time to stop playing golf, he decided he wanted to start a golf company. He had a vision that he could make a better golf club than what was being offered by the other manufacturers at the time. He got together with a few of his friends and raised some capital and formed the Ben Hogan Golf Company. It was a small operation, and Ben applied his expertise to make the best irons for better players like himself.

In the early years, Ben would discover he had a real talent for designing golf clubs better than anyone else. The early years were hard, and the operation had its problems with quality and being able to make the irons to Ben's specifications. The problems with the quality of the products caused a split with the original investors. Ben remarked he did not know what would have happened if his close friend Marvin Leonard did not come to his rescue. The operations settled down, and the precision irons that Ben was manufacturing were becoming in high demand and being recognized as a leader in the golf club market.

As the company was growing, Ben always felt the pressure of the burden of financing his operations. The growth continued, and by 1960, Hogan sales reached $1,870,000 per year, and his company was making a generous profit of $193,000 on these sales. That's when AMF came calling. AMF was very interested in adding the Hogan line to the other product lines that AMF carried to become a major player in the sporting goods business. They made Ben an offer of a little more than $3.7 million for the Ben Hogan Company. The deal would include cash and a trade of Hogan Company equity for AMF equity. This was the opportunity Ben was looking for. He wanted to continue designing clubs, but he wanted to eliminate the financial risk of owning the company. He also had ten investors that would be able to make a profit on the deal, and he could also pay back his very close friend Marvin Leonard.

Ben's share was about $1,000,000 total, but he also signed a royalty deal that would allow him the ability to continue to office at the plant and be able to continue the development of the product line under the AMF umbrella. This was the best of both worlds; his financial security was protected, and he could continue to be instrumental in the company designing and producing products.

Ben also felt very good that he was able to return a profit to his friends and, in particular, Marvin, who had bailed him out and saved the Hogan Company from early disaster when Ben had to buy out his first partner over a disagreement about the quality of the clubs Ben wanted to ship to the golf professionals. Without that early help, Ben would have lost his company, and very few people would have any memory of the exceptional products the Hogan Company would produce for over thirty-five years.

Hogan's legend of overcoming obstacles made him a survivor. He had survived his difficult childhood to become one of golf's brightest new stars when he turned pro at the age of seventeen. He wouldn't join the tour until two years later, where problems existed, and then again two years later. His winning prize money improved so much so that he was the tour's top money winner for the years 1940, 1941, and 1942. Hogan's golf career was put on hold when the world went to war against the Axis powers. Hogan served as a lieutenant in the Army Air Corps from March 1943 to June 1945. He was stationed in Fort Worth, where he performed as a utility pilot. He would not see action on the battlefield like his friend and rival Sam Sneed. His two other rivals, Lloyd Mangrum and Bobby Jones, both were awarded for their bravery in combat. These obstacles fueled Ben's fire to succeed with his business as he did with his golf game.

The coming year at the Hogan Company would present some new challenges in regard to what steps needed to be made to continue improving. I was still toying with some needed organizational changes, but in the back of my mind, the ball manufacturing situation lingered in my brain. The Hogan ball plant was not yet a major operation for us, but one of the directors of marketing was previously with Titleist, and he was pushing to increase the ball revenue with the introduction of new products.

As the New Year rolled around, my feelings on the ball plant began to bubble to the surface. My experiences prior to Hogan allowed me to see the capabilities of other leading ball manufacturing companies like Bridgestone and Wilson. I knew Hogan did not possess the capabilities of those companies to handle the requests that were being demanded by the marketing director. We had very little engineering capacity and expertise to handle new ball introductions. I was aware the marketing department was pushing hard for new golf balls, not just tweaking our design but a brand-new two-piece product. One of my last jobs at Wilson as general manager of the Walter Hagen Plant that was producing two- and three-piece golf balls. The Hogan R&D department gave me nightmares in this regard. I felt we were way behind the times, and if we were going to introduce more products, I needed some hired help to make sure we were successful with the introduction. This would become a political fight with R&D as they felt they did not need any help and could compete with anyone. I did not share these sentiments, so I put a plan in place, knowing I could not bring in another outsider to my organization without a backlash from the manufacturing and engineering departments. The progress with my staff made me feel as though they trusted me. I needed to build a consensus with them as to how we could effectively handle a new two-piece ball technology by relying on R&D for technical assistance to set up the ball process.

Our Hogan president came with a marketing background, so he naturally favored the marketing department. Thus, rarely did anyone ever bring up a problem with marketing or sales in our monthly staff meetings. After several months, it became apparent that the VPs of finance and sportswear were not fans of this relationship. It appeared to all that whatever marketing wanted, they got. The first sign of improvement came when we eliminated the grip department with the blessing of R&D, which came with it, the president's approval. The Hogan Company could not progress without the marketing arm and, more importantly, the president's support.

We were beginning to behave as any successful company should. The improvements in delivery, lower manufacturing costs, introductions of new woods, irons, accessories, sportswear, and soon golf balls made for a more complete company, along with a more inclusive company dynamic. We were gaining steam. I was feeling good about my job and future.

This was now the Christmas party season, and the Hogan Company held its Christmas party for all the office personnel. Each VP had a party for their staff at the local country club. The president had a party at his club, Shady Oaks Country Club, which enjoyed Mr. Hogan's membership. The final party of the season was held by the VP of marketing and sales, and I was surprised with an invitation, as in the six months with the company, my interaction with the various VPs was very minimal. This was also considered to be the elite party of the year. I have never attended this many parties in my life. At the Walter Hagen plant, their Christmas celebration was held in the plant by serving a wonderful turkey dinner for all the employees, both hourly and salary. No country clubs were involved, so you can imagine how great I felt with all these perks.

As the new year started, I was invited to the PGA merchandising show. Every year, the golf pros would travel to Florida to play golf, and all the manufacturers would have large sales booths to show off their new products and any sales programs they were offering for the coming year. After the show, the Hogan Company would hold their national sales meeting at Bay Hill Country Club. I was to speak at the meeting to inform the salesmen how we were doing in regard to delivery of the Apex persimmon woods, which were still in such demand. I was a little nervous about my reception, as I knew we were still 20 percent behind in deliveries to the field, but we had made tremendous progress in improving on deliveries and reducing the backlog that was created during the previous summer months. The warm reception from the sales force surprised me as I expected to be ridiculed about the late deliveries. I was further shocked when the top salesman of each region was announced and finally the salesmen of the year. It was announced that the top salesmen performed at 130 percent of the quota. How could that be as my team missed our schedule in woods by 20 percent? We had been blasted all year for that performance at every monthly staff meeting, so how could any salesmen beat their quota?

It became obvious the number they had been given was a lot lower than the number manufacturing was trying to produce. This bit of knowledge would serve me well down the road. The sales force over shipped the numbers of clubs to reach their sales goals. The manufacturing department only made 85 percent of the scheduled production for woods. This meant we produced and shipped 15 percent less clubs than we were scheduled to make. Even with this miss, the sales force sold 30 percent over their sales targets. The award for the leading region and the leading salesmen was a trip to the Masters Golf Tournament for a full week. The group that attended that celebration was the national sales manager, the regional manager of the winning region, the VP of marketing and sales. In addition, other marketing and sales personnel would be included in that trip. They would rent a house right next to the famed Augusta golf course with breakfast and dinner provided at the house. The award winners would get to play golf at the nearby Jones Creek golf course, which was built on a superb site reminiscent of the rolling hills of Augusta and were awarded tickets to attend the master's tournament.

Now with the ball plant operations in my focus, I really needed some trusted, experienced people to improve our situation. The ball operation was controlled by research and development, and the VP's engineer had a free run of the plant. When he spoke, everyone would listen, and no one even would challenge the product engineer. He usually went unchallenged with his ideas. We were in the process of designing a new Hogan ball for introduction this year, but hearing all the horror stories of the past about quality and production gave me pause. I decided to move up the hiring of the two key positions I needed to make sure we could deliver what R&D was about to introduce. The two new positions were a ball plant manager and a process engineer that both understood how to introduce a new product and had in-depth knowledge on how to run the ball manufacturing process.

After the PGA show in January of 1985, we were informed that Hogan did not make our overall profit goals, so no bonuses would be awarded for the year. Again, I questioned if I was in the right place. My family's adjustment to the southern culture was slow, and we had a problem of not being able to sell our house in Grand Rapids, Michigan. I had two boys living at home, and they both had to adjust to new friends and circumstances. The biggest adjustment was being made by my middle son, who was a junior in high school. My youngest son was just starting first grade. Back to work I went, where we needed to solve for losing market share with our player's blades, as more and more people were changing to cavity back player improvements clubs. The marketing department was now demanding a "game improvement" club to be introduced to combat Ping.

Everyone at Hogan was on board, except for Mr. Hogan. Since he started the company, he had never considered producing a casting, preferring only forgings, as history and popular opinion supported him. Mr. Hogan's forgings offered the golfer more feel than a cast club. So the company-wide push for a casted club had everyone nervous, imagining Mr. Hogan's reaction to this information. We would also introduce the two-piece ball for the first time ever to go along with the clubs. I felt really good about the club introduction process but had much less of an idea of how that would work in the ball factory. We had been making three-piece balls forever and thus fairly streamlined at the manufacturing process, but change here did not seem monumental. Boy, was I wrong? The introduction of the Hogan Magnum ball would change Hogan's placement in the "ball" game. I was able to sell my boss, the president, on the idea it was time to make the changes to improve both the ball and club operations.

It was around this time that I sought out the help of an old friend. I had met Steve Dryer back in 1976 after I moved my family to Grand Rapids to run the Walter Hagan plant there. As general manager, I got to know Steve and his exceptional talent for making a great and quality golf ball. It turned out to be the most fortuitous friendship. Steve's help would transition into his move to Fort Worth in 1985 to take over the Hogan ball plant and eventually distribution as director of manufacturing for Hogan. Now both the wood plant manager and iron plant manager reported to Steve. To form the head of the clubs, the Hogan forged clubs utilized a raw forging from the Cornell Forge Company out of Chicago. *The raw forgings come* in as a cylindrical rod which is then heated and then struck by a large forging hammer in multiple stages that helps form the initial rough shape of the head. The edges are then trimmed, and the head is struck again and again until the head is more precisely defined. After it reaches this stage, the score lines and any numbers or artwork can be stamped into the head. At this point, the craftsmanship begins to focus on the hosel. The hosel is the hollow cylindrical portion where the shaft of the club connects to the clubhead. The hosel cylinder is now spin welded onto the head in a very precise manner to make sure the correct lofts and lies are of exact nature. Now the heads have the form, the iron number and Ben Hogan stamps, the score lines and hosel that you would see on a finished club. The head is then polished and plated to protect the raw metal from rusting.

By 1970, under the ownership of AMF, Hogan had the number one iron on tour as well as the number one ball being used on tour. The Apex golf ball was also number one on the tour in the early seventies and was the number one ball on the PGA tour. At that time, Hogan was producing about 750,000 dozen golf balls per year. Wilson still maintained a strong presence as well with the Wilson Staff ball. Wilson was doing three million dozen compared with Spaulding's twenty-eight million dozen with their Top Flite ball. These days, technology has taken over, and golf balls consist of a solid core with an injection mold and cover with zero human hands were utilized. Back then, human contact was imperative.

When I arrived in 1984, the Hogan Company was known throughout the industry for the quality irons they made and the other products such as woods, golf balls, clothing, and accessories complemented the leading club maker position. Hogan never wanted to be the biggest manufacturer but rather the best club ball company in the marketplace. Hogan, after all, stood for quality first and foremost. Growth in the ball industry would come slowly for us. The Hogan ball plant made our golf balls in a three-piece manufacturing process. The center of the golf ball in those days differed depending on the ball. Golf balls generally were either a Surlyn or Balata type. The Surlyn ball began with a small half-inch diameter solid rubber core. The Balata ball, in contrast, started with a frozen half-inch ice ball which required a temperature of thirty below zero coupled with a steady supply of dry ice in order to keep the core frozen during the entire ball-making process. Next, the new cores would enter the winding department, where banks of three to four operators run machines tightly wrapping each core to a USGA rule minimum of 1.680 inches in diameter, which was the smallest you can be legally. There was no maximum size for cores, but larger cores meant shorter flying distance.

At Hogan, we always pushed the limits of the size of the ball's core without going below. We always wanted to be as close to a 1.680-inch diameter as possible so as to not fail inspection. In the audits, inspectors utilized a ring gauge to measure. The reason to keep the core at or near the minimum was to limit the potential variances in molds, heat cools, covered thickness, and moldings. Golf balls had to be consistent in their performance if they hoped for tenure on the course.

The two largest problems within the winding department were working with dry ice, which required the workers to tape their fingertips to protect against the extreme cold of the dry ice required for the frozen core of the Balata ball. The other difficulty was tying off the rubber band after it was wound around the core. The initial tie to the core was painstakingly done by hand, then the machines would tightly wrap the desired length of rubber around the core. Finally, the wound ball needed to be tied off by hand so the rubber would not come unwound. In the case of the Balata ball, the center had to remain frozen solid to ensure the core did not soften and cause a deformed ball, thus the dry ice. The Surlyn ball core was made of rubber similar to a jack's ball and required no dry ice. After the winding process came the half shells, which gave the ball its golf ball look. The bottom half shells were laid into a compression mold where the tied-off wound rubber cores were placed on top. Then the top half shells were laid on, and a compression machine, which was heated, pressed the two halves together in a cycle. The heat would imprint the customary dimples and bond the two shells together over the core. The compression of the two halves left a seam that required a buffing machine with a gritted belt. The Balata ball and its frozen core had to be refrozen prior to buffing so as not to melt during the buffing process. The Surlyn ball required just a quick buff to remove the seam. Nearly all the tools throughout the Hogan manufacturing process we had to build, making them specific to their respective operators.

We were still working on the prototype balls for Hogan. We would produce the new balls in the factory, and then the research and development engineer would take the balls to the test site. There he tested flight and performance before it could be released to manufacturing. In addition, the R&D department would hand out samples to the various department heads to perform their own testing to report back to the R&D department. My office moved to the back of the plant seemed to develop the chemistry I felt was needed. Being close to the manufacturing operation and the people separate from the executive wing brought a level of camaraderie I had not thought possible. Additionally, I was not called to Mr. Hogan's office once in the last five months. I was also able to forge a relationship with the product manager in club, ball, and sportswear that allowed a much better working relationship with marketing and sales. The monthly department head staff meetings were much more productive and kept everyone in the loop.

The Hogan club plant, in contrast, came along with its own specialized processes. The swing weight of the club was consistently our biggest concern. Golf clubs by design are designated either a D-1, D-2, or D-3 in accordance with the club's swing weight and balance point. Every 1.7 grams or the equivalent of the weight of two $1 bills equals a swing weight point and the difference between D-1 and D-2 clubs. The majority of golfers have been told through marketing efforts that the D-2 club is the best and thus the more preferred designation, but very few can tell the difference. The weight difference of 1 swing weight change is 1.7 grams. So the average player could not tell if they were swinging a D1 or D3. The weight difference would be 3.4 grams. Mr. Hogan was one of the few that could, though.

The three iron is the lightest club in the standard set. As the club number increases, the head becomes incrementally heavier. With each increase in number, seven grams increase in clubhead weight. As the club selection increases, a half-inch reduction in club length also takes place. A three-iron head weighs roughly 240 grams; thus, the four-iron head will weigh 247 grams and be a half-inch shorter club length. The club shafts tended to float with their respective balance point. At Hogan, we used the Apex shaft, which allowed for different pour models and different flexes. Hogan carried twenty-seven different shafts.

Once I understood the operational processes at Hogan, I made a few moves to put the best people in the best positions for success. I moved the golf ball plant manager over to head up Hogan iron production and narrowed the focus for the current club manufacturing manager to specifically handle the Hogan woods, as both needed separate attention. This turned out to be one of my best moves to start the year, putting an experienced manager heading up the vital processes in both plants. The club plant embraced the introduction of the Magnum woods, Magnum cavity back iron and the Magnum two-piece golf ball, and production was moving along with minimal problems. As we moved into spring, things were running increasingly smoothly in both operations. The product samples that were being produced in both woods and irons were meeting the approval of the department bosses. The ball process, though, was another matter.

My relationships with product managers around the company strengthened, which increased my knowledge of the inner workings of the company. Little did I know how important these relationships would mean in the years to come. As we approached the summer of 1985, rumors started to fly that our corporate parent company, AMF, was being raided by T. Boone Pickens and Irwin Jacobs from Minneapolis-based Minstar. We were preparing for the important summer sales meeting to introduce the Magnum woods and irons and the Magnum two-piece ball, along with the hopeful new golf balls to our sales force. This was a big deal, as marketing was continually crying for a two-piece ball and a cavity back club to compete with popular Ping clubs. All Hogan products were being made on time with very few problems in delivery, so everyone was feeling confident that the Hogan company would gain back the market share we were now losing to Ping.

At the national sales meeting in Fort Worth, the salesmen would play in a golf tournament at River Crest Country Club, one of the most exclusive country clubs in town. Samples of the two-piece Magnum ball were given to each salesman to play the first two-piece construction ball that the Ben Hogan Company ever made. So they would play with the balls, and they would see the clubs at the sales meeting that would be introduced in the fall.

The Magnum ball was an absolute smash hit. Everyone was elated at how well the ball performed. It could not have gone better with this introduction. The sales for the year were improving even as sales dropped on our staple Apex player blade. Sales of the newly introduced Radial model, which was Hogan's first attempt at a player's assist club, helped offset the Apex iron drop.

Minstar was only interested in AMF to buy the yacht company Hatteras. When AMF would not sell the company to Minstar, they raided AMF, and that is how they came to own Hogan. They never intended to keep any of the AMF companies other than Hatteras. As the news of the Minstar sale started to spread, the Hogan president decided to get a group of the VPs together to see if we could put together an offer that would compete with Minstar. Rumors came back that Mr. Jacobs only wanted was the Hatteras yacht manufacturing part of the deal. The Hogan component was of no interest to him. The department heads and I made a presentation to some local equity managers to come up with an offer that we could take to Minstar to buy the Hogan company from Irwin Jacobs after he completed the sale with AMF. We all knew all he wanted was Hatteras yacht, so Hogan might be available to us for the right price. We were instructed not to mention this to the other heads of finance, sportswear, and human resources.

After a couple of meetings with the financial people, it became very apparent why I was included in the deal. In order to get the financing needed, we would have to double the profitability of the company at the present sales level to support the debt. The hard goods manufacturing margins were in the middle 60 percent profitability, and the ball, sportswear, and accessories were in the low 30 percent profitability. So it became quite obvious, the best and quickest method to increase profitability to get the financing done was slashing manufacturing costs of material and labor. The financial people looked at our presentation and started cutting costs to put together a budget they could support in order to finance the deal. The biggest cuts were made to the inventory levels we had in manufacturing to support our schedule. We left the meeting and headed back to the plant with this new charge. All eyes were on me to see if I had any way of guaranteeing I could make these changes and still provide the products for delivery. After much discussion, I was unable to provide a guarantee that I could run manufacturing with those cuts and still provide the support necessary to meet the sales objectives and profit goals that they demanded.

In 1984, the Hogan Company only made about 2 percent profit on sales of about $50 million. Profit for 1985 looked better on paper if we met our sales goal and the Magnum ball and club were the success that was projected. The profit projected for 1985 was about 4 percent where the finance people were looking for double digits. As much as I tried, I was not in a position to provide the cost cutting necessary to secure the financing we would need to approach Minstar. So the effort to secure the financing stopped, and we all went back to work like nothing had ever happened. Amazingly, this subject was never discussed again, and the department heads that were not included never found out about this effort by the president. As the year progressed, more and more rumors started to be spread about the eminent sale of the Hogan Company. Nearly every day, someone would come into my office and want to discuss the sale of the company. This seemed to go on forever; it was hard to get through a day without having several conversations about the sale.

Then out of the blue, one day, in the middle of the summer, our marketing and sales departments started to get calls that our Magnum golf ball was falling out of the sky. Most of our salesmen got their product samples and distributed them to potential clients. When these clients began hitting the balls, a large percentage of them would drop like a big bird that had just been shot. Emergency meetings were called to determine what was wrong. The initial testing of the samples was outstanding. Thankfully, I had my engineer in place, so we met with R&D, quality control, manufacturing, and manufacturing engineering to go investigate the problem and fix it. R&D quickly blamed the manufacturing of the ball as they did not have the process set up correctly, so that is where the investigation started. I sent the process engineer to R&D to get the correct specifications. He was to check to see if the manufacturing operation was following the recommended process. We stopped production and inspected the entire process. We then took a recent batch of the new Magnum balls to the test facility to see how they would perform off the hitting machine. We knew each batch we tested went through the current manufacturing process to specification. The test proved we had a problem as the failure rate or performance problem of falling out of the sky was observed on about 70 percent of the samples. This shocked everyone who bore witness.

During the further investigation, we discovered that the R&D engineer had cherry-picked through the balls so as to get the best ones which were given to the salesmen during the golf tournament. Of these, 50 to 70 percent of those balls performed badly. After many further tests, we learned that the core was moving around during the manufacturing process, causing the cover to be irregular or too thin on one side and too thick on the other. We now had the problem identified, which unfortunately turned into an all-out battle between the R&D team and my manufacturing team. Everyone was sure the other side was to blame. Once the data was collected and evaluated, it supported a failure in the design that was turned over to manufacturing to unknowingly produce an inferior product. We also skipped the new products meeting for the Magnum ball, as was customary in the club department, which fell on the feet of R&D. No ball design should ever reach the manufacturing process without R&D first approving it, so as to eliminate what we were now going through. This blunder allowed us to become equal partners with R&D in regard to the development and introduction of new golf balls. The VP of R&D had become a friend of mine, but this battle had strained our relationship. He also headed up quality control, which would initiate many battles for us in the future. The good news was we had answered the ball problem and were taking the right steps to correct the design flaw.

As we were solving the internal struggles within Hogan, we were carefully being scrutinized by Minstar. I had no connections to our parent, AMF, so I had to do my own research on Minstar. The first thing that popped up was that the owner of Minstar, Irvin Jacobs, had earned the fitting nickname of Irv the Liquidator. That certainly did not give me or any of us a warm feeling about our suitors. I also learned that Minneapolis financier Jacobs became wealthy by taking stakes in Fortune 500 conglomerates to unlock value by breaking them up. There was little history of Jacobs operating companies for profit. My research found that Jacobs started at the age of thirty-three, purchasing the Grain Belt Brewery in 1975 for $4.1 million with his company IJ Enterprises. He worked at that for eight months, trying to turn around the company, which was losing around $200,000 per month. He then liquidated the company, selling the brand to G. Heileman Brewing Company, and profited $4 million. He later sold the property that accompanied the brewery to the city of Minneapolis in 1989 for $4.85 million.

He made money not operating a company but rather by breaking it up and selling off the pieces. Jacobs's next big success was buying the W. T. Grant consumer accounts receivable after they filed for bankruptcy. He sold off the parts of the company, earning him a healthy profit and supreme investor status. History would show deals Jacobs made with Kaiser Steel, Walt Disney Productions and Avco, Pabst Brewing of Milwaukee, and Castle and Cook. He also bought Larson Boats in Little Falls, Minnesota, out of bankruptcy in late 1977 and nursed it back to profitability. So his background, while significant, spelled caution in regard to the Ben Hogan Company. AMF nor the Ben Hogan Company were nowhere near bankruptcy and had been profitable for many years.

A few months later, we received the memo informing us that Minstar did, in fact, acquire AMF and thus was now the owner of the Hogan Company. We were scheduled to meet representatives from Minstar as they would come to kick the tires of the new company. Walt Mahanes, Minstar's vice president of operations, came to visit with us and explain their plan for the rest of 1985. They started to meet with the president and the VP of finance to understand the financials and what to expect the performance for the year to be. Behind the scenes, they were interviewing all the department heads to get a clearer picture of the Hogan Company. People inside of the Hogan Company began speculating on who would be terminated and who would survive the reorganization that was coming. Much emphasis was over if our president would be terminated and replaced by the VP of sales and marketing. As the interviews took place, the big question was always the last question. What do you think of the president and the job he is doing? I had a little experience with this type of situation at Wilson and Walter Hagen when they replaced plant managers. That experience taught me you are always loyal until the leader is no longer the leader. For you to assist in his demise would never be in your best interest. So I was ready when the question was asked, "So what do you think of the president and the job he is doing?"

My answer was "It is not for me to evaluate, but rather it is your job to determine what kind of job he is doing."

The interviewer rebutted, "But don't you want to be president?"

My answer was "Yes, someday down the road but not by stabbing my boss in the back."

With the interviews over, the Minstar representatives returned to Minnesota. But that did not stop the speculation and with people taking sides on who to support when the shake-up came. The VP of sportswear thought he had the ear of Irwin Jacobs, claiming he was talking with him every week and letting him know what the problems were and how to fix them. Outside of these conversations, we had a business to run, products to produce, and sales to make. The yearly schedule and deliveries were no longer a problem. The Radial clubs, Magnum clubs, along with the Magnum ball, were all being shipped on time, maintaining the quality that was expected of the Hogan Company. However, sales of our Apex irons were slipping as the market was moving away from forged irons that were intended for the really good golfers to cast cavity back irons that were intended for use by the broader golf market as they were more forgiving clubs. Player's blade was slipping, and the new Magnum and Radial sales were not enough to offset the loss. A larger percentage of our sales were coming from accessories like balls, sportswear, golf bags, gloves, etc. While this increase in accessories sales can be seen as a positive, the 30 percent gross margin of these products was less than half of the nearly 65 percent gross margins that the Apex irons earned. So even though we were making our overall sales goal, we were not making the profit that was forecasted, and there was fear that we would miss our number again, putting us in the red. As this information was communicated to Minstar, the heat was turned up in regard to how we fixed this and who was to blame.

The intensity was increasing between the department heads as everyone was on edge and did not want to be viewed as the problem. Early fall brought another crisis to manufacturing between quality control and manufacturing. After completing the manufacturing of two hundred Magnum woods, the clubs were submitted for inspection. These clubs were on the shelves of a truck to be delivered to our warehouse facility on Montgomery Street. The last step before the club's head to the warehouse, as well as the first step when the clubs enter the warehouse, is a quality control audit. The call came in from the warehouse supervisor, so I got in my car and headed over to the warehouse. When I arrived, the supervisor took me to the back of the warehouse to show me the clubs that were rejected. I started to inspect the clubs and could not find anything wrong with the clubs. I telephoned the VP of finance to come over to see the clubs, as a big fight was brewing and our monthly staff meeting later that day. The VP of finance found no problems either with the inbound clubs. When I told him that these clubs had been rejected by quality control, he was as perplexed as me. We weren't sure how to fix something that didn't need fixing. I was keenly aware that the VP of R&D had recently reported to our VP of marketing about the quality problems that they were having with Magnum woods. Neither one of these VPs knew I had inspected the clubs and was well aware of the rejection. So I decided to take about five of the rejected clubs with me to the staff meeting that afternoon as evidence.

I arrived back at the plant with my evidence and walked to the back of the plant to find the inspector that approved the release of the clubs in the first place. I asked her to inspect the clubs and let me know if anything needed to be repaired. It did not take her long to fully approve the quality of these clubs. I was as prepared as I could be for the staff meeting that afternoon when the quality issue was brought up. I knew the department heads would raise the quality issue without checking to see for themselves what the problem was. Just as I expected, the VP of R&D covered a few regular items about testing of the golf balls, along with his report that manufacturing and R&D have settled on a process to produce a substantially larger percentage of pro-grade balls through a new molding process to increase the yield. Then the mood turned sour. The issue with the Magnum woods arrived. The R&D VP stated the quality problem, which resulted in the VP of marketing and our company president turning their attention to me. As all the focus in the room turned to me. I was ready and waiting. I asked if anybody had inspected the clubs to see what the stated problem was and what, if any, repair was needed. I knew the only people in the room that had seen the clubs were the VP of finance and myself. The VP of marketing and R&D both responded in an expected negative fashion. They did not need to look at the clubs as it was my job to ensure the quality standards set for the Hogan Company. I let the discussion go on for a while.

The president then spoke up and stated that I needed to get on this and make sure it never happens again.

I snapped back, telling them, "It's hard to repair something when no one tells you what is wrong with the product." It was time to produce the five clubs I had with me for the room to inspect. The clubs were passed around for everyone to inspect. I again asked for guidance as to determining the problem that needs to be fixed. The head of R&D began accusing manufacturing of making garbage. I stopped him mid-sentence and presented my findings, showing the quality audit rejecting clubs that had just previously passed with flying colors. I presented the clubs as evidence with their most recent quality inspection. I turned to the president and the VP of R&D and asked them both what I should fix. At this point, the friction in the room was palpable. I did let them know whatever he needed from me to help with the situation, I would help, but I made the case that quality control was most assuredly the problem. The meeting finally ended, and all went back to work. The VP of R&D and I stayed behind to speak privately, where I let him know that the inspectors were playing games with each other, creating fictitious problems creating dissension among the executive staff. I shared with him about my morning tours of the plant and how I had become close with the hourly workers. This relationship created awareness of the deceit the quality control staff and the manufacturing staff would engage in, resulting in a bevy of internal problems.

Hogan's product lines at that time included irons, woods, golf balls, golf bags, golf gloves, umbrellas, and a variety of sportswear. Minstar's new oversight of the Hogan Company created a lot of friction between the marketing, sales, and sportswear, and as everybody knew, there would be some changes. The fear within the organization was at a peak level. One of the first things the Minstar people did was meet with the president and review his organization. Minstar was very critical about all the VPs as sales were below the $50 million at that time. Hogan had a VP of sales and marketing, VP of research and development, VP of manufacturing, VP of sportswear, VP of quality control, VP of warehousing, VP of embroidery, VP of finance, and VP of human resources. It was very clear that somebody had to go. The Hogan president seemed to be steering the chopping block. Minstar was asking questions, and the president's answers would guide the cutbacks. After a couple of meetings with Minstar, the president held a staff meeting to determine where cuts could be made to improve the profitability of the company. This really did not go very well as no one was going to volunteer cuts to their departments. So this exercise produced few results. The local press was writing articles, including things such as Mr. Irwin Jacobs stating, "We have no plans to sell Hogan or any other properties remaining from the AMF deal. Minstar is slightly more focused, following the AMF buyout than we were previously. We are more solidly a consumer products company now."

Reading this gave the nervous Hogan management some comfort that perhaps there would not be any major changes if we kept our heads down and just did our jobs. The articles made the sale sound like an amicable business deal, but in reality, it had been a very nasty corporate raid. AMF had fought Minstar to the bitter end. Jacobs decided, possibly as a strategy, that holdover AMF managers were milking the operating division's profits to support a high-end lifestyle, and thus he took his case to the stockholders. He stated what AMF spent redecorating their corporate headquarters was enough to have built a few more factories. This was just ridiculous as none of the former AMF operating plants required any more space, and the capital budgets that were provided allowed us to expand whatever operations we needed. The stockholders, though, took it to hook, line, and sinker. Minstar was created to be a holding company over its companies and did not have the operational expertise to manage them, especially the Hogan Company. Minstar sent their general manager along with staff members to manage our Hogan situation. We were made to justify our respective budgets and staffing to the new owners. We had to explain how and why we did things as well as justify each position within our organization. They would grill each vice president of their respective departments why they needed each position and then ask them what they felt about the other vice presidents and their performance. This created a tremendous amount of stress within the executive ranks, putting everyone in survival mode for the cuts that were on their way. Each vice president evaluated their operation and recommended any changes they thought would improve their operation.

Hogan had several corporate trainees that would spend time in each division and eventually become the future executive pool for the corporation to use to fill future vacancies. They were all working in marketing and sales at the Hogan Company. Minstar did not have any of those positions anywhere in their corporation and did not have a need for them because Minstar was not interested in operating the company. They were getting it ready to sell to someone else. This was all speculation at the time, but the reality would eventually be realized. Some of the managers had come to that conclusion, and some did not. After the reorganization, the trainees each filled a full-time marketing position within the company. Dick Lyon would be promoted to director of marketing for clubs, balls, and accessories. Peter Cobb would be promoted to international marketing manager, and Bill Zietz was promoted to marketing director for sportswear and reported directly to me. The biggest concern we all had was how the president would react to this new direction. In the staff meetings, it became apparent to some he was fighting this new approach, and this new management team was not like AMF, and we needed to change or perish. The Minstar team began sending directives and subsequently what would happen should we refuse to comply.

After the staff meetings were over, we met with the president one-on-one to discuss what changes we would recommend for our operation. He would ask us about the changes he was going to recommend for the other operation to get our feedback. I had only been at Hogan for about eight months, so I did not have a lot of skeletons in the closet that I needed to reveal. The closing of the grip operation and the restructuring of the manufacturing operation had been completed just prior to the Minstar takeover, which created cost reduction efficiencies and increased the gross margins of both balls and clubs, which were now being realized. So as I reviewed these items with the president, we both agreed, manufacturing should keep doing what we are doing. He then asked about the position of VP of sportswear. If that position was eliminated, could I assume the management of the warehouse without the addition of any more people? The first cut was the VP of sportswear as that department's low margins coupled with product delivery problems made them an easy decision. In addition, the president discussed some changes he was thinking about by splitting the sales and marketing positions into two positions, essentially reorganizing the managers to reduce the overall cost and create a balance of power in the company between sales and marketing. These seemed to be reasonable adjustments that could streamline the organization and reduce cost, which I was sure Minstar would approve. Several more Minstar visits were conducted, and it appeared they were keying in on these changes in sales, marketing, and sportswear with some minor moves in the other departments.

Those moves were finally made in the third quarter of 1985, and Minstar stopped sending people in to interview Hogan staff. The task at hand now was to deliver the results that were budgeted to the new owner. This started to become a real problem as the sales for the year were dropping below forecast, and the cuts implemented by Minstar were not making enough of an impact on our numbers. Nearly all the top executives were quietly out, looking for their next opportunity as they saw the writing on the wall. Everybody, though, was still working hard to find cuts that could be made to at least show a breakeven by year's end to make up for the loss of sales. We were all sure expenditure for travel, golf tournaments, and country club memberships were going to cause a major problem if we came in with a loss. In many of my conversations with the president, I would remind him that these guys were not fooling around, and should you not make the appropriate cuts, they may just cut you. That seemed to fall on deaf ears because those hard cuts were never made. It did not help the company's morale. It was very disappointing to accomplish all the manufacturing goals and significantly reduce costs with the knowledge bonuses had been cut. I started in July of 1984. In January of 1985, no bonuses were awarded at the division level, and now this would make two years in a row since I started that no bonuses were awarded at the division level.

December rolled around, and the GM from Minstar was coming down to Fort Worth for a year-end meeting and talking about a prospective bonus program that Minstar would be using going forward. In addition, they would review the projected year-end finish to determine if Hogan Company would show a profit. The dinner with the Minstar brass was held at Mac House, an exclusive Fort Worth restaurant, which was a regular locale for entertaining out-of-town guests. The dinner was fantastic, with everyone on their best behavior, but the cocktails wore down the group's inhibitions. When the restaurant was closing, the GM of Minstar offered all of us down to the downtown Worthington Hotel for a nightcap. He could sense some of us had a few things on our minds, and this would be a good time to hear them. It wasn't long for the gloves to come off. Our Hogan president, who was in attendance, became the source of everyone's complaints. His failure to address most of the internal problems left most with plenty to say. Several VPs believed we should not have spent so much effort on sportswear with its 25 percent to 30 percent gross profit margin (compared to the 65 percent gross profit margin on the irons).

Additionally, the vice presidents suggested to the GM that the money being spent on sales meetings and marketing was excessive when we were losing money and bonuses were affected. The evening was trending poorly when suddenly, a shouting match broke out between a couple of the VPs. The alcohol and the tempers tipped the scales as the verbal fisticuffs ensued. As the tempers finally wore out, the night came to an end. Everyone was exhausted and ready to go home. The president was visibly inebriated and clearly upset but refused any and all attempts from us to drive him home. I crawled into bed at three o'clock in the morning, knowing I had to be up at 6:30 a.m. to go to work to finish the year. To make matters worse, tonight, I had my staff Christmas party at Ridglea Country Club. The next morning, I made it to work on sheer willpower. The hangover I suffered from made all movements painful. Luckily, many of the personnel at Hogan were on vacation, so the plant was slow-moving. I struggled mightily to stay alert, knowing this would be a long and grueling day.

About nine that morning, my phone rang from the general manager of Minstar to ask if I would come to the Worthington Hotel and have breakfast with him. I took a deep breath and answered, "I will see you in about thirty minutes." Panic quickly set in. What could this be about? I had refrained from any of the arguments last night with any of the staff or the president. I had no idea what this could be about; then I remembered the last time I was invited to a hotel to meet a company official, and it resulted in me getting fired. A thousand things were running through my mind.

Should I call my attorney to make sure I was prepared to respond to the termination, which I was not prepared for the last time? Who else could I call to see if they had been invited to the hotel? I called each of the VPs that were at last night's meeting, and no one answered their phones. I walked in totally unprepared for whatever my fate was. As I pulled into the entrance, the attendant took my car, and I entered the building and went upstairs, where breakfast was being served. The room was very crowded, and I had to scout the room for a minute before I saw the GM, and to my surprise, the VP of sales, who had just been promoted when they reorganized the marketing and sales VP responsibilities. Having a friendly face at the meeting calmed me down a little. If they were going to fire me, they would have a representative from Minstar or human resources present at the meeting. My mind was still racing, trying to remember if I said something terrible that now I don't remember saying. Did my consumption cause me some personal or company embarrassment?

There was nothing I could do about that now. I eased into my seat, exchanged some pleasantries, scanned the menu, and then ordered some breakfast. We made some small talk for a bit as I waited for the bad news. Then the GM's mood got serious, and he looked at me and dropped the bomb. "Jerry, we have decided to terminate the president and would like to offer you the job."

My jaw hit the floor. I froze for a moment, not knowing what to say. Finally, I muttered, "Of course! I will accept the job."

He then said, "We will work out the details later, but I do not want you to tell anybody because the president has not yet been terminated. That will happen this morning. We have someone at the plant, and they will call me when he arrives. I will then head in to inform him and then make the company announcement. Here is what I would like you to do. We have seen next year's budget proposal, and it is not acceptable to Minstar. It needs to show more profit. I will be back in town in the middle of January, and I would like you, between now and then, to look at the budget that was presented and accept it or change the numbers that budget will be the goals for golf. All I have heard from all the interviews is the reason for this company's poor performance is the president. He was the problem. So if he was gone, so was the problem."

The only people that knew what I now did were the new VP of sales, the GM of Minstar, and me. The breakfast was adjourned. I thanked the man for his trust in me, and I went back to work. My mind was racing a mile a minute. I am now president, and I am not really sure about the job I accepted. We did not talk about compensation or any other details at the breakfast meeting. I had absolutely no experience with marketing or sales. The only operations I have ever managed are manufacturing plants. My tenure with the Hogan Company was a mere eighteen months, and in that time, I saw Mr. Hogan just four times, and two of those times resulted in me getting chewed out for the bad quality the plant was producing.

My mind turned to Mr. Hogan. Who could I talk with to find out what Mr. Hogan's relationship was with the past president and staff? What, if any, was Mr. Hogan's involvement with the operation? I got back to my office on Pafford Street and shut the door. There I sat down and waited for the announcement to be made. I busied myself, trying to figure out what my first steps should be to accomplish this turnaround. Once the present staff was informed, I would have to meet with them as a group and then individually to determine what other changes I would have to make. The executives that I was concerned about were the VP of marketing and the VP of R&D. They had not been easy to work with, but now I found myself as their boss. The day was December 20, 1985, a Friday, and my world had just been thrust into the spotlight. I had so much to do and say, but that night, I still needed to host a Christmas party for my staff. They would surely have questions, and I would have to confirm my promotion at that time. I also decided that once the announcement was made, I would ask my staff to meet the following Saturday morning to review the budget and update them on what is expected of us by Minstar for the upcoming year. I felt overwhelmed with the new responsibility and very uncomfortable with my lack of knowledge of marketing and sales. No one was going to step forward and train me in these two functions, and Minstar was only interested in one thing, profitability, so they could sell it off. I knew manufacturing backward and forward, but I needed to find a way to become comfortable with marketing and sales while I turned the company around and delivered a profit for Minstar, or I would be gone.

As the workday was reaching a closure, a few people started to come into my office to congratulate me on the promotion, including the VPs of marketing and R&D. These would be my two biggest concerns going forward. Could I trust them, and could they accept me as their new boss? The Saturday morning meeting would shed some light on their mindset. I was getting ready to go home and get ready for the manufacturing Christmas party when I remembered I had not called my wife to tell her the news. She remained quite upset with me for coming home at three o'clock in the morning after a long night of drinking. In addition, her parents were at our house to celebrate the Christmas holiday. I arrived home with very little time to change for the party and drop my big news on my wife. The manufacturing party was a big success, and everyone felt that manufacturing would be treated a little better now because I was the new president. This dinner would not last as long as the executive staff dinner and with far less alcohol consumption.

On the way home, I finally had a real discussion with my wife about the new job and how unprepared to handle this new experience I was. I could not believe they had offered me the job. What could they have been thinking? After a long discussion, the decision must have been due to controlling costs which I was in a better position to do than any other executive. My wife and I agreed that I had to rely on my strengths of working with people and being able to define problems and their respective causes. By the time we arrived home, she was feeling much better about the night before, and she was able to celebrate my promotion. How incredible to think, I was very close to leaving the company and returning to my old job at Keeler Brass, not that long ago. I recognized this promotion as a once-in-a-lifetime opportunity. I honestly could not look in the mirror and tell myself I really earned this promotion. It felt more like being in the right place at the right time, and I was comfortable with that assessment. In order for me to succeed, I would rely on my strengths of problem-solving that worked so well in my manufacturing career.

There was no one working in the plant Saturday morning, other than some maintenance people and a few guards. We seemed to have the place to ourselves. I was not expecting very much from the meeting other than presenting my staff the goals that Minstar had laid out for us. I started the meeting with the comments that the GM had made to me and the VP of sales at the Worthington Hotel during yesterday's breakfast meeting. Minstar is not happy with the Hogan profit for the year, and they all suggested during the interviews that the main problem was the president, so he was eliminated. Minstar wanted me to revisit the budget for any improvements, and the GM would be back in two weeks to review. There was silence in the room. I had been on the job for forty-eight hours and wasn't prepared to take any action at this time. I decided to give the staff the following week to review their budgets, and I would meet individually with each department head to prepare the new budget we would present to Minstar. I decided I would give them some direction on what I was looking for in this review. We looked at the most profitable year we had at Hogan and used that as the benchmark to establish each department's budget. The manufacturing departments were all based on the direct cost to produce the product. All other departments were considered indirect costs not directly associated with production. So whatever those changes in percent happened to be, they had to justify any increases and why support was needed. This also gave me a framework to build my understanding in regard to all the elements of the sales and marketing budgets. The Minstar GM called to share that he had notified the president of his termination as well as shared the news with Mr. Hogan.

The first thing I did Monday morning was met with the president's executive secretary, Fannie Meyers. I asked her if she would have a problem with staying on as my executive secretary, and she said that would be fine. I also asked her if she would have a problem moving to a new office away from Mr. Hogan's office in the manufacturing conference room next to the VP of finance. She again responded that it would be fine. She had been with the Hogan Company for many years and served many presidents, so she knew the drill. Nobody else knew as much of the history of the company, nor did anyone protect Mr. Hogan from the outside world as she did. My next move was to meet with the outgoing president. I was not comfortable with this meeting at all. I had worked for him for eighteen months with a very good relationship, but I was sure he was not going to be happy I was the one that got his job. To my surprise, he was very calm, as he had been through this before. He asked me if he could have an office to work out of as he conducted his search for a new job. I did not see that as a problem but asked him to move out of his office and over to the Montgomery Street plant, a long way away from the basic operations and Mr. Hogan's office. After the meeting with the president, I asked my new executive secretary to set up a meeting with Mr. Hogan. I needed to meet with him before his daily arrival of friends began.

Later that day, the time came to speak with Mr. Hogan. I had spent a lot of time thinking about our few meetings and what I would say to the man now that I was in charge of the company he had founded. This meeting would be crucial in establishing the relationship I would have with him for the foreseeable future. I needed for this relationship to blossom as I felt he would somehow be the main character in the turnaround of the company and restoring it back to profitability. The meeting, for maximum effect, had to be brief and to the point. I needed him to keep an open mind to my ideas in order for us to move forward on the steps that I would take to accomplish this turnaround.

Fannie finally alerted me to Mr. Hogan's availability, and it was go time. I walked in at my scheduled time and said hello and let him know I was the new president as of last Friday. I informed him what Minstar told me about profitability and how that needed to change. Lastly, I asked Mr. Hogan if he would have a problem if I met with him every morning before his day got started to brief him on our progress, answer any questions or suggestions he might have. The room fell silent, and I wanted to jump in and say something else, but Mr. Hogan had not responded to my question as yet. I waited patiently for his answer, not sure what else to do. He finally replied, simply, "Okay." That one word ended our successful meeting, and I went on my way back to my office. I was now to hold daily meetings with the greatest golfer ever to play the game.

As the day neared its conclusion, the VP of R&D asked to speak with me. As he walked into my office, I could see he was very nervous. We had some very heated battles recently over club issues and the Magnum ball introduction, which gave him concern about any bad feelings that might be between us. He just so happened to be the friend from Wilson Sporting Goods and one of the main reasons I ended up at Hogan. He got those concerns off his chest and asked me if I had a problem with him as VP of research and development. I stood and walked to the blackboard and erased everything that was on the board.

I then sat back down and said, "You and I are now starting from scratch, so whatever happens from now on will be what our relationship will be based on. One of the most important things I need from you is trust. I need to know I can trust you and to always be honest and tell me the truth. Together, we will deal with whatever that is to turn around this company. If you can live with that, we can start fresh today."

He was very relieved and even smiled. We shook hands, and he left my office.

The next concern I had about my staff was the VP of marketing. You will remember he was the one that was supposed to replace the president with the AMF succession plan. There were some rumors that the VP was looking for a new job after his responsibilities were cut in half with the separation of sales from the marketing function. No one knew for sure, and I was not very close with him to have any idea what he would want to do.

I needed to meet with the VP of marketing after Christmas to ascertain what he was thinking about his new role. The majority of my time was spent reviewing budgets in preparation for the upcoming meetings to improve the profitability of our forecast. I also used this time to set up my new office in front of the manufacturing plant, still a good distance from Mr. Hogan's office as well as the old president's office. The new office would still allow me to tour the manufacturing plant every morning before I started my day. In addition, I would set up tours of the Montgomery Street operation to get familiar with how the customer service and embroidery functioned at least twice a week to get familiar with those operations. This would also give me a chance to visit with the employees at this plant like I did at the Pafford Street operations, where I became very comfortable with the employees there and the operations. I was very excited to begin the daily meetings with Mr. Hogan.

The meeting with the VP of marketing took place the day after Christmas, on a Thursday, and caught me by complete surprise. We sat down and shared a few words between us, but before I could express just how I understood the disappointment he must feel, he cut me off and blurted out, "I am turning in my resignation, as I have accepted the VP of marketing position for Bridgestone Golf operations in Atlanta, Georgia."

I was surprised how quickly he was able to put that together, as he must have been looking after Minstar made their first cuts in September of 1985. These kinds of jobs don't come easily for most, and he had done it in short order. The VP had decided it was only a matter of time before Minstar sold the Hogan Company, and the change would be made for him. I wished him the best, and he parted ways with the Hogan Company. The only management personnel left in marketing now were three young men who were hired by AMF as trainees but with solid educational credentials in marketing. I also knew Minstar was not going to let me go out and hire another VP of marketing at this time. So I had to get the fledgling group together and figure out how we were going to turn the marketing of Hogan products around. I met with each trainee individually and promoted each of them to directors, one for clubs, balls, and accessories, another for sportswear, and the third for international affairs, all reporting to me directly. As the year wound down, my team was in place with the exception of the VP of manufacturing, and I still needed to replace myself. That would take a couple of months to solve.

I ran my new team by the Minstar GM, and he quickly approved them. We had a lot of energy but very little experience. The best part was that everyone got along well and didn't participate in the politics that existed previously. The first problem we addressed was the profitability question. The Minstar GM was due back the second week of January, and I needed to present the new budget to him with an improvement in profitability. With all-new department heads, none of them created the issues that eroded the profitability of the company, but they all now had the responsibility to fix the problem. The budget submitted under the old president showed about a 3.6 percent profit on fifty million in sales. I sat with each department head to look at the historical profitability percentage measured against sales and asked why that percentage has increased and ask what changes you are going to make to get back to that performance. It was important to get to the bottom of these questions so that we could understand what went wrong in the prior year and how we were going to overcome these issues to get the business back in line with expectations.

These meetings took about ten days at roughly ten to twelve hours a day to get everyone to buy in, but we created an initial profitability forecast at 10 percent. No one was going to believe that number, so we had to massage it a bit down to 5 percent. Also, the changes we implemented in manufacturing improved the performance of the group, and that added the additional efficiencies that increased the profitability percentage we needed as a cushion. Now we were going to go from near 5 percent loss to a 5 percent profit in the next twelve months. How believable would that number be and is everyone on board to deliver that performance? I spent a lot of time with the VP of finance, so I knew the numbers like the back of my hand. Minstar would need convincing that we could deliver the plan. The cost reductions that we accomplished with the elimination of the grip plant impacted manufacturing costs substantially, and those cost reductions were not loaded into the new standards for production.

Every time we produced a golf club with a purchased grip, it was at a much lower cost than the standard cost that was in the production and accounting system. These figures would be excluded from the cost until the end of each month, where we adjusted the standard by the number of clubs produced. If we had included the variance into our new budget, the profit would have been calculated to be 10 percent which would bring along some certain scrutiny. My initial visits to Mr. Hogan's office entailed going into detail about the new staff and their background, so he was aware of each department head and their role in turning the company around. I felt it extremely important that he knew all the entire department heads. Hopefully, anytime Mr. Hogan was at a meeting, he would feel comfortable with the marketing directors. As I talked about each department head, I would mention a point about that person that Mr. Hogan would be familiar with, like the director of hard goods that worked with Mr. Hogan on the design of the Radial, Magnum, and Apex irons. Once I felt he was comfortable with the organizational plan, I offered up my background to him. I was waiting for him to say, "Who in the hell do you think you are to be wasting my time with stories about yourself? You're a nobody, and do you know who I am?" Thank God that never happened.

One morning early on, I was updating Mr. Hogan on the company. The topic moved to my background. I was glad I had a chance to discuss this so Mr. Hogan would know from where I came. We, after all, both came from meager beginnings. I was from a poor family on the south side of Chicago, and no one in my family attended college. I believed sports would be my way out of poverty. My dream to play professional baseball would be this way out. My father instilled in me that. If you want something bad enough, go earn it. Mr. Hogan then shared his experience working at Fort Worth's Glen Garden Country Club as a way of earning some money. It was there where he learned how to build and recondition clubs that would open a door for him that led to one of the greatest golfing careers of all time.

On the next daily visit to Mr. Hogan, I informed him of our progress in pulling together a budget that improved profitability at Hogan that was accepted by Minstar. Most times, I would do most of the talking in our meetings. He would not say much except "Okay" or "That's fine." I knew I needed to discuss the Hogan club lines with him. Before I could have a discussion with Mr. Hogan about clubs, I had to find out what his thoughts were about our products and why we were losing market share. Our iron clubs' gross margin was a healthy 65 percent, so replacing that with anything other than another club would be foolish. This promulgated our discussion about the design of a new club. Hogan was always talking about the product lines, the club's leading edge, and the club's top line because he felt that is how one aimed the club. Hogan also felt that a club should look beautiful and elegant, like a piece of jewelry. Ben was adamant that forgings were the best method to use because he believed that the softer metal of a forging versus a casting would provide more feedback to the golfer on how well he was making contact with the ball. Without this feedback, Ben did not see how the player could improve his or her swing mechanics. They gave the golfer the feel no other metal would on the quality of shot that you would be making. The club's loft, lie, and length, as well as the overall weight, is what makes a great golf club.

Coming out of those meetings with Mr. Hogan, I now knew what a great club should look like but with no idea why the clubs Hogan was making were not viewed collectively in that light. In order to increase our sales, we had to find out why our current clubs were not selling better. In our monthly staff meeting, everyone shared their opinions which included reasons such as delivery issues, poor quality, price, lack of efficient advertising, and the need for more pro endorsements. In formulating the plan, we had severe budget constraints on expenditures. How should we respond? Delivery had since improved, quality was being monitored on a daily basis, the price did not seem out of line, advertising dollars were severely limited, and professional endorsement was needed, but that required money. We struggled mightily to define the actual problem, which made fixing it even more troublesome.

Inside, I was still stunned by the promotion and what that would mean for my family. All my background was in manufacturing and quality control. I knew those operations like the back of my hand. I was very comfortable with each part of the manufacturing process required to run a successful business. Marketing and sales, on the other hand, were quite foreign to me. The only experience that I had with that function was at Wilson Sporting Goods when I performed field audits at the pro shops. I sought to measure the quality of the pro-grade clubs Wilson was producing compared to the other products in the marketplace. Many times, I was comparing Wilson's clubs to Hogan's clubs. Other than that small exposure, I was in the dark about the Hogan's marketing strategy and other strategies to increase our market position and sales. I was also quite familiar with the PGA shows, where most manufacturers would come to show their products off to the golf world. I pulled out some old data that I had kept from the marketing activities at Wilson to try to glean some knowledge on the subject. I found an old marketing report from a quality audit done at Wilson. It listed all the major golf competitors of the time—Mizuno, Titleist, Daiwa, Dunlop, MacGregor, Spaulding, ProGroup, Ram, Tommy Armour, Ben Hogan, Taylor Made, Walter Hagen, and a couple of new entries into the market, Cobra and Ping.

The marketing most utilized by the companies was the PGA Tour players' endorsement contracts. Wilson was clearly number one with over sixty-one victories from their sponsored tour players. Some of the greatest names in golf were playing Wilson Staff irons and winning tournaments with the product, and these wins were heavily marketed in their advertising program. The Wilson Staff golf ball stood as a favorite on tour as I started to wonder, with all that going for them, why did they consolidate their two pro plants into one and reduce their manufacturing capacity by 50 percent? I did not realize it at the time, but they must have been losing market share to make that decision. I still kept in contact with some of my friends at Wilson, and the rumors were being confirmed that Wilson again would consolidate the pro plant into the one remaining golf plant that made commercial clubs in Tullahoma, Tennessee. One thing was surely true; their volume had to be shrinking just like we were at the Hogan Company ten years later. The report detailed some specifics about each competitor. Everybody was making a forged player's blade, and everyone was trying to sign a big-name tour player to showcase their product. MacGregor had one of the best names in golf with Jack Nicklaus. A small company in Chicago, Ram Golf, had Tom Watson to showcase their brand. The Lynx Golf Company hired Fred Couples and Ernie Els, both major champions on tour. These were the companies that I would be competing with at the Hogan Company, and they had substantial marketing budgets. This old marketing report did show the market was changing, and some new companies were emerging that might challenge us in the market. The three, in particular, were Cobra, Taylor Made, and Ping. Nearly every company was making players forged blades as tour players continued to influence the golf companies to make products targeted at the better players and sold through the country club pro shops to their members.

Cobra made a splash in the golf world through innovation. They were the first company to offer graphite shafts for both woods and irons. Almost all the other manufacturers used steel shafts from a few select vendors. Cobra was able to sign Greg Norman, one of the greats on tour at the time, which helped them introduce a newly forged blade. The Ben Hogan Company used a forged iron instead of a cast iron because a forged iron is constructed from a single piece of steel. A forged clubhead is more consistent than a cast iron club. It is thought the casting process creates air bubbles in the mold and eventually becomes a part of the finished product. This difference is what a skilled golfer refers to as "feel." A forging does not have these air bubbles; therefore, the product provides a more solid fell back to the golfer at impact. Taylor Made was gaining ground as they were the only company featuring the new metal woods. The Taylor Made company started in 1978 and had but a few senior golf tour players, Ron Streck and Jim Simons, putting the metal drivers into play. Streck was the first player on tour to win with a metal driver, which gave the company supreme momentum to continue. The major companies still resisted, as did the main tour because all pros were playing with wood woods and felt the metal wood was just another gimmick. The third new entrant company was Ping, which to many of the major companies was just a putter company and thus not a threat. Ping would introduce the first game-improvement club, which advertised that the club would perform better for off-center hits versus the player's blade. While this might have been true, the tour players typically rejected anything that could be construed as an improvement to their game other than their own hard work and talent.

This helped to answer some questions about our competition but did not give me any answers why we were losing market share when we had one of the best player's blades in the market, along with our solid tour representation. Some of the other companies might have a more famous tour player, but our quality and numbers were high on the leaderboard. I could fix the manufacturing problems and bring the cost back in line, but I had no idea what plan or strategy we would need to increase sales and gain market share. I wanted to be as prepared as possible when I would meet with my staff to be able to have an intelligent marketing discussion so I could determine if we were going to change our strategy to improve our market share. Minstar was not planning to add any further expertise that would help in the marketing area. It seemed obvious when they promoted me that they were only concerned about cost, not growth, as they were remolding the company so they could flip it for as much money as they could get.

    I was able to call some contacts I had at the National Golf Foundation and have them send me some data about the companies that were on the main floor of the PGA Merchandise show. To my surprise, two names popped up that were not previously considered major competitors to Wilson or Hogan. They were Taylor Made and Ping, the putter company. With the exception of a few players, everyone was doing the same thing. The golf industry was producing player's blades influenced by the PGA Tour players made of forged material with steel staffs and wood woods for everybody, with the exception of Taylor Made, Ping, and Cobra, who were not considered major players at that time. It certainly was easier for a start-up company to venture into a radical new product, whereas it would be quite difficult for an established company to take that step. The market was undergoing change, and rumors were swirling that quite a few of the major companies were in trouble as their sales were continually shrinking. Dunlop, Daiwa, MacGregor, Spaulding, Ram, Tommy Armour, and Wilson were rumored to be having major problems. I was acutely aware of Wilson's problems as they had now closed two of their three golf plants. Would this be the fate waiting for Hogan should we not rectify our situation?

    I reached out to our advertising agency to request some market data about golf club sales, for my review. It hadn't been long since my promotion, and I was not sure whom I could trust to provide me an unbiased look at where the market was headed and how Hogan was aligned with that direction. This type of information could fill in some of the holes I needed to plug. I needed grounds and facts to support any changes in the company's direction that I implemented. The data I procured opened my eyes to what was happening in the marketplace. Sales of forged irons across the board were down 30 percent, and wood sales were down almost 40 percent industry-wide. This supported the sinking sales of so many golf companies. Metal woods sales, on the other hand, were up 22 percent, and game-improvement clubs were up even higher at 33 percent. Was this the reason that Ben Hogan lost money in 1985 because the market was moving away from the types of products we were offering for sale? With this helpful information, I could have a discussion with our marketing folks to determine what corrective action was needed to improve our market share. I concluded, we lacked a metal wood in our line as well as a game improvement club, and our most popular product was the Apex Staff blades. These player's blades were influenced by the tour and by one of the greatest players to ever play the game, Mr. Hogan. The market analysis considered our player's blade the number one choice for a player's forged blade being sold, yet players were saying it was the hardest club to hit. Something had to change here.

Mr. Hogan started his company with the notion to create the best players clubs in 1953. He did not start the company to make game improvement clubs for anybody. Technology and the times had changed, so I had to formulate a plan that took this into account. So I made a list of questions I wanted to get answered from a focus group of customers before any changes would be made to our product line and our marketing approach.

1. Is the Apex blade #1 in the marketplace?
2. Do we need metal wood in our line?
3. Do we need a game improvement club in our line?
4. Do we have the best names in golf representing us for tour credibility?
5. How does our tour staff stack up to our competitors?
6. Are our products priced competitively against our competitors?

7. Can we increase sales without a major product line overhaul?
8. What impact, if any, should Mr. Hogan play in our future?
9. Should we move away from forgings to a cheaper casting product?
10. Do we need more advertising spending to get our message to the public?
11. Should we offer graphite shafts in our product line?
12. Should we open up our sales to off-course specialty shops?

These questions formed the foundation of the discussion with my staff. I also knew that whatever funding we required had to come from the Hogan operation as Minstar was not going to increase any spending as their sole interest was to show a profit. The Hogan belief had been that if players wanted to play better, then they needed to practice more rather than utilize a player improvement club. When I started at Hogan, I was playing with a set of Walter Hagen Ultradyne male hosel golf clubs. My change to Hogan clubs, out of company loyalty, sent my game to hell rapidly. I could not play Hogan's Apex blade. If I hit a shot slightly off-center, the ball would travel about 10 feet from the point I made contact. The Apex blades had absolutely no forgiveness when you did not hit it in the center of the club. If you hit a cavity back club off-center, the shot would travel about 80 to 85 percent of the distance a center hit ball. That is one of the major advantages for an average player versus when they strike a player's blade. Hogan then came out with its Radial club that was a little better but still not a very forgiving club to hit. So if I was not a Hogan employee and looking to buy a set of clubs, Hogan would not be the brand that I would spend money on. Our Hogan product line had a good player brand reputation, which kept all the hacks from trying them out. Almost everybody I played golf with felt the same way but did not dare to say anything out loud. You certainly would not want to sit in front of Ben Hogan and tell him his clubs are not worth the money. I decided to spend some money to do some focus groups to reinforce the decisions we would potentially make in changing our product line and our marketing strategy. I also knew that some of the marketing information was very positive about our products.

The Darrel Survey Club counts on tour that is taken every Thursday of a golf tournament to show the golf manufacturers which pros are playing which brands. I found the club count for the 1984 Colonial Golf Tournament, and the top three clubs were Hogan with seventeen players, Wilson with ten players, and Ping with three players. So the leader in the tournament club count was losing money, and the second most popular brand had recently closed two of its three main plants that were building golf clubs. The third most popular club count was a new innovative company that spent on marketing. We were missing something because this club count number would suggest we should be growing, not shrinking and losing money. With all this data, we were missing something to tie it all together. The evidence was there, and with data to support it, we needed to innovate or die. I had already concluded, we needed a cavity back game improvement club made from a forging with Ben Hogan's blessing to take back market share and grow the company.

Then it happened. At a nationally televised golf tournament, tour-pro Mark Calcavecchia, who was playing a Ping 2 iron, hit a ball out of deep rough and onto the green. The ball landed, took two hops, and stopped on a dime next to the hole, completing a most remarkable shot. The announcer, Ken Venturi, went wild on the air, shouting out loud how incredible a shot that just was. He stated for everyone watching that Calcavecchia's shot had to be the club that enabled him to pull off that kind of shot because Mark doesn't have that kind of talent. This set the golf world ablaze with excitement about this new phenomenon called a game improvement club. This sort of publicity is the type you cannot buy. Ping instantly became the new buzzword in the marketplace, and for the first time, it peaked the ears of the other pros. They certainly did not want to be left behind if someone had found a legal advantage that would help them win golf tournaments. Someone sent a Ping Eye 2 to the USGA for further inspection, and the groves were under investigation for potentially being illegal. The longer this controversy continued, the more clubs Ping was selling. The Ping groove advantage, illegal on the tour or not, would allow Ping to gain significant market share from the old guard of club makers. The media would publish many articles proving the Ping grooves were not much of an advantage at all, but that did not seem to convince the public to stop buying Ping cavity back clubs. The image of a touring professional hitting the ball onto the green from heavy rough and stopping the ball coupled with the commentator's comments in real time overwhelmed the golfing public. That incredible shot is still talked about today.

Every manufacturer was calling the USGA to make a ruling. Either declare the clubs illegal and take away Ping's advantage or let the market follow the specifications Ping has pioneered. Finally, the USGA had their big meeting at their headquarters in Connecticut, and every golf company was invited to give their input in regard to the Ping grooves and what action was to be taken. Everyone presents expected the USGA to declare the Ping clubs illegal and banned from the tour. That move would have ended the controversy and the market advantage that the grooves provided to the Ping clubs. What nobody knew at the time was Ping had filed a lawsuit against the USGA for the damage this would cause their brand. The meeting lasted all day, and everyone in attendance read their official company statement to the committee, stating what action they recommended to be taken. The meeting concluded with the committee saying they would issue a ruling in the next couple of days. Everybody, with the exception of Ping, was disgusted with the lack of action to enforce their rules. We all expected them to stop Ping from continuing to produce illegal clubs.

The very next day, we learned that the USGA settled the lawsuit with Ping and modified the standard for all manufacturers to use the Ping technology. Everyone felt Ping got away with this one. The controversy and subsequent ruling created a tremendous buzz in the marketplace. Ping, though, reaped the most benefit as their brand exploded and became the leading consumers brand for a cavity back game improvement club. Ping could no longer be ignored by the major players. It became obvious to me, we also needed to venture into this market if we wanted to continue to stay relevant in the golf industry. We could not continue to be a major player in the club market unless we were able to compete with Ping and other innovators.

Minstar made it simple for us, reducing costs, increasing sales, and getting our budget under control. Still we needed to do more, and somehow, we could not come up with defining these sales decline internally. We decided to create an outside focus group through the University of Minnesota graduate school for a fee of $5,000 for a project to answer the question, "Why are the Hogan clubs losing market share?" Between the marketing folks and our advertising agency, they would prepare the questions and guidelines that we wanted the group to pursue. Once these results were in, I had hoped it would give us the direction we needed to go to reverse this trend. As the year progressed, Minstar gained confidence with the direction Hogan was headed, and they publicly announced my promotion as president and chief executive officer. Also, the Minstar GM informed me that they were adding another executive, who would become my immediate supervisor as his role in the sale and cleanup of the Hogan Company was completed. This new person will be coming down to visit with me in a couple of weeks. I was acutely aware that Minstar had me on a short leash.

With my objectives outlined, it became quite clear how we would operate over the next twelve months. Each problem was identified, and the appropriate corrective action was implemented. For example, sportswear's biggest problem, aside from being a low-margin product, was the number of overruns of embroidered golf shirts. Typically, an order came in for logo'd Hogan golf shirts, but whenever the buyer, usually a country club, did not want the product for any number of reasons, we could not resell a brand-new shirt with a country club logo embroidered on the shirt. In order to fix this problem, we added an overrun percentage of 10 percent to each order to assure we would deliver 100 percent of the order at all times and got agreements from the account that we could ship up to 10 percent more to assure completion of the order, and we would give the account a 20 percent discount on any additional orders on the same item. By fixing that problem, we would be able to improve the overall cost of the product line and thus meet our profit objectives. But these were small steps, as the club business and mainly irons were where our Hogan future success would be determined. We all knew the club industry was moving to cast products. We also recognized the needs as all the Hogan woods were made either of persimmon or strata block, without a single metal wood. Our big chances had to be made with clubs, and I wanted to have Mr. Hogan embracing this new direction. The arguments to convince him of the change we needed to make would come straight from the focus group results. I was gaining more comfort in our morning meetings, as we would cover many different subjects, all pertaining to improving the Hogan Company's profitability.

The focus group report would take some time, but early reports came back, suggesting what needed to be changed with our present product line and our marketing strategy. I was hoping we would get some clear answers about the twelve questions that we were looking for validation. The feedback suggested our Apex blade was number one in the marketplace. As well as the Hogan company needs to develop a metal wood line to replace the loss of revenue from our wood products. The feedback on our tour program and the tour players reinforced my opinion that our staff was as good as anybody in the market but would not necessarily increase our revenue in the near future. The consumers all supported continuing with forged irons. The report also indicated we needed to spend more on advertising in order to get our message out to the consumers, but that was not an option I had with the Minstar budget constraints. The one question that got my attention was what impact, if any, Mr. Hogan would play in our future. Every single one of the responses was favorable to seeing and reading more about Ben Hogan and his validation of our product line. The reviews we received from the tour pro were clear to me that Mr. Hogan would be the only one that could create the buzz we needed in the marketplace to elevate our company and our product line. So the conclusion was made very quickly that

Hogan needed a metal wood line, a cavity back forged iron, and the great Mr. Hogan to be the face of this effort to the public.

In our next morning meeting, I would ask him about the tour and what he thought of the players of today. He felt too much money was being paid to the players from sponsors without winning the golf tournament. I came away with the impression Mr. Hogan did not value endorsement contracts very heavily. So one morning, I asked my executive secretary Fannie Meyers if she was aware of any endorsements that Mr. Hogan had in his early years on tour. She thought he had a few, but she could not remember. Fanny had been with the Hogan Company from the beginning and worked for every one of the presidents during the early years with AMF. Then one morning, after my plant tour as I was going to see Mr. Hogan, Fanny came into my office with some new information she found; here was this big poster with Mr. Hogan smoking Chesterfield's cigarettes. I rolled up the poster and headed to Mr. Hogan's office for our meeting and a discussion with him about how the tour started. At some point in the meeting, I would bring out the poster and ask him if this is the kind of endorsement we were discussing the other morning. We started talking about how the tour got started way back then. He stated that the golf professionals from up north got together when the country clubs would close for the winter as they had nothing to do. They called the three major golf companies at that time, Wilson, MacGregor, and Spaulding, to ask them if they would care to sponsor some golf events in California over the winter months to keep them going until their respective country clubs would open back up in the spring.

This made a lot of sense, as these pros were the biggest customers in buying golf equipment from them each year. Once they got the sponsorship, the next major problem was getting the country clubs to open up their courses to nonmembers in an effort to increase revenue and potential membership. In those days, Hogan shared that the pros typically came through the back door for tournaments, and as soon as the event was over, they were gently ushered out of the club. When he finished, I expressed to Mr. Hogan how interested

I was in the story behind this poster I now held in my hand. All I got was a slight smile as only Mr. Hogan could do, with no supporting comments or story. This signaled the end of that day's meeting. The wonderful thing about Mr. Hogan was when you were in his company, being the greatest golfer to ever play the game, he never once flaunted his celebrity nor enjoyed particularly talking about it. A humbler man there was not. I felt our relationship was getting stronger by the week, and I was getting to know him much better with each visit.

Over the next few weeks, I visited many pro shops with our salesman in their respective territories. I would ask them about the tour and the impact that it has on selling clubs. The responses were all over the map, but one thing became very obvious to me. Everywhere I would visit, everyone would ask about Mr. Hogan. Is Mr. Hogan alive? What is he doing? How is he doing? Does he have anything to do with the day-to-day operations of the plant?

This convinced me that we needed to utilize Mr. Hogan more to take advantage of his influence in the golf industry. The funny thing was not once did I hear of or see any pro playing our product. In fact, when we quizzed the club pros about which current Hogan touring professional had influenced them the most, no one could list a single name. Most could not even name a single current Hogan touring pro. When we asked which touring pro had the most influence with their customers, the pros did not have a name to give me, such as Don January, Larry Nelson, John Mahaffey, Mark O'Meara, or Lanny Wadkins, but they *all* knew Ben Hogan! I had become increasingly more comfortable with the idea of reducing our tour representation sponsorships as I believed Mr. Hogan would replace them when we featured him in our advertising.

We finally got the comprehensive focus group results in early 1986 and spent a lot of time reviewing the responses to the questions. The opinions from the focus group were very favorable in regard to the quality of products we were producing and the reputation of the company. Questions about the Radial, Apex, and Magnum irons were very positive, but not one person looked at these products as game improvement clubs. In regard to the Hogan woods, the Golf Shop Operation Survey indicated persimmon woods sales had dropped by 50 percent. The iron market for forgings had dropped by 31 percent. It was clear to me what we needed to do in order to maintain and grow. If Hogan was to have a prosperous future, we must introduce new products that incorporate new technology and maintain our perceived leader's position. We met as a staff to review the focus group study and get everyone's reaction to the feedback. I also knew that Mr. Hogan might not be willing to accept this information. The decision to innovate was not a safe one. What if the study was wrong and we needed to stay the course? Our staff was mixed about the results, with some believing we needed to change and others thinking we could make minor shifts and accomplish the same results.

The first big obstacle was convincing everybody we were going to use Mr. Hogan in our advertising instead of touring professionals. Many questions were raised about how we would maneuver Mr. Hogan if we featured him in an ad and he decided he did not like a particular ad. The toughest question we all had. What would happen if he passed away in the middle of the campaign? He was certainly of the age where it was conceivable. These were all risks, but I felt we needed to take them. Now I needed to convince Mr. Hogan because we needed to have him featured in every ad we did from now on. The campaign featuring him would hopefully initiate in 1987. This would include a now-iconic commercial that would serve as the foundation for this campaign.

While the impact of the current Hogan touring pros may have been lost on most of the country club pros, there still existed a legendary legion of Hogan-sponsored pros, past, present, and future. One such touring pro who existed on the Hogan register long before my arrival had come into the fold through the most honest means. Ed Sneed joined the Hogan team at the end of 1977. He had become a great ambassador for the Hogan branded clubs for the next eighteen years, which included several years on the Senior Tour. Sneed, a former caddie for his grandmother hailed from Roanoke, Virginia, had met Mr. Hogan back in 1972 while lunching and playing golf at Fort Worth's Shady Oaks Country Club with then Hogan tour rep, Lynn Price. At that time, Sneed was a McGregor-sponsored player with whom he had begun his career with. It would take him a few years to convert over to Hogan as he had grown accustomed to the MacGregor sticks. He did, though, slowly begin to add some Hogan irons to his bag. Mr. Hogan would occasionally invite Sneed to visit him at his factory. Each trip to the Hogan factory pulled him closer toward Hogan.

It was in 1976 that Sneed made the decision to switch to only Hogan equipment even though he was still under contract with McGregor. He made a deal with McGregor to finish out his contract but was allowed to use the Hogan clubs on tour. The following year, his Hogan contract was made official. The quality improvement was very apparent to Sneed early on. It was around this time that he was changing the shafts on his McGregor irons, and he discovered a bunch of lead weight dropped down into the shafts of each iron as an ad hoc solution to their underweight iron. This would be the end of his McGregor clubs. Sneed knew without a shadow of a doubt that Hogan didn't operate this way. They ground the clubs accurately to weight, and the finish was better, which sealed the deal. Every club in Sneed's bag, including the bag, became Hogan from that point on except for the renegade Walter Hagen, one iron that he had found in a barrel for five bucks years ago and couldn't part with it. Sneed's Hogan contract was renewed year to year with the typical Hogan perks as well as a bonus program which would earn you more based on your accumulation of points from playing. His Hogan contract lasted twenty successful years, including the time with me as CEO. Sneed's love for Hogan clubs only intensified after meeting with Gene Sheeley, the legendary Hogan master model maker. Every trip to the Hogan factory in Fort Worth would entail a visit with Gene in the back room. Sneed would watch Sheeley at his craft create the quality that Hogan was known for. He learned so much about his clubs, the whys and hows.

On one particular visit to Fort Worth, we met with Mr. Hogan and his Hogan players representative, Chip Bridges, at Shady Oaks for lunch and a few swings. After lunch, Mr. Hogan drove Sneed in a golf cart to the par-three course to hit a few, but Sneed quickly found himself just watching Mr. Hogan for more than an hour. Hogan never said more than a few words to Sneed during the practice session. Sneed did finally step up to the tee box when Hogan backed off to watch him. It wasn't the golf shot that interested Hogan but rather the stiffness of the shafts Sneed was using. It didn't take long, but Mr. Hogan found that Sneed needed to play stiffer shafts as well as replace his three-tipped driver shafts. The half-inch and full-inch tipped shafts weren't helping Ed's performance. He recommended that Sneed visits with Gene in the morning. The next day, my clubs all received specially created Hogan Apex shafts from Gene's special reserve, which made me the stiffest shaft on tour. My play on tour improved as well. Sneed and Hogan never were able to play an actual round of golf but managed to practice a number of times.

Gene Sheeley was a superior craftsman in every sense of the word. He would first always check the loft and the lie as forged clubs are softer and will bend sometimes, especially if hit on a hard ground. If the clubs were bent, Gene had nearby an old block of lead and its accompanying hammer, which he would use to pound the clubs back into the correct position.

On the way back of the Hogan factory, there existed a private room where all of Mr. Hogan's clubs resided. One day, Gene Sheeley invited Sneed back there as he wished to show him something. Behind the locked door, Gene handed Sneed a six iron that Mr. Hogan had put on his desk that very morning. Gene went on to explain that under each of Mr. Hogan's grips, Gene had carefully laid a small string on the underside of the grip as a sort of reminder that fit into the grooves of his knuckles. Most golfers would have considered the angle of Hogan's grip to be fairly weak. His right hand especially would be turned over on top of the club. Gene made every set of Hogan's clubs this way. He would tape the string down to the shaft before wrapping it with the grip. Gene, on that day, had recently made a new set of irons for Mr. Hogan, which met with his approval except for this six iron that now sat in front of Sneed for examination. When he pulled off the new grip, he found that the string was slightly out of line by the tiniest of measurements. This showed just how sensitive Mr. Hogan was to the smallest increment or variance in his equipment. Sneed was perhaps one of the most dedicated Hogan-sponsored players and fully vested into the craft that Gene Sheeley pioneered for Hogan.

Ed Sneed's often unabashedly shared Hogan memory took place back in 1978 at Shady Oaks when he again was invited to lunch and some practice with the legend. Hogan, who was in his late sixties at that time, asked his caddy to go downrange from him to act as his target. The caddy showed no reservation about Mr. Hogan hitting balls in his immediate direction. Sneed simply stood by and watched as Hogan dumped several dozen balls on the ground in front of him. Next, Mr. Hogan began hitting balls repetitively at his caddie some hundred- and seventy-five-yards downrange. For the next twenty minutes, Mr. Hogan proceeded to land his shots 5 to 10 feet from his stationary target. Each shot landed slightly in front of the caddie, never over or left or right, always right in front. A few shots came out thin, but never could Sneed remember a fat shot. Sneed would witness this type of practice session four or five more times, and he always left in amazement. This story has been shared by other witnesses over time but never were exaggerations needed as the exhibit was entirely true. Hogan's command of his shots, even at an elevated age, only proved what we all knew to be true. He was once and always one of the all-time greats.

Back to Work

Convincing Mr. Hogan to become the face of his company as well as getting him to see the merit of innovating the Hogan company would serve as my two major objectives. With each morning visit, the meetings never lasted longer than twenty to thirty minutes, so I needed to manage that time with him efficiently to accomplish any of my goals. The advertising seemed to be the first thing I needed to address as our budget for the tour representation was shrinking, and Hogan needed to advertise our products more directly. Prior meetings with Mr. Hogan had entailed discussions about the pro endorsement contracts and how that was ruining golf. Whenever one of our Hogan touring pros would win a golf tournament, we would run an ad featuring them and showing our equipment but without any noticeable increase in sales.

Minstar's limited advertising budget forced me to accept the fact that we could not play very well in the touring pro endorsement game. There was no better marketing option out there than the man whose name was imprinted on everything we do. The cost would be negligible and the impact unmistakable. I felt it was time to address Mr. Hogan as an equal in this venture, so I needed to ask for his permission to address him as just Ben.

In our next morning meeting, I explained things as I knew them. The company was in the red last year. Minstar has asked me to cut costs and improve profitability. I explained the approach I used when the company was profitable, where we maintained each department's costs as a ratio to sales, with the exception being manufacturing which was a direct cost. I explained the current market and our advertising as our next greatest expense. I then relayed to Mr. Hogan that we needed the validity of the tour but could not afford the hefty endorsement contracts. I told him that it was tough to justify the large sums of money spent on endorsement contracts for the current roster of pros playing Hogan clubs. It was a business decision and had nothing to do with the likes of Larry Nelson, Mark O'Meara, Kurt Byrums, David Frost, Mark Brooks, Lanny Wadkins, Phil Blackmore, Don January, Bob Tway, John Mahaffey, to name a few. These large sums of money, which pale in comparison to today's endorsement deals, were dragging the financials down and why we needed Mr. Hogan to become the voice for our company as we go forward. Mr. Hogan was generally very reluctant to speak to the media as they would exploit him for their benefit. I assured him we would shield him and utilize him only for the good of the company that bears his name.

The campaign we had in mind with his inclusion would be used to turn around the Hogan company and restore us to profitability. As I finished my comments, I waited for his response. He sat silently expressionless for what seemed like twenty seconds as if he was contemplating his response. My eyeballs were affixed to him, awaiting the fate of my discussion. The silence was finally broken when he announced, "Yes, I will."

My heart almost fell to the floor. As I sat there jubilantly, I decided to push further and ask the big question, "Mr. Hogan, as we are going to be working together on this project, it is important to me that we are viewed as equals, so if you have no objection, I would like your permission to call you Ben from now on. Would you have a problem with that?"

Again, silence took over the room. It seemed like forever with no response. He broke the silence with a simple, "Okay." I almost jumped out of the chair on my way out of his office. I thanked him for his belief in what we were doing and his commitment to work with me. Walking out of Mr. Hogan's office, I was on cloud nine, knowing the opportunity that now stood in front of me.

The marketing folks took the news well that Mr. Hogan would become the face of a company he founded. Minstar raised the question about what would happen if Mr. Hogan passed away. He was seventy-four years old and not in the best of health. As with the times, Mr. Hogan smoked a lot of cigarettes. It became apparent to me that even though I was comfortable, many people in our organization and at Minstar had some reservations on this approach. So I asked our director of marketing to contact our advertising agency, Tracy Locke, and request them to assign someone to put together a contingency plan just in case something happened to Mr. Hogan. This assignment was given to a young man named Blair Franklin. The plan considered the awkwardness of the first twenty-four hours after his passing, the next forty-eight hours, media materials for this future event, and outlining executive and staff responsibilities and protocol in order to manage this tragedy. Once the contingency plan was completed, I kept the thirty-eight-page binder in the top right-hand drawer of my desk. Fannie Meyers, my executive secretary, was also coached on what to do if I was not available to follow the steps outlined in my top drawer. We were now prepared for this emergency if needed.

The next steps were to schedule the commercial filming to be used to kick off the advertising reintroduction of Mr. Hogan to the golfing public. As that plan was being developed, the next order of business was to dig into the focus group findings in detail and determine our next clubs. In addition to the focus report, I requested marketing to get market data from the golf magazines that conducted annual surveys and market trend reports. This data would support what we were doing.

The answer was not as easy as it seemed. After all, Hogan clubs were perceived to be the best in the industry. Our quality, price, and performance were additionally rated very high. So if all that is true, why were our sales not increasing? We found our answer in the golf market statistics, which pointed out our major problem. Our iron products, the Apex, Radial, and Magnum, were not considered game improvement clubs by the consumer. Hogan R&D would dispute this, as the Radial and Magnum clubs were, in fact, designed as game improvement clubs. So the answer was this is a marketing and sales issue, not a design issue. Research was correct from a design standpoint that the Radial and Magnum clubs were game improvement clubs, but marketing had missed the mark with the public's perception. The number one selling game improvement club in the market was Ping, which was cavity-backed. Everyone came to the same conclusion. We needed a Hogan cavity back club. The public's perception of the cavity back club being a game improvement club was proof enough. The forged iron market had dropped by 25 percent in favor of castings. Forgings were softer than castings, and many believed one could feel the shots better. This public perception factored heavily into our decision.

The answer was that we needed a cavity-backed iron made from a forging. R&D said that sounds good, but we do not have a process to make a cavity-backed club from a forging. They suggested that Mr. Hogan would never allow this company to make a product that looks like a Ping. That was probably true, but what other option did we have? We can tweak our present product line and add metal woods, but without a breakthrough iron, we will continue to lose market share and possibly our jobs. All the game improvement clubs in the marketplace were cast products. I was convinced that the only way forward was to develop a forged cavity back club. This would also give us the ability to market ourselves as the first company to introduce a forged cavity back club.

As we approached the end of the year 1986, it was apparent we were going to make a significant increase in profit from the previous year's loss. In Minstar's eyes, they seemed to make all the right moves. An article appeared in the *Fort Worth Star-Telegram* (November 1986) discussing Minstar's Irwin Jacobs, owner of the Ben Hogan Co. of Fort Worth, which dipped into the red last year but will be profitable in 1986. The article also stated that Jacobs's principle move at Hogan was to replace the Hogan president with Jerry Austry, who had been with the company for two-and-a-half years as vice president for manufacturing. The article was very positive about the future of the Fort Worth company. As the year grew old, I planned to attend the 1987 PGA show in Florida. My boss at Minstar informed me that I would be attending after the PGA show, a meeting in Malaga, Spain, with all the presidents of the Head ski and Head tennis, Tyrolia ski bindings, and Mare's scuba diving equipment. All these presidents worked for AMF before the sale to Minstar, and I was the only new addition to the group. Nothing was said about what we would be discussing or how long the meeting would take. I was planning on taking my wife to the PGA show, so we just extended our time a few days with this trip to Spain.

I was also notified that *Golf Shop Operation Magazine* wanted to do a story about the turnaround at the Hogan Company for the January edition. Things seemed to be all headed in the right direction. The magazine would be distributing a special edition all about the Hogan company with a printed interview with Mr. Hogan, as well as Irwin Jacobs. Everybody attending the PGA show would see this gleaming advertisement for our company. The cover of the magazine said it all. "The Golf Business and Ben Hogan: Exclusive Interview with Mr. Hogan, the Man and the Company and the Men behind Ben." The back page of the magazine featured a full-page ad for the Hogan Radial irons that was marketed like a fine piece of jewelry.

The incredible traction of my life was not lost on me. Less than twelve months ago, I was unsure of my place in this company or industry. Now I found myself running one of the premier golf companies in the world and on a first-name basis with a golf icon. I would frequent events, such as the Masters, US Open, British Open, and the PGA Championship, as part of my responsibilities.

The year concluded with a Hogan open house just for employees, the first type of event for the employees and their families in its thirty-five-year history. A turnout of over eight hundred guests enjoying themselves and their fellow workers. The employees took turns on a dunking stool as their pint-sized future club makers chased after circus clowns passing out balloons. It was remarkable to see some of the factory personnel showing their families what they actually did at the Hogan Company. The workers spent as much time showing their spouses and families how they built clubs and balls as they did any other activity. The highlight of the day was the appearance of Mr. and Mrs. Hogan at the party, shaking hands with everyone he could.

WELCOME TO
THE BEN HOGAN CO
OPEN HOUSE
EMPLOYEES AND
FAMILY ONLY
PORT-A-SIGN

THE HOGAN EDGE

JEROME AUSTRY

THE HOGAN EDGE

JEROME AUSTRY

THE HOGAN EDGE

JEROME AUSTRY

The PGA Show 1987

The year was off to a great start, and the PGA show kicked it off. The excitement was everywhere about the Hogan Company and Mr. Hogan. Everybody that visited our Hogan booth at the PGA show carried a copy of the *Golf Shop Operation Magazine*, and each brought many questions about Mr. Hogan. Everyone would ask me, "How is it working with Mr. Hogan each day?" They could not get enough of him. This only convinced me that making him the face of our advertising program would be a smashing success. Once the PGA show concluded, I skipped the Hogan sales meeting at Bay Hill as I was on my way to Malaga, Spain. The flight was long and anxious but exciting nonetheless. Once we arrived at the hotel, I received a note to meet for a dinner meeting that night on the oceanfront. All the wives were invited to the dinner as well. I had never met any of the presidents before, so the dinner functioned as a meet and greet for me.

At the end of the dinner, the Minstar general manager informed us all that we were going to meet on the beach at nine the next morning. For some reason, I did not think this was a real meeting, as the locale was a nude beach. I was in my room when the phone rang, and my boss's voice questioned if I was coming to the meeting, which caught me by surprise. I said, "I am on my way." As the meeting began, it became obvious the purpose. Minstar had been publicly stating, since the day they bought AMF, that they had no plans to sell the giant sporting goods company which held the Hogan Company, among many others. That would change that morning, as the general manager informed us that every one of the former AMF companies was now for sale. I was the youngest of the presidents and had only been in my job for about one year; the rest of the presidents had been with AMF for a long time. Little else was said that morning, and the meeting broke up. That announcement shocked the whole group. Hogan was now for sale. We just turned the Hogan Company around from a loss to a healthy profit in just twelve months. I was stunned and did not know what to say or do. Not knowing any of these presidents made it hard to talk to them about what, if anything, they would be doing. My boss informed me he would be coming to Fort Worth in early February to inform our staff of the Minstar decision, and we said goodbye until then.

My wife and I spent another two days in Malaga on this vacation, but we really did not enjoy ourselves as our future was now in jeopardy once again. Once I got back to Fort Worth, I had to keep this news quiet, as per instructions, and get back to work with the turnaround plans we already had in process.

The Hogan master plan entailed Mr. Hogan becoming the face of advertising as well as introducing an updated Apex player improvement iron that was easier to hit, along with some Lady irons, and our first venture into metal woods for 1987 with a major iron product introduction in 1988. Step one was to get Mr. Hogan to participate in shooting a commercial. It was my job to set this up with Mr. Hogan, and if he agreed, we were off and running. In our next morning meeting, I shared that we thought it was time to shoot a commercial featuring him. I asked him if he wanted us to contact Shady Oaks or Colonial Country Clubs to arrange the shoot. A silence came over the room, and I waited as usual for his reply. Ben, moments later, said, "Jerry, Jerry, Jerry, no one is going to believe a commercial of a golfer hitting shots off brown grass."

It was the middle of February, and fairways in Texas looked less than idyllic. I responded, "Oh my god! I completely forgot about that. You're right, Ben. Where would you like to film the commercial?"

After another long silence, he chirped back, "Seminole in Florida, Augusta on the master course or Riviera." I had heard all I needed.

"Thank you, Ben. I will get that set up and let you know."

Little did I know how much of a problem this would be. I called our marketing director into my office and let him know what was going on so he could get with our agency to get this set up. Seminole Country Club outright said no. Augusta gave a polite no, stating if they allowed Mr. Hogan this, then they would not be in a position to refuse anyone else that might want the same. That left us with Riviera. It came out later that they had also turned us down, but our marketing agency, Tracy Locke, sent the head of creative for our account James Dalthorp on a plane to sell them on the idea of the commercial. When he got there, they started yelling at him because Mr. Hogan had turned them down on attending a PGA tournament at their course, which had been dedicated to him a few years earlier. I am not sure what we would have done had James not been successful. One of the major pieces of our strategy was almost lost before we even got started. We were also on a tight time frame as we wanted to introduce Mr. Hogan in the 1987 advertising campaign to bridge the gap until the new iron would be introduced. Somehow, James convinced the Riviera people how important this was, and they ultimately capitulated. The relief was short-lived as now I would be accompanying Mr. Hogan for three days to California to film an ever so important commercial. One of my biggest fears was keeping the silence filled with conversation with a man known to hardly speak.

The other major concerns I had were, what would happen if it leaked out Mr. Hogan was at Riviera shooting a commercial? What about the plane ride? Would he be mobbed at the airport? Mr. Hogan received thousands of requests for interviews and invitations to appear at events to which he turned them all down. What if I am not able to control the crowds that surround him at the golf course? How would I handle dinner each night? Would he expect me to join him, or would he prefer to dine only with his accompanying wife and her sister? Additionally, the behavior of the agency personnel and the filming crew was a big worry for me. How does one handle a problem with them? All this ultimately landed on my feet should the bottom fall out. Mr. Hogan was a recognized celebrity still many years after he left the competitive players world. Luckily, Mr. Hogan had agreed to cooperate with this endeavor, so that gave me some confidence we might be okay.

Worry as I did, Minstar's public announcement of a sale of the Hogan Company loomed much larger in my problem file. I could not control the sale or my future, but I could control my daily activity and the development of the new irons. I wanted to prove to everyone that I was capable of completing this turnaround, and once completed, everyone in the industry would recognize this accomplishment. The results of the focus group study had been very positive in regard to the Hogan brand and the irons we were offering to the public. So why was Ping outselling us three to one? The industry kept telling us that forgings were softer than castings. We knew the new Hogan irons needed to be forgings, but why did the Hogan Radial iron not accomplish this for us? It was a game-improvement club and was advertised as "The Club That Was Made That's Easy to Hit." What were we missing? Further study of the report kept leading me to one question. The focus group was asked, "Which of these identified clubs are game improvement clubs?" Time after time, the answers came back, identifying game improvement clubs as the clubs with cavity backs. No one in the group picked the Hogan Radial or the Magnum as game improvement products simply because they lacked a cavity-backed feature. Our new product had to be a forging with a large cavity back large enough that anyone could identify it as a game improvement club.

If there was any chance to introduce our hopeful game improvement club with its legendary namesake spokesman telling our customers of its worthiness, then we had to get started immediately. I called a meeting with the director of marketing and the VP of R&D to discuss this idea. In presenting my position to them, they were lukewarm to the idea. They did not make any strong arguments against it, but they just were not totally on board with it either. The biggest concern was how Mr. Hogan would respond to this new direction in our club department. Everyone knew the master model maker, Gene Sheeley, had been groomed by Mr. Hogan and thus had to be on board in developing this model, or Mr. Hogan would not be. I quizzed the meeting attendees. Once Mr. Hogan approves the design, is it full steam ahead getting the iron developed for its introduction next year? (1988).

I then looked at the VP of R&D and asked him if he could meet that timeline and develop the process to manufacture this new product. He answered, "Absolutely." As the meeting ended, I remember thinking to myself that they both didn't believe Mr. Hogan would approve this new product. The pressure mounted. How am I going to present this to Ben? I decided to pitch the idea in two meetings. I would break down our sales and market share so that he understood where we were failing. Then I would challenge his competitive nature to take on Ping and beat the hell out of them and reclaim the number one club maker title in golf. This felt like the biggest challenge of my career. I still had not informed my staff about the Minstar decision to sell the company. This fueled my need to get this product on the drawing board, which certainly would enhance a prospective buyer's interest. The next morning, I entered the distinguished office of Ben Hogan. Our discussion followed our product line, along with the golf data outlining the benefits of forgings and metal woods. Ben offered his thoughts regarding the basics of design, lines on a club, leading edge, top line, and sole. He made a point to add that forged clubs must look like a piece of fine jewelry. Every club we were already producing had that ingredient. Ben would agree. He had concerns that the market seemed to be falling away from forgings as he believed the softer forged product was much better and would allow feedback to the player on the execution of his shot. Without that feedback, the player would not improve.

A couple of days later, in the next meeting, I brought a Ping club and one of our Radials with me to review with Ben. As I walked into his office, he could see the clubs in my hand. I said, "Good morning, Ben. I would like to discuss the design of these two clubs with you. Is that okay?" He said that it was. "Which one of these clubs has better lines?"

Ben responded, "The Radial."

"How about the leading edge of the club?"

Again, Ben said, "Radial."

"Which one looks like a golf club you would be willing to put in your bag?"

Again, Ben answered, "Radial."

"Which club will provide the golfer more feedback on off-center hits?"

"Radial."

"If I asked any consumer which one of these clubs is a better game improvement product and will make hitting the ball easier, which would they pick?"

Ben had no other option. "Radial."

"Ben," I finally shared, "that is not the answer that we are getting from our customers. The public does not accept the Radial as a game improvement product or a better alternative to the Ping." I held up the Ping club and said, "If we cannot build a better forged game improvement club than this, we shall go out of business." I went silent, waiting for his answer.

He finally replied, "Jerry, I agree with you. We should be able to do that."

I then said to Ben, "In order for us to do this, I need your help to develop a product with all the best features. Additionally, I would appreciate it if you could test the models as we develop the prototype to release to production." The ask was over. I felt very good at that moment as Ben seemed ready.

"I will help you," he told me.

I told him, "Thank you, Ben," and left his office.

As I left his office, my feet hardly touched the ground. I called the VP of R&D and the director of marketing and asked them to come to my office. When they walked in, I shared that Mr. Hogan is on board, and he will test the model clubs to help develop the first forged cavity club ever produced. They could not believe it. I could sense the relief on the VP of R&D's face as his model maker always previously involved Mr. Hogan, which often led to its dismissal. We just eliminated that complication. We were starting to develop a new forged club no one else in the industry has ever made. What a relief to have Mr. Hogan aboard for advertising and to have his support with the company's new direction. Our staff seemed to have developed a genuine respect for each other's talents. The staff meetings once a month were no longer a political minefield. Each executive would share the department's progress and shortcomings toward our total effort to make Hogan relevant again. There was no longer any finger-pointing. We had become a team.

At the end of January, the GM from Minstar arrived for the big announcement. As he explained that, we are now for sale. The air just gushed out of our balloon. We would now be expected to exhibit our company to prospective buyers, some of whom might be some of our competitors. This bomb would be one of the hardest to overcome. We were all pulling together, and now all our efforts could be for not, as a new owner could come in and change everything or worse, fire us all. There seemed only to be one winner in this game, Mr. Irwin Jacobs.

We finally got approval to shoot the Ben Hogan commercial at Riviera Country Club for three days on March 2, 3, and 4. The new model development was underway, and the Hogan commercial was scheduled to be completed by March 16, 1987. One of the last Hogan ads we ran without Mr. Hogan was a full page for our game improvement Radial forged iron.

Once the commercial was completed, the golfing world would see a completely different look at the Hogan Company. The golf world would be reintroduced to one of its patriarchs. He had been missing in action for some time, but now he had returned. What impact that would have on sales at this point was unknown, but we wouldn't have to wait long if we had made the right decision.

The Hogan marketing problem wasn't the message we put out but rather the dollars we weren't budgeted to spend. We simply weren't reaching enough eyeballs as the marketing budget had been too tight. Now with Ben Hogan as our poster child, coupled with his free cost of labor, we could fully share our message with the world. In hindsight, we should have advertised our Radial clubs as a significant game improvement club. Ben felt strongly that if any golfer ever tried our Radial club, then there is no way they would choose a Ping. We certainly did not advertise in *Golf Digest* or *Golf Magazine* at the same level as Ping. Would that have enough difference to matter? Even if we doubled our marketing efforts, there was no guarantee of increased sales. We needed to go and take back market share. We were then selling about fifty thousand sets of Radial a year. Although we were now headed in a new direction, there were still many people both at the Hogan Company and the Tracy Locke Agency that felt this could be a mistake.

The Riviera

I arrived at Dallas/Fort Worth International Airport, accompanying Ben Hogan, his wife Valerie, and her sister Sarah Jeanette Fox Harriman to California for the commercial. My first surprise was that no one at the airport made any fuss at all, no crowds, and no autograph seekers. We met at the gate, which was allowed then, and we boarded the plane. For this trip, we found our seats in first class. Valerie was seated with her sister, and Ben and I sat behind them. It was a Sunday afternoon, March 1, and the commercial was scheduled for the next three days. I would serve as Ben's chaperone for the next three days. I had been meeting daily with Ben now for over a year but never for more than half an hour. This trip would change all that. It was a midday flight, and it did not take long after takeoff for the drinks to start flowing. Ben asked the stewardess for a vodka tonic, and I followed his lead. The plane was very loud, which made it quite difficult to hear Ben's voice. He began a story, which over the years became one of my favorites, on how he got started in the game of golf.

Ben quietly began, "I came from a poor family and had to work to help our family. I was always searching for ways to make the most money I could. The first job I had as a boy was selling newspapers, but that did not pay very much. One of my friends told me I could make 65¢ a day by caddying at Glen Garden Country club. So I gave up the paper route and became a caddy. Part of my responsibilities besides caddying for the golfers was to keep the members' clubs in perfect condition. All the clubs had wood shafts, and they needed constant work. The pro taught us what to do, and we would sand and polish these shafts every day. The irons were not plated back then, so we had to polish them to get the dirt off and keep them from rusting. From time to time, the shaft would break, and the pro would show us how to replace the shaft with a new one. Each morning, before and after each round, the caddies would hit the ball down the fairway and back and back up until a member was ready to play. That is how I started to play the game."

We ordered two more vodka tonics. Ben asked me how I started the game. I shared that my first round didn't happen till after I graduated from college when I was twenty-four years old. He was shocked. He quizzed me, "Why did it take you so long to try the game?"

I explained, "I was a baseball player, and my dream was to become a professional baseball player. I lived in a poor neighborhood in Chicago, and I had never seen a golf course until I got to college, which was made possible by baseball. In the beginning, I would swing the golf club so hard sometimes that I would miss the ball."

Ben laughed. He replied that having the benefit of watching a lot of good golfers swing their clubs at the country club gave him the advantage to get the feel of what a good golf swing looked like.

We ordered two more vodkas, causing Valerie to look back at us and make some comments, but I did not hear her. We furthered our discussion with the professional golfing tour and if Ben knew he was going to be a professional golfer. I leaned in to hear him. "I knew I could play because of all the matches I won while caddying, but there was no professional tour in the early days for those who could play." He went on to share that the PGA professionals would travel to California during the winter months when snow covered their golf courses, and they would all play against one another for money. Ben informed me they approached Wilson Sporting Goods, Spaulding Golf, and MacGregor to sponsor the fall swing and be able to earn enough money to return to their homes in the spring. These three companies were happy to do so as 100 percent of their business was sold through these professionals.

We ordered a couple more vodka tonics and started talking about the players of today. I had heard Ben did not think the golfers of today were deserving of the game. I asked him what problem he has with present-day golfers. He felt that they could only play the game they knew. They know nothing about club making or how to repair the clubs they are playing with. He believed you should know how to build a club to appreciate how it performs. I questioned him about comments I heard him make about all of today's players looking like race car drivers, with endorsements all over their clothing, hats, and bags. "Were these not available when you played? If you could have made that kind of money early in your career, would you not take advantage of that?"

He thought for a moment and then responded, "I guess my problem with the tour today is that too many people are making money by not winning or just playing golf. I believe it has diluted the quality of play. Today's players have too many distractions pulling at them, which hurts the overall quality of play for tournaments and the fans."

I pressed him further, "Are you telling me you did not have any endorsement when you played?"

"No, that is not what I am saying. My endorsements were offered because I performed well on the tour, and I was rewarded as such."

Two more vodka tonics and we were well on our way. I felt confident enough to ask him about tour players endorsing our products. "Ben, how important do you feel it is to have a stable of players playing with our clubs and carrying our bags on tour? Some of our pro staff have not won many tournaments, and I have a hard time seeing how these large contracts create any additional sales for the Hogan company."

Ben's answer surprised me when he said, "I agree with you, Jerry, but it is a necessary part of the golf business. With the right product and marketing, you must find the balance that works for the company."

"Ben, if you don't mind me asking, I have heard from a lot of people you were not very friendly when someone would ask you for help to improve their game."

This time, he replied quickly, "That impression is totally wrong. When I was playing, we all shared with each other and watched each other play. I learned to play by watching other good players, which forced me to figure out what he was doing and that impact that had on his game." In other words, Ben felt if you could not watch what a good player was doing and then see the result of that swing and the movement it created with the ball, then telling you what to do would be a waste of time. "After I left the game, many people asked me for help. I did give some advice early on, but to my dismay, I found out that my advice was being used to create profit for that person. So unless I knew what the person's reasons were for asking, I usually refused to provide any advice."

Two more vodka tonics. "How come you do not travel to the Masters and other tournaments like the other players of your time?"

"For most of my golfing career, that is all I did with Valeria night after night on the road in hotels and eating at restaurants, so I finally just wanted to stay home and enjoy my friends and family without the travel." Ben covered more stories about seeing people that he met years earlier in the service. He shared a particular story that he got all choked up about, where he approached the scoring table at a US Open Tournament, and he recognized the gentleman that was at the table. He was a medic while Ben was in the service and recalled the stories from the medic when wounded military personnel would be shipped in for treatment and to be operated on, many not making it through the operation.

As the flight to California was preparing to land, I asked him why he decided to sell his company when he did and was it hard for him to give up the control of the day-to-day operations.

Ben stated, "It did not take me long to figure out, I was a hell of a golfer and great club designer, but managing a large operation with the financial exposure was a problem for me. In the early days, things were very tight financially, and we almost went out of business very early on after a large production lot had to be scrapped. You probably have heard that most of my money partners were nervous. Nobody ever gave me anything for free. I had to earn everything I ever got, so when AMF called me, I thought this was a great opportunity to secure my financial future and still be able to contribute my ideas in regard to future designs of the Hogan product."

Our conversation had become considerably more animated as the drinks piled up, but Ben's ease in sharing with me felt sincere. We understood each other better than before. We both had struggled to make it in life, and that now bonded us together.

We landed in Los Angeles, and a limousine was waiting for Ben, Valerie, and her sister. As we parted ways, Ben said, "We will meet for dinner at the Beverly Wilshire Hotel at seven o'clock," where we were staying. That hopefully would give me enough time to get to the hotel to shower and sober up before dinner. The agency executives were staying at the Riviera Country Club. I would have rather stayed at the club, but that would have left Ben more exposed to the public, which could be an issue. I was there as a buffer that might protect this aged golf giant. The Riviera stood as one of the legendary country clubs in the world.

As we arrived the next day, we were put on notice that any member complaints regarding us interfering with their ability to play could result in our project getting shut down.

This was the biggest project the Hogan Company had ever undertaken. The pressure on the head of creative for the agency to complete this commercial on time was intense. We were to remain on a very tight schedule. I felt like a duck out of the water as I had never been involved in any kind of endeavor like this in my life. In addition, the only job I had was to take care of Ben to make sure nothing interfered with him for the next three days. Our marketing agency notified me before dinner about Ben's schedule for the next day. He was scheduled to start at 6:00 a.m. I could not believe how early we would have to get up as we were now on California time, and they were expecting a seventy-five-year-old man to be ready to go at that time. I was ready to explode, but it was too late to do anything about it. I felt bad I had not checked this out before we got on the plane so as to let Ben know what was expected of him the next day.

As we were enjoying dinner, we heard a voice from behind us say, "Mr. Hogan, I cannot believe it is you!" All of a sudden, Dave Marr, a TV announcer for women's golf, stood up from his table to say hello. After some polite greeting, Dave asked, "What brings you to California."

We waited for Ben's answer, and he got this funny look on his face because he was not going to let Dave know he was there to shoot a commercial at Riviera so as not to create a problem for us if the news media got wind of the event. Ben commented he was there to meet some people he had not seen in years. I thought to myself how savvy Ben was and how aware he was about the importance of keeping the commercial secret from the general public. We finished a delicious dinner when Ben asked me what time he needed to be ready for pick up in the morning.

I told him, "We are expected at six in the morning at the course." I braced myself, waiting for his response.

After a slight pause, he said, "Fine, I will see you in the morning."

The Hogans left, and I stayed in the bar area to have a nightcap and ponder the day. I was truly exhausted from the day and wondered how Ben could handle such a rigorous schedule at his age. As I was reviewing my day, my thoughts again shifted to Ben. He seemed to know exactly what was expected of him and how this shoot was supposed to go. I saw a completely new side of him outside of the Hogan Company. He apparently had a lot of experience with commercial shooting schedules, which became a great relief for the next three days. The next big worry was the weather and would it cooperate and let us complete this on time. This new advertising campaign with Mr. Hogan would air two months later at the Colonial Invitational golf tournament in Fort Worth, Texas. The new print ads would start once this commercial was completed and approved.

The next morning, I got to the golf course before Ben did, and they escorted me to the back of the property, where a trailer was set up for Mr. Hogan. A personal assistant was there to make sure Ben was comfortable while he waited to be called to action. I had a chance to look at the storyboards that the agency had outlined for the shoot. After reviewing those boards, I thought to myself, *This shouldn't take that long as they are only looking at doing fourteen to sixteen different shots.* How long could that take?

A few minutes later, Mr. Hogan arrived, and everybody introduced themselves. Ben came over to the trailer where his personal assistant asked him if he needed anything at all, to which he said no, thank you. What an experience this was becoming for me. The biggest golf icon in the business is sitting here, and what a gentleman he was. I have never seen a humbler human, let alone a celebrity. Mr. Hogan was so welcoming to everyone that was there. He treated everyone as his equal and made them all feel as an important part of the shoot. He also let everyone know we were guests of the Riviera Country Club, and they have been gracious enough to let us use their course, so let's keep that in mind. As I was walking around in awe of how well he was treating everybody, I kept remembering the critical stories about Mr. Hogan that most have read, such as a story by Bob Oates of the *Los Angeles Times* on June 19, 1988, that described Mr. Hogan in as many words, "As a person and as a golfer, Hogan was reportedly cold, calculating, distant, antisocial, uncooperative, preoccupied, and obsessive in his drive for perfection." There was not a person involved in this shoot that would consider any of these words to describe the man they were working with on this commercial.

Me, on the other hand, was perhaps a different story. I was ready to go. What the hell is the delay? We had already wasted a good hour while they were checking lighting and all kinds of other details that didn't make any sense to me? How long is Ben going to be sitting there waiting? Finally, we got the word. They were going to start shooting. Ben was asked if he would like to warm up first, and he said yes. Ironically, this would be the first time I had ever seen him swing a club. When asked how much time he would need, as today was the filming of the iron's shoots, Ben responded, "I will need about fifteen to twenty minutes."

The first day went off with minimum disruption. The crowds were minimal, but as the first day progressed, some people started to congregate around the sight. As we started the second day of shooting, we all noticed a lot more people were watching and trying to get a glimpse of Ben. The fans were very respectful and kept their distance, but it was apparent something had leaked out about the commercial. Later that day, I found out that Jim Murray, a legendary sportswriter for the *LA Times*, had published a story about Ben Hogan at Rivera and what he was doing. My stress triggers were now realized. How would we be able to control the crowds? That fear turned out to be unfounded as the Riviera was a private club, and no one could get onto the course without being with a member. The members made sure the behavior of their guests did not embarrass them. The second day, the crowds grew larger, but again, they kept their distance and just watched Ben execute each shot for the camera crew. The spectators couldn't help but applaud each shot he made. The final portion of day two would be the iron shots to the number four green where the crowd could actually watch him strike the ball and see it land on the green. He was never very far from the pin, which only helped keep the crowd more engaged. We estimated several hundred people standing nearby at a safe distance by the green.

After several directed shots, Ben started to hit different shots just for the crowd. He would fade several shots into the green. Then next time, he would draw several shots into the flag. It did not take long for everyone to realize that the golf legend was performing for them, and the crowd loved it. He would hit it high and then hit one low at the target, showing off his still sharp skill set. After each shot, he would tip his hat and acknowledge the applause. This went on for some time after we completed the filming, but Ben continued to entertain to the delight of the crowd. This moment quickly took on a life of its own as everyone realized the extraordinary event they were privy to. The powers that be at Riviera felt it so memorable that the club decided to erect a statue along with a commemorative plaque at the number four green with the following inscription:

> Greatest Par 3 hole in America (Ben Hogan in 1987). The fourth hole at the Riviera Country Club was chosen by Mr. Hogan as the site for filming his club company's commercials. It was the only time his golf swing was ever seen in the Hogan commercials.

"Greatest Par 3 hole in America"
Ben Hogan

In 1987, the 4th hole at the Riviera Country Club was chosen by Mr. Hogan as the site for filming his club company's commercials. It was the only time his golf swing was ever seen in the Hogan commercials.

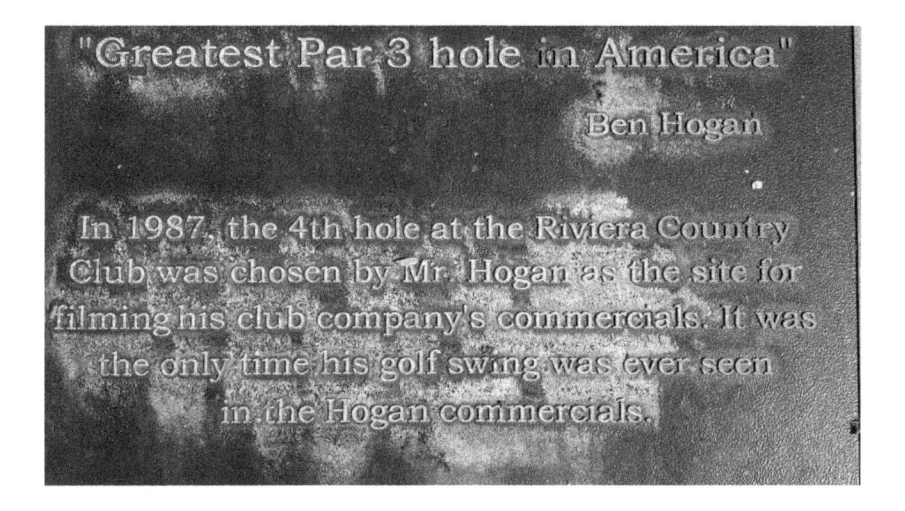

I did not find out about the plaque until thirty-three years later, when I got a call from a friend who was playing the course and said, "You will not believe what I am taking a picture of at this moment." He explained the plaque to me and how amazing it was to see. The Riviera must have felt this Hogan moment at number four was important enough to capture for eternity.

The next photoshoot called for Ben to hit some balls from a fairway onto a green. As we looked for the best place to warm up, we drove into the middle of the course so as not to disturb any member's game. Ben's assistant dropped some balls in the fairway as the cameras got into position. Ben decided himself to move the balls off the fairway and into a slight rough. We looked on with puzzled looks until he commented, "Let's not tear up the golf course for the members." Who were we to argue with such a gracious act? Everyone involved in the shoot could not help but look on in awe as this small seventy-five-year-old man hit several dozen balls out of the rough and at a practice green. The brilliance of this man was realized on each seemingly effortless iron shot he made. I could not believe what I was watching as Ben's mastery and control of his swing left me speechless. He could have passed as a current top tour player with his efforts.

After a few more iron shots, Ben asked the filming crew if he could also hit some wood shots. We all answered yes in unison. Ben wanted to be out of the way from any member playing the course, so we found a relatively quiet spot in an open field between the first hole's fairway and the second hole's fairway. He was set up high on a hill, just below the first tee, hitting down into the valley away from the club. Ben walked up to the ball and looked over his left shoulder to see if anyone was on the first tee at the top of the hill and saw it was vacant. He then lined up and smashed a towering drive over the trees and hooked the ball away from the golfers playing number two. I remember thinking, *You have got to be kidding me! Did he really just do that?* He hit a second one with the same trajectory and a slight hook at the end. The ball landed to the right of the first green but strategically far enough away not to disturb any potential golfers hitting that direction. He did this about six more times, always looking over his shoulder before striking the ball.

On the next drive, he noticed someone was on the number one tee, so instead of hooking this ball, Hogan implemented a fade away from the players on the first hole. He repeated this a few more times and then looked over to me to say he was ready. We had only witnessed his warm-up. We captured the ball striking that had become synonymous with the icon. The footage would not all make the final commercial, but we all knew we were seeing something special. The more I saw the filming, the more confident I became that this change in direction would be a smashing success for the Hogan Company. I just prayed the film would show something close to what we were seeing in person. After the morning filming was complete, we went back to the trailer as they reviewed the camera work. Ben and I relaxed as his personal assistant made sure his every need was taken care of. I was allowed some alone time with Ben while we were waiting at the trailer, and I was anxious to ask him a few more questions.

"Ben, over the years, there have been more stories written about you, but one question I have never heard anyone ask you about is your favorite nickname? Which nickname do you like better, Hawk or Wee Iceman?"

As usual with Ben, there was a long pause. I could tell he was searching for just the right answer. When he was ready, he said, "I like them both, but if I had to choose which one, I prefer Wee Iceman because I felt it would intimidate my competition, giving me the advantage to win the golf tournament." Our conversation did not last very long as the creative director informed us that it was a wrap for the day. Just before they took Ben to his limousine and back to the hotel, he waved me over and whispered, "Jerry, make sure you give that young lady a nice tip for her work today."

The second day was complete, and everyone felt good about what we captured on film.

The third and final day of shooting found a much larger crowd on hand to see the great Mr. Hogan. The crowds never posed any problems for us. We had ample opportunity to get Ben at his best. The crew even had time to listen to Ben tell a few stories. He would sit with the group and relate to them many stories about golf and his experiences with the game.

Each day, Mr. Hogan would always ask how much time he had to warm up, and we would inform him that he could take as long as he needed. He generally took fifteen to twenty minutes each day. The way the production team had organized it, a large recreation vehicle was to be parked near Riviera's first fairway each day, far enough down so as not to be in the range of members' drives. Mr. Hogan would arrive early each morning by limo, step into the recreation vehicle where his cleaned and pressed apparel would be hanging. In the kitchen would be fresh, hot coffee and a carton of his brand of smokes. He would spend some quiet time getting dressed and relaxing until the need for the day's activities.

For all the many things Mr. Hogan did know, there was one thing to which he was oblivious when he arrived in California—how much his reputation still resonated with fans. During filming, Riviera club members, their friends, and other fans started to appear out of thin air. The number of onlookers swelled each day. But the fans were consistently quiet and respectful. When he first saw them assembling around shooting locations and realized they were there to see him, he said, "Why would they even care? I haven't played competitive golf in years." Even Riviera's owners at the time, the Hathaway family, came to the course to welcome him back and to exchange pleasantries. His manners were surprisingly formal and old school, as he removed his cap and bowed in his salutation to them. He told them how delighted he was being allowed to return to the club, as it had meant so much to his career. It was a great lesson in professional etiquette and humility.

At the end of the day, everyone reconvened near the first fairway near the RV, and Mr. Hogan got ready to go back to his hotel. He was tired because the first day, he spent much of this time doing "walking shots" with his heavy brace on, so he was ready to climb into a hot tub and stretch out.

As the commercial shoot started to wind down, the camera set up was in Riviera's practice fairway between the first and second holes below the clubhouse. We learned during his playing days, he would slip down and use the location to practice without distractions. The crowd that had assembled that afternoon got to see a shot-making show. He hit draws, fades, and holds shots, some with high trajectories and some lower. Seemingly to amuse himself, he hit some long iron drawing shots that curved up and traveled over the trees that bordered the practice fairway and first fairway. Eventually, he turned to our little corporate group and surprised us by saying, "What shot do you want me to hit?" It was a little game where we could call outshot.

After the last day, several of us sat down with him at a portable picnic table that was set up near the RV. Hollywood publicist and old friend, Bob Williams, came down and brought Mr. Hogan an XL martini from the club's bar and sat down for a short chat while he relaxed and let the California sunshine work on his muscles. Before long, there was a bit of a commotion coming from up around the clubhouse. He turned around to see a couple of Riviera employees descending the hill, carrying something quite large. It looked like an oversized piece of sheetrock from a distance, but we quickly determined it was a mounted photograph of Mr. Hogan from a room in the club. A gust of wind almost caused the employees to take an unscheduled flight across the first fairway. When they finally arrived near the RV, they simply asked for his autograph for the club. As he signed, he politely told them he would have been delighted to come to the club and sign it while it was still on the wall in its frame. You could tell he was a bit amused by the effort and determination of the employees.

The commercial was a grand slam home run for the Hogan Company and us. The creative team was unbelievable in what they were able to do. We were now in a position to take the golfing world by storm with the introduction of the Hogan game improvement product. The trip back to Fort Worth would be much shorter and with a lot less stress as the commercial was completed, and Ben was very happy with how the team worked together to accomplish the task. On the way back, I felt it was important to inform Ben of Minstar's decision to sell the Hogan Company. There wasn't much we could do about it anyway, but he could expect an influx of companies coming to kick the tires to see what we were doing. I told him that Minstar never intended to own us for the long haul. Their ownership did, though, allow us to change the course of the company and gain back momentum in returning to the top of the industry. We may not be as lucky with the next owner, but we would do the best with what we could. I asked him if any of the Fort Worth money wants to get involved in buying his company and guarantee its stay in Fort Worth. Now was the time to let them know what is going to happen.

Ben said okay and made no other comment. I did ask why some of his close friends did not make a move when Minstar raided AMF and ended up with Hogan Company. He never did answer that question, so I did not pursue it any further. I had learned that whenever Ben does not give you an answer, you can assume he has no intention to answer. One of our last discussions was about the airing of the commercial before we actually aired it on television. I informed him that we were planning to show the commercial at this year's Colonial Invitational in May. The Colonial Golf Tournament stood as a very big event for the Hogan Company. We typically had eight spots in the pro-am tournament. We also buy enough tournament badges to give our entire workforce a couple of tickets to watch the tournament. So with Ben's approval, we organized an open viewing at Shady Oaks Country Club and invited the Hogan executives and their spouses for a private viewing hosted by Mr. and Mrs. Hogan. Ben also picked out the welcome gifts that were presented to everyone to say thank you for a job well done. I also invited a few from Minstar, but no one was available to attend. This was another opportunity for a lot of people to see Mr. Hogan in a different light. He could not have been more kind and welcoming to all the guests. He spent time with almost every guest, thanking them for coming and showing his appreciation for all the hard work everyone had done to complete the commercial.

Two months prior to Colonial, we ran the new Hogan ads in the March edition of *Golf Digest* and *Golf Magazine*. In *Golf Digest*, we ran two single-page ads—the Series 56 with Ben Hogan as the centerpiece and a full-page ad for our Hogan Radial. In *Golf Digest*, we ran the two pages for better player ad and a single page for the Series 56 with Ben Hogan. The month before the 1987 Colonial Golf Tournament, we released a family of print ads, changing the face of our advertising to be Mr. Hogan. We ran four pages in *Golf Digest* and *Golf Magazine*, which we had never done before. One common theme was Ben Hogan was in every ad in all his iconic glory. He was everywhere. His two-page spreads had a headline of "Hogan, Not Just Clubs for a Better Player but Clubs to Make Any Player Better." Mr. Hogan stood proud in a suit and tie, inspecting his clubs in the center of the ad in tournament form along with a picture of Apex, Radial, and Magnum irons. The next single-page ad read, "Why a Golfer Known for Consistency Builds a Club for Golfers Who Aren't," and finally a full-page advertisement, "When It Came to Making Metal Woods, Ben Hogan Was His Own Best Inspiration." We had never run ads in both major golf publications at the same time, and thus the hopes were very high for the impact.

HOGAN. NOT JUST CLU BUT CLUBS TO MAK

In 1953, Ben Hogan began his equipment company because he believed that he could design and manufacture better clubs than were then available.

In the 34 years since, Hogan clubs have earned a singular reputation for quality and performance that makes them among the most sought-after clubs in the world.

Unfortunately, they've also become known as clubs exclusively for "better players."

An understandable mistake, given Ben Hogan's own legendary playing status, and the Ben Hogan Company's long association with the PGA Tour through our tour blades.

But, in fact, for the past several years, we've offered an excellent choice of clubs for golfers of all handicaps willing to make a serious investment in their games.

© 1987 Ben Hogan Co.

S FOR BETTER PLAYERS,
ANY PLAYER BETTER.

At Hogan, we offer this selection because we believe quality and sound design are fundamental to better and more consistent golfing. Or, as Mr. Hogan puts it, "with the right equipment, a player of any skill level can improve."

In 1987, the "right equipment" includes Apex, our traditional irons and persimmon woods preferred by low handicap and scratch golfers. Also Radial, our popular cambered-sole, easy-to-hit club. And Magnum, our most forgiving club ever, for golfers who want to put more good hits in every round.

You see, Hogan clubs aren't exclusively for the better player. But they're an excellent idea if you'd like to work on becoming one.

Ask your pro about the right Hogan club for your game.

Hogan
PLAY THE BEST YOU CAN PLAY

The new ad campaign was taking shape, and the look and feel of each ad captured Mr. Hogan's personality to a tee. Reviewing each one, I could imagine Mr. Hogan saying the taglines, and I could not have been more pleased. They were not just ads; they had the future of the company riding on them. I could not have been happier with how the Tracy Locke Advertising agency responded to this new direction. The chemistry between their group and our marketing guys could not have been better. Their hard work and understanding of our new vision helped to form a very beneficial partnership that benefited both company and the agency. As we were under a limited advertising budget from Minstar, an interesting new partnership was formed. Hogan did not have enough money to advertise in both major golf magazines, so we required a little assistance to pull off the Hogan campaign. We felt it essential to cultivate a partnership with the magazines. The needed assistance came in the form of *Golf Magazine* and its publisher, Peter A. Bonanni. The local agent for the magazine, Joe Kelly, had been a close confidant of mine over the years, and he introduced me to Mr. Bonanni early in 1987.

Mr. Bonanni had shared a dream he had to organize a Hundred-Year Centennial Celebration of Golf to be held in 1988. One of his biggest problems was how to have a celebration of the first hundred years of golf without the assurance of Ben Hogan's attendance. Initially, Mr. Hogan had not warmed to the idea of attending the Centennial Celebration in New York City. It would take more than one meeting with Ben to convince him how beneficial this would be to impact our marketing efforts. Joe had briefed Peter about the Hogan strategy to get Mr. Hogan involved in the new advertising campaign, along with the development of the new Hogan iron that was underway. Joe became a very close friend with whom we would spend time together on family vacations. On one of these vacations, Joe asked me about the possibility of Mr. Hogan attending the Centennial of Golf Celebration, being planned in New York City in June of 1988. Would it be possible for him to agree to come? Both of us knew Mr. Hogan's reputation for turning down requests of this sort.

I remarked, "You know, Joe, if Ben believes the motive is truly positive in nature and would be beneficial to the Hogan Company, he might probably go." I suggested he put together a proposal to present to Ben. Joe said his boss, Peter Bonnani, would come down to make the presentation to Hogan at any time. I told him that I was not sure that would work. Ben doesn't know Peter, and his coming to his office for a brief morning meeting would not give him enough time for Ben to become comfortable enough to accept Peter's proposal. We decided to give it some thought on how to accomplish the mission. As Joe and I discussed how to get Ben to agree to come to the celebration, we brainstormed how our attendance and Ben's attendance could increase our exposure in the magazine for free. That would certainly be a selling point to Ben.

WHEN IT CAME TO MAKING METALWOODS, BEN HOGAN WAS HIS OWN BEST INSPIRATION.

Introducing Series 56. The new line of metalwoods from the Ben Hogan Company, based on one of Mr. Hogan's most successful club designs ever, our classic 1956 woods.

Why did we adapt a traditional wood design to metalwoods?

Simple. We believe it makes a better club. Shaped by Ben Hogan's years of playing experience, the 1956 Hogan wood became a classic because of its excellent playability. It was the natural model for these metalwoods.

Borrowing from the traditional design, Series 56 metalwoods set up visually square and allow you to align the ball better.

Yet, they feature the best metalwood technology of 1987, including perimeter weighting for tremendous distance, even with off-center hits. They're also the only metalwoods available with our exclusive Apex shafts.

And, as with all Hogan clubs (including the original '56 woods), our metalwoods meet the tightest specifications in the industry for weighting, balance point, flex point, loft, and lie.

Uncompromising standards set by Ben Hogan himself.

Ask your pro about the new Hogan Series 56 line of metalwoods.

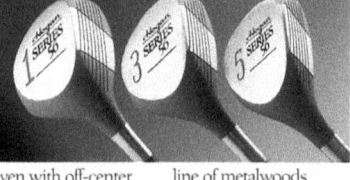

The only metalwoods we know of that've been 31 years in the making. And, we might add, are better clubs for it.

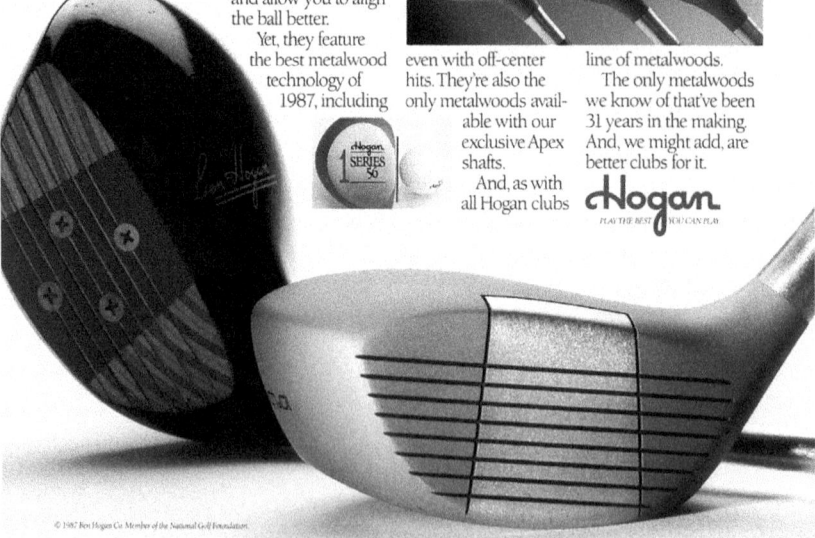

Hogan
PLAY THE BEST YOU CAN PLAY

Peter Bonanni knew that the celebration would not be the success he envisioned without Mr. Hogan. So Peter agreed to have Mr. Hogan kick off the yearlong celebration of the Centennial with an interview "The Hawk Talks." They would provide the Hogan Company a mini magazine with Hogan on the cover, and inside the magazine would be the Hogan interview, and in between each page would be an advertisement for a Hogan product. Peter would provide thousands of copies of the magazine to the Hogan Company to pass out at the 1988 PGA show. Additionally, all the Hogan sales force would be able to pass this magazine to each of their accounts during the normal visits to the pro shops, all during the fall-booking period. This offered the Hogan Company the opportunity to place six advertisements, at no cost, for the interview and Mr. Hogan's attendance at the celebration. The values of these magazine inserts allowed us to publish one two-page and six single-page advertisements with Mr. Hogan on the cover, a letter from me as the president to all our accounts announcing the kickoff of the yearlong celebration of the Centennial of Golf which quadrupled our exposure to our accounts.

WHAT THE QUAL
MEANS TO THE QUA

Y OF YOUR CLUBS
ITY OF YOUR GAME.

Recently, Ben Hogan said in an interview that he believed golf was "90% skill and 10% equipment."

Now, that may sound like the quality of your clubs means very little to the quality of your game.

But if you know Ben Hogan, or play Hogan clubs, then you know that nothing could be further from the truth.

THE QUALITY OF YOUR GAME

At some point after he's taken up golf, every golfer, no matter his ability, must decide just how seriously he wants to pursue the game. And if simply playing golf is not enough, then he'll begin investing more time and energy to play better.

This is where quality equipment becomes so important.

Poorly designed, mediocre equipment will hold you back. You'll always wonder about the problems in your game, when the problems may really be in your clubs. Well-designed, fine quality equipment, on the other hand, permits you to better your grasp of the game. You're freer to improve your concentration. Your mechanics. Your management. And ultimately, your score.

THE QUALITY OF OUR CLUBS

It begins even before we commit a design to paper. Because first, we look for good club ideas. Then we develop appropriate club designs which fill real playing needs.

One other thing: we don't offer one club model as the right club for all golfers. To us, that doesn't seem especially realistic. We understand that different golfers have very different playing skills and styles.

And that serious players come in all handicaps. Our object is to make clubs which help the golfer play his individual game better.

Currently, we offer a selection of three different clubs. Apex is our traditional tour blade. Radial, our club for easy hitting. And Magnum, our most forgiving club.

Of course, most golfers know Hogan clubs for how well they're built. We use none of the shortcuts found elsewhere. Instead, we take extra manufacturing steps which make our clubs perform so well on the course. We hold our finished clubs up to the toughest standards in clubmaking. Standards set down by Mr. Hogan himself, over thirty years ago.

If you're ready to get more serious about the game this year, then this is the time to invest in more serious golfing equipment.

To that, we can think of no better investment than the golf clubs of Ben Hogan.

You might as well get the most out of that 10%.

Hogan
PLAY THE BEST YOU CAN PLAY

Over the next couple of days, I reviewed this request with my staff to get their opinions on the idea. Everyone was excited about the idea and how this might impact the Hogan Company with a lot of free press. With the commercial and the ads all being released in the middle of the year, this should give us a big advantage over our competition. Now the task was for me to convince Ben that the Centennial of Golf Celebration was something he needed to do for himself and the company. I needed to develop a strategy within the time frame of my morning meetings to get Ben's commitment to attend.

How important would this event be to the game of golf? What impact would it have on the players that have created this wonderful business? What impact would it have on the Hogan Company? Finally, what are the motives of the people that are pushing for this event? If I could shape this properly, I was confident Ben would agree. The one big part of the celebration I felt he might not appreciate was the Player of the Century Award they were planning to announce. This had the feel of a competition, not a celebration, and Ben would approve of that type of honor for any player. I would need to downplay that part of the celebration. We were well on our way into the development of the iron at this point, and I planned to bring him some samples that he was to hit and then provide us with feedback. This was my opportunity.

One morning after dropping off some new samples to Ben, I confessed to him, "I have heard that *Golf Magazine* is talking about celebrating one hundred years of golf in this country. They believe if they can properly honor the history and the players that are responsible for this incredible game, they can separate themselves from their competition as the premier golf publication in the world. Their publisher, Peter Bonanni, is a golf historian and is the one that came up with this idea. In addition, if you were to agree to participate, this would substantially enhance our advertising effort in the marketplace." I added, "Many of our staff will be there to make sure we control the media that will obviously try to bombard you. I could also accompany you as we did for the commercial shoot we did in

March." I went on, "The event will be held at the Waldorf-Astoria hotel, so that will provide more crowd control for the attendees. I have been told all the greats of the past that are still alive and can travel are planning to attend." Finally, I said, "Ben, if you agree, this will greatly improve our ability to place our ads closer to the front cover of the magazine without paying a premium." Feeling some momentum, I launched into more details, "You will fly up there with Valeria and her sister, and yes, you will be with them during the presentation, and yes, they will accompany us to the cocktail party before the event. There is also a golf tournament to celebrate the event in which I am playing." I felt I needed him to know that small little piece of information. "If you need anything at all during the tournament, Joe Kelly, a close friend of mine whom you signed some posters for, will be available to make sure there are no problems until the tournament is over." Having barely time to catch my breath, I concluded with "How does that sound, Ben?"

The pause was short this time. "Okay, I will go."

I couldn't hold back my grin. "Thank you, Ben. This is going to be the celebration that will be talked about forever. Mr. Peter Bonanni from *Golf Magazine* will want to come down and introduce himself to you as well as present you with the invitation to attend the event. I will let you know when that will be." I said goodbye and hurried back to my office. I called Joe Kelly to give him the news. He, in turn, called Peter Bonanni and let him know that his dream was now complete. It now would be a true celebration of the first hundred years of golf. Life could not be much better at that moment.

The Hogan Company was set to make a momentous splash on the golf world even in the midst of a constant influx of prospective buyers about every other month who awaited our staged presentation to decide if we were worth buying. We were being asked to share our company secrets with our competitors and not hold anything back, which became increasingly uncomfortable for all my staff. These meetings would continue the rest of 1987, all the while the new Hogan strategy was in action. As good as life seemed to be, we always had Minstar looming over our heads.

It had been two years since Minstar raided AMF to acquire the Hogan brand, which resulted in my promotion to president in December of 1985. Irwin Jacobs had visited the company once or twice in the beginning, but then the only time I would see him was in Minneapolis, at Minstar corporate office. My general manager, Bob Sutter, would visit Fort Worth to review our budgets and strategies before leaving. Any and all contact with Mr. Hogan was left up to me. I was given the task of informing him of what Minstar was contemplating. After each sales presentation to each prospective buyer, I would update Ben the morning after the visit and give him some details about who was there. I could tell that Ben was upset about what was going on with them trying to sell the company. When Ben originally sold the company to AMF, they wanted to continue to manufacture the products that Ben started the company with. He was not happy that all this new owner wanted was to sell Hogan to the highest bidder. I often inquired during this sales process if any of his friends were interested in buying the company, and I really never got an answer to that question. The beginning of December of 1987 was the last visit of the year by Minstar's Bob Sutter to review the year's performance against the budget. He shared that early next year, we would have a sales presentation to a Japanese group named Cosmo World who was interested in buying the Hogan Company. The thought of a Japanese company owning the Fort Worth-based Hogan Company was revolting to me.

As we approached December, I decided the staff Christmas party should include Mr. Hogan and his wife, Valerie. The event was held at Shady Oaks Country Club, where I became a member. This would be a great celebration of the year and all that we had accomplished together, the good and the bad. I had a surprise in store that I hoped would make for a memorable event. As everyone arrived, I took Ben around the room to greet everyone in attendance. We enjoyed cocktails and dinner, which were fantastic. I then took the podium and made a few prepared comments to recognize all the company accomplishments for the year. I pointed out how bright the future looked for the Ben Hogan Company. I emphasized the Ben

Hogan commercial and the wonderful ad campaign we launched that had turned the company around and reclaimed our standing in the marketplace. I thanked everyone present, along with Ben Hogan and Peter Piotrowski, for creating the new Edge product. I highlighted the improvement in sales and profits that were achieved and thanked Doug McGrath for the effort of the sales department for the year. I thanked Dick Lyon for the seamless execution of the ad campaign. I thanked Doug Hendershot for helping produce the products that helped us achieve those sales goals as we dealt with a very difficult employee morale due to the upcoming union negotiation. Then I thanked Don Holland, the VP of human resources, for coordinating the Hogan open house and for updating the Hogan service award program that recognized contributions by our employees to our overall success. The final thank you was aimed at Ben Hogan himself for bringing us all together and all he had done to make this year the best we have ever had. Then I pulled out of my pocket the Hogan service award, a gold ring with three small diamonds on the plaque with the Reveille image of the Hogan swing to recognize Ben for thirty-five years of service. This would be the only ring of its kind.

    I looked over to Ben and asked him to stand so I could present him his award. There was a hush in the room, and no one said a word. As I looked at Ben, I could see he was struggling to keep his emotions in check, so I did not ask him to speak. The moment was not lost on anyone as many a tear was shed. As he sat back down, I had a few more remarks before we ended the party. After Mr. Hogan had left, Doug Hendershot came up to me with a smile on his face. He said, "You would not believe what Ben just did to me while you were completing your speech. As you were speaking, Mr. Hogan turned toward me and put his powerful right hand on my shoulder, saying nothing for a moment. Then he turned toward me and said the words that made my heart sink. 'Doug, I could smash your face in with this ring right now!' Several seconds passed, then he leaned against my shoulder. A smile appeared on his face, and he said, 'Just kidding.' Oh my gosh, my heart then resumed beating again. Yes, Hogan was the great intimidator."

It was around that time that our union contract came time to renegotiate. The Hogan hourly waged workforce was reflective of the Fort Worth labor market. We were very competitive with the larger companies in the area, like Bell Helicopter and Lockheed Martin, formerly known as General Dynamics. The union at the Hogan plant had been in place for over twenty-five years. After Ben sold the company in 1960 to AMF, the plant was unionized, and for the next twenty-five years, there was never a strike during any of the negotiations. Minstar had early on taken a very aggressive approach with the union negotiation. They let me know in no uncertain terms that they would handle the negotiation, and everyone was to cooperate with their top legal counsel, Alan Rickmond. This handler's main contact with the Hogan Company was Doug Hendershot, VP of manufacturing. Doug would brief me on how the process was proceeding. The union chief, Paul Bresnan, tended to keep most of the union contract negotiation strategy to himself.

In preparation for the meeting between both sides, he instructed the VP to interview replacement workers in case there was a strike. The Hogan representative put pressure on the union to accept the new contract. He also informed us they had hired a security force to step in if a strike happened to protect the employees that would be required to come to work during the negotiations. The back and forth between the union and Minstar seemed typical for these sorts of things. The union and its workforce to protect would make a demand, and Minstar's hired spokesman would reject the proposal. Minstar would not make any counteroffer, which seemed strange to us at that time. As the negotiations slowed down, the union made their last proposal to the management team, which again was rejected. Minstar then introduced a brand-new contract to the union to accept and go to work. The union was given twenty-four hours to accept or reject the offer.

Hogan Strike

The Hogan employee's union and their former owner, AMF, had been negotiating union contracts for over twenty years, so no one expected there would be any problem with Minstar at the helm. From a financial perspective, we knew the company was heading in the right direction based on the improved profitability in the years leading up to 1988, going from a $2.5 million loss in 1985 to $2.5 million profit in 1986, and it improved again in 1987 to a $4.0 million profit, and the union was well aware of those numbers.

There were always many preparations to support management positions in regard to the wages Hogan paid our employees. Local information would be gathered to support our wage scale, which included the cost-of-living increases. The Hogan workforce was hourly wage and was reflective of the Fort Worth labor market. We were very competitive with the larger firms like Bell Helicopter and General Dynamics (now Lockheed Martin), competing for our skilled workforce. The Hogan Company had always been able to settle the new contract negotiations without a labor stoppage. In the twenty-five years of AMF ownership, there never was a strike.

I was a part of the first negotiating team back in 1985, and the relationship between the union and the company remained quite positive. The Hogan Company was a small division under the AMF umbrella, with most of the employees working as hourly employees. The company morale was the highest it had been in a long time. The Hogan open house early in 1986 had a very positive impact on the hourly workforce. We had also improved the employee service award program to put greater emphasis on years of service at the company. Now that Minstar had control, we were about to see how they did things. This would also be the first negotiation conducted by Minstar, and we were curious to know what kind of an owner Irwin Jacobs would turn out to be.

The union contract was set to expire in March of 1988 as we were in the middle of producing our new breakthrough forged cavity back iron. All the positive feedback on this product convinced us, we had to protect our labor force from a potential labor slow down. The only way to do that with our own labor force was to agree with the union's wage demands, but Minstar was not going to increase wages and potentially damage the sale of the company. At the very least, we needed to be able to produce enough product to get samples and demos into the hands of our salesmen so they could showcase the Edge. The backup plan that Minstar directed us to have in place was to set up assembly operations outside of Fort Worth, one in Mexico and the other in California. This would allow us the capabilities to temporarily continue production lines if operations in Fort Worth were shut down.

Everything seemed normal during the first labor meeting. The Hogan Union submitted their first proposal demanding a 10 percent raise. We all felt this was a good starting point as surely Minstar would be able to settle the contract at about half that number. Then things turned ugly as the Minstar negotiator did not even make a counteroffer. He stated the Hogan wages were too high, and thus no raises would be accepted in a new contract. This created an instant problem for both sides. The union now knew Minstar was playing hardball, and they needed to adjust their position or face an all-out battle. These negotiations went on for several meetings, and it became apparent Minstar was not looking to settle the contract, but rather they were there to bust the union.

As the meetings continued, the Hogan plant and our hourly workers, generally unaware of the major momentum happening within the Hogan Company, grew into a very hostile working environment. Most of the hourly workers were outstanding employees and would do anything to make sure the company was successful, but unfortunately, we had our share of agitators that would make the situation worse for everybody. I would meet regularly with Doug Hendershot, as he would update me with any progress on the contract negotiation. The Minstar attorney felt no obligation to ever meet with me as he was taking his direction from Irwin Jacobs. After weeks of talks, the attorney put on the table their new contract for the union that they would be implementing. The wage structure that Minstar would implement in the factory would be a 40 percent reduction in the average hourly wages. This was met with outrage from the Hogan Union representatives. This Minstar contract was nonnegotiable, and if the Hogan Union did not agree to those terms, they could go on strike, which is exactly what they did.

The union contract expired on March 31, 1988, and without an agreement, Minstar forced them into a strike on April 8, 1988. No one ever imagined that Hogan would entertain closing the plant. Once that decision was made, the next move that the Minstar attorney made was to order Doug to bring in a security force named Knuckles. Knuckles's security team members were present, armed with military-grade weapons while they patrolled the grounds. Knuckles secured both the Pafford Street plant and the Montgomery facilities from any potential vandalism around the clock. They were also present to help keep the salaried employees safe during the strike as there were high tensions between the union workers and the salaried employees. At the same time, Doug was instructed to continue to interview replacement workers so we could keep opening up the production plants with this new workforce. Doug and his handful of supervisors interviewed over seven hundred prospective employees to get two hundred fifty replacement workers to start within a week. The replacement workers were also promised, once the strike was over, they would keep their jobs.

I felt helpless as there was little I could do to help solve this problem. The plant workers were the lifeblood of the Hogan Company. All the marketing, Ben Hogan commercials, and new technology clubs in the world could solve the absence of plant workers to make our products. The disgruntled employees of the union called the strike, and all the union workers left the plant. They set up picketing lines that would block Pafford Street traffic and try to keep the salaried employees from coming to work! The armed guards would create a path through the picketers so the salaried employees would have access to the plant. On a daily basis, both coming to work and leaving work, the salaried employees were yelled at and were on the receiving end of profanity-laced tirades and chants from the picketers. The replacement workers moved in on cue and started their new jobs. They were accompanied in and out of the employee parking lot by security as the picketing employees did not take well to their presence. Tempers flared, and many threats were yelled out at the new workers. It wasn't long before some of the picketing workers saw the writing on the wall. They knew they had few options here.

In the first week of the strike, three employees crossed the picket line and returned to work. This first week was also when Doug Hendershot and I would start to receive a series of frequent terrifying calls, threatening our livelihood, including threats to our family. I received my first death threat on my home phone in April of 1988. One call in particular hit heavy with me and my wife. My wife answered the call at home, and the caller went on to tell my wife that they knew where we lived, and they knew we had a child in elementary school. "If your husband doesn't settle this strike, he would be punished severely."

Doug was the most visible face of the Hogan/Minstar resistance, and he received the majority of the anger, but as the head of the company, I was also deemed responsible, and thus I got my fair share of threats. The representative from Minstar would also take on threats, but he was only seen during the meetings, and he would fly out right after meetings. Doug would ride to work each morning in a bulletproof van fitted with solid rubber tires to guarantee his safety. I was able to come to work unescorted, but the security remained very tight around the facility. The Fort Worth Police Department would be monitoring the situation, and more than once, the Fort Worth Swat team was summoned to clear the streets of demonstrators, with several being arrested. One incident was particularly disturbing for me. I was at a city baseball field, watching my youngest son, eleven-year-old Mark, play baseball. About halfway through the game, as I looked around between the action, I noticed this guy watching me and every move I made. I would move to another section of the stands, and he would move to be able to see me. From that point in time, I recognized this "shadow." The charade went on for about another forty-five minutes, and I was getting worried for my wife and son. I went to the bathroom, and he followed behind me. He kept his distance and did not approach me in the restroom or at the field. I looked for any type of security but found none. Could he have been one of the people that were calling my house with death threats? I felt the onset of panic creep over me. How would I protect my family? I was trying to figure out what to do and knew the parking lot was very dark. Would that be his place to act? How did you leave? Did you grab Mark's bat as a weapon?

After I made it home safely, I decided to call Steve Dryer, my golf ball plant manager, who was in charge of security and hiring the security team Knuckles, to alert him to the situation. Steve asked me to describe the guy that I witnessed at the ballpark. I gave him the most detailed description I could as I had studied him quite clearly.

Steve replied, "Jerry, that is your personal security guard!"

"Wow, someone should have told me that you had a security guard on me when I went out in public."

Steve replied, "I am so sorry, Jerry, with all that was going on, that was an oversight on my part."

That night still weighs heavy on my heart today, and thank God it wasn't something more.

As the strike continued with daily picket lines, chants, and threats, I received the next big bombshell of news. I was informed that Minstar had found a buyer for the Hogan Company in Cosmo World International. As part of the closing process, Minstar was required to negotiate a new contract with the Hogan Union before the new ownership took effect. The new Japanese company sided with Minstar's position and therefore had little interest in considering the union's ask. The strike would continue for about three weeks until April 13, 1988, as the hourly employees were in an increasingly difficult position not earning a paycheck. The pressure on them only mounted as the replacement workers threatened their return ever happening. The pressure grew so great that the union representatives decided to accept the unfavorable contract just to get to come back to work. When that decision was made, all the replacement workers were terminated, and the promise that they would have a job went up in smoke. The union decided they would fight the contract through the national labor board with lawsuits for unfair bargaining by the ownership group.

No one knew much about Cosmo World and whether or not they knew all the facts of the strike. We all assumed they had been fed their knowledge from Minstar, so they may not have had a positive view of the strikers and their reasonable requests. We heard later that Minstar sold Hogan to Cosmo World for $53 million. All that talk from Irwin Jacobs in the media not looking to sell Hogan seemed to be a little shallow now. The mess he left behind would have to be cleaned up by someone else. I would always feel a knot in my stomach when I would think that this all happened under my leadership.

In the twenty-five years that AMF owned the Hogan Company, at no time did they ever create such a mess for the company with their negotiating strategy. Irwin Jacobs turned out to be whatever everybody claimed he was, a corporate raider. No one ever did a follow-up story from the original raid to determine how Minstar's purchase of Hogan would affect the future of the Hogan Company and all its employees. The simple truth is, one man walked away with $53 million and left everybody at the company holding the bag. He made a significant business deal but left in its wake a hostile working environment that would linger for years to come. Now that the smoke had cleared and the union contract negotiation was over, the question was, could we come out of this and still realize the momentum we had created? Would we survive the strike and new ownership?

As the plant workers came back to work, we began to notice several instances of sabotage of some of our machinery. One particular frustrating instance of sabotage involved the nickel-chrome plating tanks. We would discover pennies had been thrown in the tanks where the copper from the penny would ruin the plating bath. The entire tank would require draining, which was an expensive and time-consuming process. Many of the union workers came back to work very disappointed in what the Hogan Company had done to them. But they had families to feed, bills to pay, so back to work they would go, some more reluctant than others. A few would try to slow down the operations, thinking this would put pressure on the company to open up negotiations again. The biggest problems we were having were procrastination on the ball painting lines and the plating of irons. This was the last process for each of these lines; therefore, any time there were delays at the end, it would shut down all productions for balls and irons until the lines and plating tanks were cleared. We would be fighting this battle all summer and most of the fall of 1987 as other instances of sabotage slowed down our ability to ship irons to meet our sales forecast.

1987 RANKINGS: GOLF Magazine's 100 Greatest Courses in the World
GOLF
September 1987
$1.95
$2.50 Canada
THE HAWK TALKS!
Ben Hogan shares his keys on "playing smart"
...and kicks off our year-long Centennial celebration with a revealing one-on-one interview
Ben Hogan

Moving Forward

The strike was behind us, and we were making a concerted effort to heal the wounds that were created with the union, and slowly our production capabilities were improving to support our sales. As we got the company back in the right direction, we felt the worst was behind us. The sales forecasts were looking good since the Ben Hogan marketing had done its magic. This was the most exciting part of the year for us. Sales for Apex tour blades were up, the new Hogan iron exploded in the marketplace, the Series 56 woods sales had doubled, and the introduction of the new Ayn Young Sportswear line had been received very well by the market. No one knew that we were about to introduce a new revolutionary product in 1988 that would become the most successful club in the history of the golf business.

As a part of our partnership benefits for having Ben agree to go to the Centennial of Golf Celebrations, *Golf Magazine* pulled together all the ads we placed with them in 1987 and then asked Ben for a personal interview to kick off the start of the Centennial celebration. Then because they were kicking off the yearlong celebration of their event, the golf insert would be published just like their magazine with a September 1987 date, and now they could include the five advertisements we placed with them in this insert, framing the interview. This reprint would be provided to all our sales associates for a leave behind during the fall-booking program. This was the most impressive piece I have ever seen about Mr. Hogan; Ben was on the cover, and it was labeled September of 1987, addition with "1987 Rankings: Golf Magazine's Greatest Courses in the World publication." The magazine would provide us with thousands of copies to distribute to our accounts and at the 1988 PGA show. The inside cover had a letter from me to the trade about what we were able to accomplish with their help in 1987. In addition, the reprint would have the exclusive interview with Mr. Hogan and all the ads we ran during 1987 Ben Hogan's Sixth Fundamentals, two-page spread and single-page ads for Radial, Magnum, Series 56, and the new Apex iron. Peter Bonanni would later inform me of all the complaints he would receive from the rest of the trade about how their magazine was favoring the Hogan Company. Once this reprint would be circulated, my phone was ringing off the hook. How did you guys get that done? That must have cost you a small fortune to get the magazine to run that exclusively for the Hogan Company. This was so out of the ordinary for our company, and the sheer volume of these ads and the quality of each one set us apart from the rest of the industry. The quality of the ads and framing them all with Mr. Hogan with his reputation for quality and craftsmanship no one could come close to what we had done. When I gave my answer, most people could not believe it, as I would say, "I did not do this. Mr. Hogan was the one that put us in this position to pull this off. Without him, this would never have happened."

Hogan

BEN HOGAN CO

J. M. AUSTRY
President

January 10, 1988

Greetings:

I'm pleased to announce that 1987 was a fantastic year for us at the Ben Hogan Company. The success of several new products in 1987 created the momentum for us to maintain a leadership position in the industry.

Leading the way was, what is our most popular tour blade introduction ever, new Apex Irons. Also a big hit was the introduction of our new Lady Hogan clubs. Extremely popular products such as our Series 56 metal woods and our Fall introduction of the all-new Ayn Young women's sportswear line were also major contributors to a successful year.

In 1987 we were also very proud of Mr. Hogan's involvement in our advertising. With his help, our message was very clear. At Hogan we believe we design and manufacture the best clubs in the industry, and that's what we proudly told the golfing world. Mr. Hogan would have it no other way. It was the basis of his company in 1953 when he opened shop, and it will remain that way in 1988 and for many years to come.

We also owe each of you a special thanks for all your help and support. We couldn't do it without you.

Looking at the coming year, we are expecting even more success and excitement. We are doing all we can to make Ben Hogan the Company of your choice for 1988. As the year unfolds I think you will agree that, Now as Then, Ben Hogan Is The Name To Watch In Golf. Good luck in the coming year.

Sincerely,

Jerry Austry

Jerry Austry
President

2912 West Pafford Street,
Fort Worth, Texas 76110 • 817/921-2661

Centennial Conversation

Ben Hogan

The "Hawk," now 75, looks back on his career, debunks several myths and shares the keys that made him golf's shrewdest tactician

This interview, conducted by Editor George Peper, is the first of a series of Centennial Conversations between GOLF Magazine and 10 of the game's most prominent figures.

GOLF: Next year we'll be celebrating the 100th anniversary of golf in America. You've been around for 75 of those years. What's your first golf-related memory?
HOGAN: I guess it goes back to about 1920. I was nine years old and selling newspapers in Fort Worth to make some money when one of my friends told me I could earn more by caddieing. The word was you could make 65 cents just by packing a bag around 18 holes. So one day I walked the seven miles from my home to Glen Garden Country Club to see what it was all about.
  The established caddies at Glen Garden ran sort of a kangaroo court. For a new caddie to break in, he had to win a fist-fight with one of the older, bigger caddies. So they threw me against one of those fellas and I got the better of him. It was through the caddie experience that I got the golf bug.
GOLF: You were a natural left-hander who took up the game right-handed, weren't you?
HOGAN: No. That's one of those things that's always been written, but it's an absolute myth. The truth is, the first golf club I owned was an old left-handed, wooden-shafted, rib-faced mashie that a fellow gave me, and that's the club I was weaned on. During the mornings we caddies would bang the ball up and down the practice field until the members arrived and it was time to go to work. So I did all that formative practice left-handed. But I'm a natural right-hander.
GOLF: So many top golfers say they've learned the game by studying your swing. From whom did you learn?
HOGAN: I used to caddie for a fellow named Ed Stewart. He was 21 or 22. He wasn't the best tipper at Glen Garden, but he was the best player. I'd wait around to caddie for

continued

"You hear stories about me beating my brains out practicing, but the truth is, I was enjoying myself."

Reprinted with permission, GOLF Magazine, 1988

Late in 1987, we finally got a model approved by Ben that he would endorse to the world, and we could order the molds to make the forgings for production. We would also have to come up with a name for the product that would best describe the magnitude of the introduction. Before that would happen, Peter Piotrowski, the VP of research and development, would come into my office and inform me that we had a slight problem. The tooling and the manufacturing process were untested at that time. He felt it would be better if we went into production with a casting. I almost exploded. How can we do that? What kind of introduction would it be as another cavity back iron from Hogan? How would we distinguish our product from Ping? Why would ours be better?

"Pete, we cannot do a casting. If any of the features of forging are true, to be softer than a casting and everyone believes that, why not give everybody what they believe to be true?" Finally, I said, "I have been able to get Ben to agree to a lot of things this last year, but there is no way he would ever buy endorsing a casting over a forging. It has to be a forging! I don't care what it costs!"

> *"The tee shot is the most important in golf. You have to hit the fairway before you can put the ball close."*

day. And the next day, too.

So I said, I've got to take this out on Tour and put it under some pressure. The next week was the George May Tournament in Chicago—and in those days he had two events, back to back. A big field of players competed the first week, and then the top 12 from that tournament went on to play for big money the following week. Well, I went up there and won both of them.

GOLF: What was that inspiration?
HOGAN: *(smiling)* I'm not telling.
GOLF: Did it relate to one of the fundamentals in your book, "Five Lessons: The Modern Fundamentals of Golf"?
HOGAN: Yes, it did.
GOLF: It was the part about pronation and supination, wasn't it?
HOGAN: Well, yes it was, but it all gets back to the grip. You can't make those moves unless you have the proper hold on the club. It's like steering an automobile. You don't steer to the right all the time, you also steer to the left. That ability has to come from the grip, which is the transformer through which the juice flows.
GOLF: Are those "five lessons" still as pat as ever, or would you like to change any part of that book?
HOGAN: I think the book still contains my best thoughts. It's a mechanics book, and no matter how people may differ anatomically, the mechanics are the same, assuming no physical deformity.
GOLF: But you're also a believer, are you not, that once those basic mechanics are learned, good golf is 90 percent mental?
HOGAN: That's right, it's all management. Even as I practiced the mechanics, I practiced visualizing shots and making the ball move in different ways on the range. Otherwise, it's nothing but calisthenics. When the shot I visualized didn't come off, I might hit 20 more before I got it right.

But once you've learned how to hit those shots, golf is all management. Certainly, if you can't manage your game, you can't play tournament golf. You continually have to ask yourself what club to select, what sort of shot to play, where to aim it, whether to accept a safe par or to try to go for a birdie. You can't play every hole the same way. I never could.

GOLF: Today's Tour players seem to play more mechanically, especially with regard to judging distances. Every pro has a yardage book in his pocket.
HOGAN: I know it, and I think that's terrible. When I played, we never had those cards that told us the pin was 20 feet from the front edge and 15 feet from the left-hand bunker. Those things have taken away about 80 percent of the feel of playing golf. Heck, they give them the answer to the foot. They've taken the creativity out of professional golf.
GOLF: What sorts of things did you routinely compute on every shot?
HOGAN: The lie and the wind, to begin with. But you also have to consider the slope of the terrain you're hitting to, the presence of hazards and, above all, the pin position.

At The Masters, for instance, there are easy, hard and moderately difficult positions on each green. On a given day, they'll set up the course with six easy spots, six hard ones and six that are so-so. That's true at most tournaments.

What was strange, however, was that during practice rounds the pins were always set toward the front-middle of the green to keep traffic off the putting surface. But when I played those rounds, I'd direct my shots at the areas where I

Peter Read Miller

WHY A GOLFER KNOWN FOR CONSISTENCY BUILDS A CLUB FOR GOLFERS WHO AREN'T.

During his years on Tour, Ben Hogan was known as a golfer who spent countless hours on the practice tee honing his competitive edge. The author of the definitive book on swing mechanics. The man with the classic swing.

As clubmakers, we at the Ben Hogan Company recognize that not all golfers are ready for the Tour. And that many of you play for the sheer pleasure of the game. But that doesn't mean you can't play better and even enjoy the game more, by playing a club gifted with Hogan quality and performance. In this case, Magnum, our most forgiving club ever.

Magnum's head design distributes weight toward the toe of the clubhead, creating a generous sweetspot, and producing more solid impacts, even with off-center hits. The design also helps reduce slicing.

The full offset promotes a "hands ahead" position to help you hit down and through the ball. Each Magnum also features Hogan's exclusive Apex shafts.

And, as with every Hogan club, Magnum is subject to the tightest weighting, balance point, flex point, loft, and lie specifications in golf.

Uncompromising standards set down by Ben Hogan himself.

Now that you know that the Ben Hogan Co. makes a club for golfers like yourself, talk to your pro about playing Magnum irons and woods. The clubs for players who'd like to be more consistent, from the man who wrote the book on the subject.

Hogan
PLAY THE BEST YOU CAN PLAY.

© 1987 Ben Hogan Co. Member of the National Golf Foundation

The tooling with Cornel Forge Co. was just one of the problems we incurred. This club would be impossible to plate and polish to get the proper weight to make the swing weights necessary with the final assembly and control the hand polishing So the cavity back would not be eliminated in the grinding operation. In addition to the hitting test performed by Mr. Hogan, Peter's group performed mechanical "golfer" testing in the summer of 1987. Once we thought we had the design we would introduce, we tested this model against comparable cast cavity back irons for accuracy and distance. The machine was set to strike golf balls at nine points on the clubface: one-fourth-inch below center, on center, and one-fourth-inch above center from heel, center and toe hitting positions. In on-course tests, golfers were asked to compare the playability and appearance of the new iron with leading cavity back clubs.

BEN
SIXTH FUNDA

Chances are, if you've ever tried to improve your game, you've come across Ben Hogan's *Five Lessons, The Modern Fundamentals of Golf.* Though it was first published in 1956, it's still considered by many one of the best instructional books ever written.

Now Mr. Hogan offers another fundamental. One that goes hand in hand with the other five: "With quality clubs, a player of any skill level can improve the quality of his game."

Of course this isn't exactly a new idea. In fact, it's been the clubmaking philosophy at the Ben Hogan Company for over 30 years.

But to many golfers, this idea remains an abstraction. And all our talk about uncompromising clubmaking standards, so much overkill. After all, every club is made pretty much the same, right?

Well, not exactly. And so, if you read on, you'll understand why.

HOGAN'S MENTAL OF GOLF.

In a game with as many variables as golf, we believe the equipment maker's role is to remove the variables from the equipment, so that the player can use that equipment with confidence. Otherwise, he's like a tennis player using a warped racquet. Or a race car driver running on five cylinders.

That leaves us with the challenge of not only designing sound clubs, but also maintaining the integrity of these designs on through their manufacture.

We accept that challenge every day at the Ben Hogan Company. And we build our clubs accordingly.

HOW WE BUILD BETTER CLUBS

We do it every step of the way.

For example, to meet specified swingweights on our irons, we use a computer machining process to remove weight from the back of the clubhead. This maintains the original face-to-hosel design relationship, which is one way of keeping the clubs looking consistent throughout the set.

Other clubmakers grind the entire clubhead, including the face.

We're just as conscientious about the top lines of our clubs.

Our forged clubs are profile trimmed and grooved along the back to control the thickness of the top line.

It only makes sense to us. Because the more similar your clubs look throughout the set, the less of a distraction they become. This lets you concentrate on your game. Remarkably, we know of no one else who takes this step.

We also take special care to give each club the proper loft and lie. Most clubmakers adjust for loft and lie just once, after the club is built. At Hogan, we make two adjustments. The first, during the initial grinding process. The second, after we align the grip

and hosel. Two separate, smaller adjustments help guarantee correct loft and lie for each club, and progression throughout the set.

And unlike clubmakers who pneumatically force their shafts into the clubhead, we insert each shaft by hand, to ensure the proper shaft step pattern for each club. This is how we can promise frequency-matched clubs throughout the set. You'd be surprised how many clubmakers can't meet that promise.

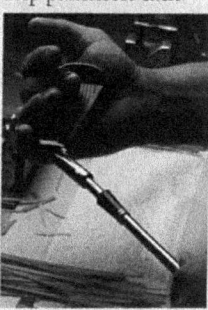

Another thing: we pin the club through the hosel and shaft, eliminating the chance of the blade becoming misaligned. This may seem like a small detail, but not if you've ever had a clubhead loosen and twist on a shot.

Finally, we don't make the radical weight adjustments you'll find with other clubs. No counterbalancing. No slugs. No powder down the shaft. Any of these measures can play havoc with our flex points. And your shots on the golf course.

HOW YOU BUILD A BETTER GAME

In the end, we build better performing clubs because we refuse to compromise our quality standards in any of the steps we take. And the way we see it, that's not overkill. That's the way a golfer gets clubs he can believe in.

So if you're serious about improving your game, get yourself a set of clubs that are equal to the task.

Ask your pro about Apex. Radial. Magnum. The clubs of Ben Hogan.

Hogan
PLAY THE BEST YOU CAN PLAY

Getting Our Edge

We learned firsthand how stiff our competition was, but months of testing consistently showed that the new iron produced greater accuracy, equal or better distance, and a more sensitive feel when hitting the golf ball. This would reinforce the softer feel claim of a forged cavity back club. The testing gave us further confidence. Now we had to come up with the name for this new product. We did not have a budget for an official naming process, so I met with the director of marketing, Dick Lyons, and requested a list of the names we presently have trademarked. We started eliminating the ones we knew would not represent this innovative club first. We also reviewed the Minnesota focus group notes to see if anything jumped off the page at us. During this review, we thought of the many ways that Mr. Hogan would be described by the news media to see what advantage they would attribute to him. What did they think gave Ben his edge during tournament play?

Ben Hogan has been written thousands of times by hundreds of writers all over the world. He was often described as cold, calculating, distant, antisocial, uncooperative, preoccupied, and obsessive in his drive for perfection. He also acquired several nicknames over the years, which factored into our discussion—the Hawk, the Wee Ice Man, Bantam Ben, the Little Man, Blue Blades. What word captured what Ben Hogan embodied more than any other? Then it jumped off the page. One word seemed more appropriate than any other for the new club—the *Edge*! How fitting that most people felt Ben had the edge over his competitors. This is a description that would also fit our story line and blend in perfectly with the tagline for the first forged cavity back club ever produced. It combined the feeling of a forging with the advantage of the cavity back to provide the golfer with an *edge* against his competition.

Dick and I both agreed, and now I had to sell the name to Ben. We did not have a second choice, so getting his approval would be extremely important. We felt good about the name, so off I went. I walked in the next morning and said good morning to Ben. "We have the model you have approved, along with machine and player testing results that confirm this product has the edge over all the other cavity back cast clubs in the marketplace." I explained about the testing and stated, "Our club gives us the edge with performance on and off center as well with toe strikes. We also receive the edge for how soft the feedback is to the player on miss hits. Therefore, we would like to name the product the Hogan Edge."

There was a long silence, and finally, Ben said, "Okay, that is the name we should use."

Thank God he agreed. Another monumental decision has just been made that will reverberate through the golf industry with the *Edge* introduction.

On January 14, 1988, a gentleman named Dick Babbitt showed up in Fort Worth, representing the Japanese company Cosmo World. My first impression of him was of an arrogant, pompous, overbearing, and condescending fellow. As we started our presentation, he would often interrupt, showing his impatience and disregard to all others in the room. The presentation went off terribly because of this. He was not interested in learning anything. He looked over to my boss and said, "All I need is the financials we talked about." He told us after he reviewed them, he would be back in touch. After the presentation, my boss and I had a brief meeting. I let him know that this group and that guy, in particular, would be a disaster if they ended up owning the company. The next morning, I briefed Ben about the visit with Babbitt and Cosmo World. Ben did not appear happy about that possibility. Ben had served in the Pacific during

World War II against the Japanese, which left him bitter toward these people. This seemed like a recipe for disaster.

The next day, we were back to relative normalcy. We decided to expand our advertising program for 1988 by using the famous Hogan one iron shot at the US Open in the ads for the new year but discovered that the Hogan Company and Mr. Hogan did not own the rights to those photos. James Dalthrop, the head of our creative team, used a little creativity to secure the rights to use that photo in a mailer to our major accounts with Mr. Hogan's signature on the photo. We decided we would produce two sizes for distribution, a 16×22 that was able to be framed and a larger 20×32 size that could be framed and hopefully mounted in each pro shop for everyone to see. Then we armed our sales force with this picture for distribution to their respective golf pros, as a leave behind from their sales call. This photo of Hogan is widely considered one of the most famous photos ever taken in golf. It did not take long to figure out this was an unbelievable success as our entire sales force was calling in for more photos. The supply of photos was kept in Fort Worth and controlled by marketing and myself. After a short meeting with the marketing director, we decided to send an ample supply of the smaller photos to salesforce. The larger photos would be mailed to the head golf pros with a special thank letter for supporting the Hogan Company. We always used the opportunity to leak to the head pro about the revolutionary Hogan product that would be introduced this coming year.

The retooling for the Hogan Edge was well underway, and the face-to-weight machine was purchased to assure we could produce the new product and maintain the tight swing weight standards. In the final budget setting process, we now had to commit to how many sets of Edge we would sell. This was a little harder than you might think. We were also to complete our budget submission to Minstar, so we now had to agree to a number that reflected our enthusiasm about how great the Edge would be. The first projection suggested we would sell fifty thousand sets for our high number. Marketing and sales had to agree to the number. I stated that if we really have found the secret of a forged cavity back, then how can we project a number that was typical for previous product launches. No one else was able to claim what we were touting regarding our new Edge club. Mr. Hogan has also put his endorsement on this product, so wouldn't we want to shoot for the stars? These were difficult meetings as our forecast had to be signed off on by Minstar/Cosmo World people. The previous labor negotiation and strike had not left a great taste in anyone's mouth as far as production increases. Both the VP of sales, Doug McGrath, director of marketing, Dick Lyons, came up with the number of sixty thousand sets which equated to a 20 percent increase in irons sales for the year. The international marketing director, Peter Cobb, did not request any sets until the first quarter of 1989. So the number was set at sixty thousand sets.

I was feeling pretty good that we would exceed that number based on the feedback I was getting on the design, manufacturing, marketing, advertising, and from Ben himself. I started to believe that something really special was happening here with the introduction of the Edge clubs. I also knew that with any new idea, there needs to be a champion for it to succeed. The 1988 PGA show was another big success for the Hogan Company. We were able to continue the momentum we generated the year before. We also received wonderful feedback about using Mr. Hogan in the advertising campaign. Every visitor to our sales booth would rave about the ads and Mr. Hogan.

A few months later, as we were preparing for the Centennial Golf Celebration in New York, I walked into Ben's office after my morning tour. Ben spoke first and asked, "Is the company making a profit now?"

I told him, "Yes."

"So why were the union contract negotiations so contentious?" Apparently, someone from the plant had talked to Ben about the large pay cut that was made with the introduction of the new contract. Ben would tell me, "Jerry, why did you do that? We have been negotiating contracts for forty years, and we never had one that was adversarial between the union and the company. I hear there are a lot of bad feelings in the plant about the way they were treated."

I calmly responded, "All I can tell you, Ben, is Minstar felt they needed to increase the profit in order to better market the Hogan Company for sale." He nodded his head, but his disappointment was clear in what we had done.

The company had also been preparing for the news conference where we would introduce the Edge club to the world. I had several meetings with the marketing director, Dick Lyons, discussing how we can maximize the introduction of this product. No one in the golf industry has ever called a news conference to introduce a new product to our knowledge. We weren't even sure how that worked. Would anybody bother to show up? I asked Dick to get with the agency to see what ideas they may have in how we should do it to maximize the chances of success. I was convinced of our revolutionary product and its status as the first of its kind in golf. By working with the creative staff at Tracy Locke Advertising, we developed a three-prong approach. The plan would include local and national news coverage, golf trade magazines, and international coverage. It was suggested we have a meeting at the Hyatt Hotel at DFW in early August as all the writers would be passing through DFW going to the PGA Championship in Tulsa, Oklahoma. Our objective was to get the golf writers to write headlines about the Hogan Edge and its first line of forged perimeter-weighted golf clubs with a full cavity back.

Every day, something exciting was happening at the Hogan Company. Everybody was pulling together to make sure the Edge introduction would surpass anything Hogan had ever done in the past. Unfortunately, the resentment that was left over from the union negotiation was still a real problem. Due to Minstar's cut of the union wages, some of the members were going to create as many problems as they could to make us pay for those actions. This caused delays and missed shipments of products that were sold and a shortfall in sales. As a reaction to these problems, we had to briefly close the operation and carefully monitor everyone entering the operation on a daily basis to eliminate the opportunity for sabotage.

One morning, I asked Ben if there was a union when he started the original company. He said no but did not remember when the plant was unionized under AMF leadership. I asked Ben if they ever had a strike during those years. He thought for a minute and replied that he didn't think so. He shared that the workers were considered a part of the company, and whatever the going rate for skilled labor in Fort Worth was is what Hogan expected to pay. Fort Worth also had several large firms producing military hardware, so that kept wages high as the competition was high for qualified employees. Ben told me he did not believe AMF would have cut the hourly rates like Minstar did when they were already making a profit. He felt it would be hard to sell the belief that, to double the profit, you need to slash hourly wages.

The sale of the Hogan Company was imminent, and thus it had been hanging in the balance. Then late one morning, I got an urgent call from my boss, Bob Sutter, at Minstar. He needed to meet with Hogan that day at three o'clock. I let Bob know that Ben would be at Shady Oaks relaxing and enjoying a few clear ones and thus not a good time to meet. I told Bob, "I usually do not meet with Ben in the afternoon because I can never count on his mood." Bob insisted on the meeting because the announcement of the sale of the Hogan Company was going to be announced in tomorrow's papers. "Holy shit!" I said. "It really is happening again?" I asked for confirmation, and Bob said, "Cosmo World, the Japanese company represented by Dick Babbitt." My heart sank as I recalled how horrible the experience had been with Babbitt.

When Bob arrived, we got in the car and drove off to Shady Oaks. When we got there, we went over to Ben's private table, where he sat alone with a clear one sitting in front of him. I asked Ben, "You remember Bob Sutter from Minstar?"

Ben shook his head. "Yes, I do."

I said, "He has something to tell you."

"Okay, please sit down."

Then Bob carefully informed Ben that Cosmo World had purchased the Hogan Company and that he wanted Mr. Hogan to know before the announcement was in tomorrow's paper. There was a long pause as usual before Ben responded, "Is the company Japanese?"

Bob stated, "Yes," before another pause.

Then Ben said, "Well, it's your company, so you can do what you want with it, but I cannot be a part of the sale. I have too many memories of the war, and I would be unable to function with Japanese leadership." He then rose from his chair and walked away.

Bob then looked at me, and I panicked about what had just happened. Could this destroy the deal? What the hell are we going to do? I was quietly feeling pretty good because I thought this was a terrible deal for everyone in Fort Worth and eventually would destroy the company as we know it.

Bob looked at me and said, "We need to get Ben aboard. How can we do that?"

I shared with Bob about our morning meetings and how I would see him in the morning. "I will go down there in the morning and see if he brings it up."

The next morning, I went down to Ben's office with a couple of clubs to discuss. The meeting was short and productive, and no word was ever mentioned about the sale. I informed the nervous Bob, who said he would let me know when the new owners wanted to visit the facility. I told Bob that is great news for Minstar but not sure if that is good news for my staff or me. More than likely, I would not make it through this transition. After Bob left, I kicked myself for not telling him that Ben was going to kill the deal, but I could help it along.

The next morning, I saw Ben again, and this time I would share with him my feelings about Dick Babbitt and the Japanese. I said, "Ben, I am going to need your help, as I believe these new owners are going to make a lot of changes, and I am probably going to get fired." I wasn't sure what, if anything, Ben could do, but he said he would back me all the way, whatever that would turn out to mean.

The next few mornings, we would discuss the production problems in the plant and how we were progressing with the Edge production. The master model maker, Gene Sheeley, retained his close relationship with Ben, so he was updating him on the mood and sharing with him how we were progressing. After the second day, the subject of Cosmo buying the company was never discussed again. Amazingly, Ben never brought up the subject again. Even after I went into his office and let him know Minstar has made the official announcement that they now own the Ben Hogan Company, Ben didn't say a word. No mention of his statement to Bob that he could not be a part of the sale. It was like it never happened. Ben would never say another word about the new owners.

Then the magic moment arrived with the Cosmo World executives paying a visit to the Fort Worth plant for the first time. We were told they wished to meet with the Hogan executives and, more importantly, Mr. Hogan. We put together a PowerPoint presentation for the new owners to show them what we had been working on. I was prepared to present our company to the group as part of my job. They'd go crazy when I explained the dynamics behind the new Edge club. The Japanese had no idea how good a company we really were and were about to be.

What a disappointment that first meeting turned out to be. Just before their arrival, we got a call that Mr. Isutani, the Cosmo World president, and his entourage would be coming to the facility. We were instructed to gather all the management team and salaried personnel to line up in a single file line. When Mr. Isutani walked by, we were to bow to him without uttering a word. I still can't believe that shit to this day. After that five-minute bowing session, the Japanese procession then wanted to meet Mr. Hogan. As I had told Dick Babbitt, Ben would be found at Shady Oaks Country Club. So we all loaded up and drove out to the club. I drove myself, and the Japanese drove in limousines to the club. I arrived early and beelined to the pro shop and alerted them who was coming. As the Cosmo World group, I led them to the men's club, where Ben was sitting by himself at his corner table with a clear one in front of him. As they crowded around the table, I introduced them to Mr. Hogan. One designated person began to speak in English. No one else said a word. The English speaker introduced the group and let Ben know how proud they were to own the Hogan Company. This introduction took only a few minutes. When he concluded, Ben looked at the speaker and asked him if Mr. Isutani could understand English. The translator replied, "Yes, he can."

Ben then turned to Mr. Isutani, raised his index finger at him, and declared, "You know you just bought the family jewels! Now don't fuck it up!" There was a hush over the table as the perturbed Mr. Hogan stood up, said a pleasant goodbye, and walked away from the table.

Dick Babbitt, who was in attendance, spoke up to let me know someone would be in contact that represents Cosmo World and to give them an office and any cooperation they need. He concluded with "I will see you in New York at the Centennial of Golf, where we can talk about the next steps in the transition." Away he and the Japanese went. They did not tour the plant nor sit for any presentation about the company they had just purchased. They did not seem to care about anything that was happening at Hogan on a daily basis. After they left, I sat down at the bar and ordered a stiff drink. What do I do now? Do I need to get my résumé in order? I sat by myself and reflected on the peculiar day. Now only time will tell what new changes this ownership group would bring.

The next morning, Ben and I couldn't avoid discussing the sale of the company and the idea of the Japanese owning the Hogan company. I could tell Ben was distressed by this set of events, and for the first time in three years, I saw the frailty of this seventy-five-year-old icon. What could he do? For the first time ever in the presence of Ben, I could see sadness on his face. In the subsequent morning meetings, Ben would ask how we could have stopped them from taking over. The answer was simple—nothing.

Our morning sessions then became more about the direction of the company. I related to Ben how Cosmo World and, in particular, Dick Babbitt, was questioning our advertising direction. Cosmo World, we would learn, was more interested in what they felt was the impact a heavy tour sponsorship would bring to sales. They were very critical of the sportswear product line and felt we could achieve double or triple our sales with the right product and tour exposure. Ben and I both felt this would be a disaster for the Hogan Company. I asked Ben if he had met Dick Babbitt, and he confirmed he had. I paused this time for more of his reaction, but none were forthcoming.

The Hogan Company was now controlled by a man none of us cared for. It is true that almost every corporate president I ever worked for had an ego taller than the Empire State building, but they did have a degree of humility dealing with subordinates, not Dick Babbitt. Beyond a brief encounter at the Centennial would not see Dick again until just before the national Hogan sales meeting in July when he arrived with his entourage of Cosmo World executives. On the rare occasion that I would hear from Dick, my executive assistant would tell me Dick has requested us to send upward of one hundred sets of golf clubs to various people in California and Hawaii, free of charge. We all felt he sure was playing the big shot now. The good news is we did not have to contend with this bullshit every day. We had too much happening and needed to keep busy. I was able to keep my staff isolated from most of Dick's bullshit. There wasn't much he could do to impact 1988, as all the wheels were in motion with advertising schedules and funding committed by the time Cosmo purchase was consummated. We would, after all, realize the fruits of our labors, at least for the time being.

As the Centennial of Golf Celebration in New York approached, I decided to prepare Ben by reviewing the progress we have made. So I put together a little PowerPoint program that I would review with him on the plane. I wanted everything to be fresh in his mind as we attended the celebration. I shared how well the public is responding to the ads he helped us create. Our total bookings are up 20 percent from last year. Ball sales are up 41 percent from last year. The new Apex iron sales were up and had garnered a 4.1 percent market share, its highest in five years. The Series 56 metal wood's sales doubled from last year, and the new Lady Hogan clubs had also doubled from last year.

I continued, "You remember the classy Radial ad we did in January? It certainly looks like a fine piece of jewelry." Ben did nothing but smile. Then I showed him the spread we did in March, with the tagline "What Does the Quality of Your Clubs Means to the Quality of Your Game." With Ben featured in every ad, the ads captured the essence of the man himself. Then I covered the 1988 Golf Yearbook ad, showing him his famed one iron shot as one of the greatest shots in the history of golf. Next was the single-page ad for the Radial woods and iron, as well as the Series 56 ad. This meeting turned out to be the longest time Ben and I ever spent together talking business outside the Riviera trip. I could see Ben was very pleased with the quality and character that was captured in each ad. I also got the sense Ben was very comfortable and was well informed in case anyone would bring up the ad campaign. He was as ready as the man could be.

FROM A GOLFER WHO MADE HITTING LOOK EASY, THE CLUB THAT'S EASY TO HIT.

Few golfers have ever understood the art of striking a ball as well as Ben Hogan.

A student of the game, Hogan spent years learning about shot-making, from the mechanics of the swing, to the design of the club itself.

This is the experience that shapes the Hogan Radial. A club specifically made to be easy to hit, for golfers who don't find hitting that easy.

When we introduced Radial five years ago, it represented a breakthrough in club design. The four-way sole gave golfers better contact from any lie. And it offered the traditional look and feel of a forged club.

This past year, we've made significant improvements. The long irons have wider soles and are weighted lower, to help you get the ball up, when typically it's the most difficult. So now, we can boast long irons that are truly easy to hit.

At the same time, our short irons are even better scoring clubs. They feature progressively smaller soles and higher weight distribution, and play with improved accuracy and control. All the clubs are also progressively offset, to better position your hands and set up more solid shots.

And as with all Hogan clubs, Radial meets the industry's tightest specifications for weighting, balance point, flex point, loft and lie.

Ask your pro about our latest edition of the Hogan Radial.

We can't promise that you'll hit as easily as Mr. Hogan. But by playing Radial, at least you'll be off to a good start.

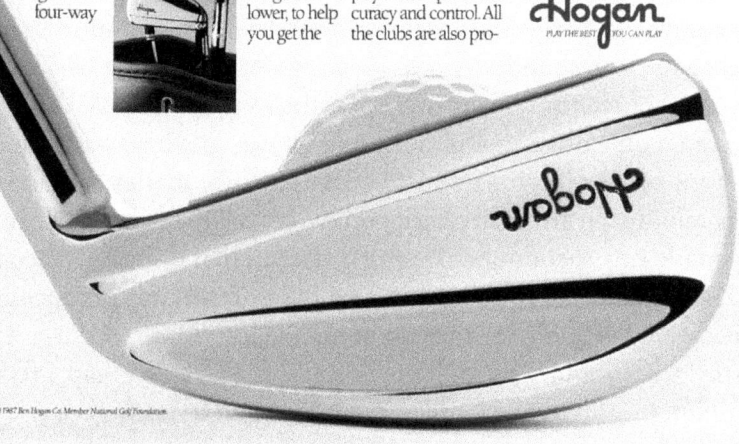

Hogan
PLAY THE BEST YOU CAN PLAY

The conclusion of this presentation was a brief outline of the schedule of upcoming ads for July and August. We ended the meeting with the pending introduction of the *edge*. After the presentation, I couldn't help but realize the projected impact these ads would have on the Hogan business. Seeing one ad in one magazine was impressive enough, but having them all together just blew me away. There was no wonder why I was getting calls almost every day about this campaign.

That presentation served me well as a company performance review which would be helpful with our new owners. About a week before we left for the Centennial celebration, I received a call from Dick Babbitt. He wished to discuss the direction of the Hogan Company. I was well prepared with all the numbers in front of me, so it should be easy to defend the marketing strategy we had selected. It did not take long for Dick to tell me the company and this brand is going in the wrong direction. "With a name like Hogan, you should be double your size." He did not give me a chance to respond as he went on, "Whose decision was it to use Mr. Hogan in your ads and move away from tour sponsorships? What happens if Mr. Hogan dies? Everybody else in the industry is using the tour players to create the impact on sales." He went on for a few more minutes before he asked me to respond.

I started by saying we used the National Golf Foundation research on clubs and found the market was moving away from good players blades, forgings, and wood woods. The market was also moving rapidly toward cavity back perimeter-weighted clubs. No amount of marketing spending was going to correct that problem. The money Hogan spent in 1984 and 1985 on the tour did not produce results that were favorable for the company. We lost $2.5 million as a company with about fifty million in sales in 1985. We had fifty-three million in sales in 1986 and made 2.5 million in profit. We also completed a marketing focus study that provided us with the information that there was nothing wrong with our products. We just didn't have a cavity back product to compete with anyone. That study also pointed out that we had the most visible, invisible tour player sitting in a corner office that everybody wanted to see and interview. That is why we choose Mr. Hogan as our new spokesman. Our strategy was eventually to transfer Mr. Hogan's image to the company, and after a while, the public would not care if it was Mr. Hogan speaking or the Hogan Company, as to them, it was all the same, and the advertising reflected that image.

The new Hogan campaign began in 1987, and our sales have grown to sixty million with a net profit of four million. We are forecasting about seventy million in sales for 1988 with the introduction of the *edge cavity back perimeter-weighted iron*.

Dick retorted, "I think the brand has been under-marketed, and I am not convinced this is the right direction for the Hogan Company."

I fired back with "If you have the wrong products and wrong message, then no amount of tour support or marketing dollars are going to solve that problem."

Dick then ended the call by saying goodbye. He would see me at the Centennial of Golf Celebration in New York in June.

I also discovered that Dick Babbitt was very critical of the advertising campaign we were using, which had won more awards than any other program Tracy Locke Agency had ever worked with. They had placed fourth place in the Magazine Publishers of America's Kelly Awards, which honors advertising campaigns that demonstrate both creative excellence and effectiveness in meeting campaign objectives. The award honored firms like Nike, Mercedes-Benz, and American Express. The Mr. Hogan campaign was named as a Kelly Award finalist. That had never happened before. They also had several ads accepted onto the One Show, which was the biggest ad show in America. The winner received a gold pencil paperweight. In the Dallas marketplace, the Tracy Locke Agency swept the *Tops* awards sponsored by the Dallas Society of Visual Communications for best two-page color spread, best single-page color, and best campaign. I was told they won a dozen Tops awards for Hogan alone. The Art Directors Club in Los Angeles also included several ads from our campaign in their awards show.

JEROME AUSTRY

RARELY HAS A CLUB FIT ITS NAME SO WELL.

Not that Apex wasn't already one of the most respected names in clubs. But with the introduction of our latest edition, Apex has taken on an even greater stature.

Already, it's our best selling Apex ever. And once you've seen this club up close, it's not hard to understand why.

Under the guidance of Mr. Hogan himself, we've designed this club to be a more playable Apex, without sacrificing the feel and performance you'd expect from a traditional forged blade.

To do this, we've redistributed the weight more evenly from heel to toe, for improved feel and more consistent shotmaking. We rounded the heel to prevent digging on uneven lies.

On the club face, Apex's new groove configuration produces more backspin than any Hogan club before; yet it absolutely complies with USGA groove specifications.

We also offer Apex in a choice of shafts: Apex and Apex Extra. All in all, 1987 was not bad for starters. With word of mouth, and continued advertising support, we expect 1988 to be another big year for this club.

Call your Hogan District Sales Manager or our Customer Service Department **1-800-433-2031** to stock up on Apex. It's an excellent way for you to make a name for yourself.

Not to mention a few dollars.

Hogan
PLAY THE BEST YOU CAN PLAY

© 1988 Ben Hogan Co. Member of the National Golf Foundation.

These were strange times as Cosmo World now owned the Hogan Company, and not a single person from their operations had visited the Hogan Company. The only contact we had with Cosmo World was my friend, Dick Babbitt, and no one knew what his job was and what authority he had running the Hogan Company. This continued like a bad dream. The phone call with Dick, however, was very disturbing as his opinion of what we were doing was all wrong, and even though the company results supported the new direction, he made it clear he did not agree with the marketing strategy that was in place. My options were severely limited, but my hope rested on the results to show him we weren't going in the wrong direction. I would stay the course and finish what we started to show Dick and the golf industry what a market-changing product introduction could look like. The buildup of advertising was well on its way to the September introduction of the Edge.

I would take the time after each month's publication to cut out the ads and make sure to review them with Ben. I could tell by Ben's reaction that he was pleased with how he was presented in the ads. I would also use this same approach with Dick Babbitt, trying to reinforce how popular our ad campaign was with our salesforce and our green grass accounts. In May of 1988, we had the front-page cover of *Golf Magazine* featuring our Series 56 metal woods and, in the middle of the magazine, a single-page ad for Radial, and as always, Ben was the main feature of the ad. The position of the Series 56 ads meant everyone would see it the minute you opened the magazine. The ad featured Ben, the Series 56 clubs, the Apex shafts, and the 392-golf ball. The copy would state Ben's club, making ability was as great as his touring career. We suggested the same detail went into making a club as what he did in planning his round of golf. When I reviewed this ad with Ben, I pointed out the comparison we were making, and he nodded his approval.

INTRODUCING THE LATEST PRODUCT OF ONE MAN'S CLUBMAKING GENIUS.

It's Ben Hogan's gift. His ability to grasp the mechanics of the game and translate them into simple, handsome, and efficient clubs.

During the past 34 years, this gift has been the inspiration for the Ben Hogan Company's most memorable clubs, including some of the genuine classics of the modern game.

To that select group, we proudly add the new Hogan Apex.

Under Mr. Hogan's direction, we have made this Apex more playable, without sacrificing the feel and performance you'd expect of a forged blade.

First, we redistributed weight more evenly from heel to toe for improved feel and consistent shotmaking. The heel has a more rounded contour to prevent digging on uneven lies.

Apex's new groove configuration also hits with more backspin than any Hogan club before, yet absolutely complies with USGA groove specifications. Apex is even available in two different shafts: Apex and Apex Extra.

And as with all Hogan clubs, the new Apex is subject to clubmaking's tightest specifications for weighting, balance point, loft, and lie.

So before you buy your next clubs, ask your pro to show you our latest Hogan Apex.

And see how extraordinary a golf club can be, when someone like Ben Hogan puts his mind to it.

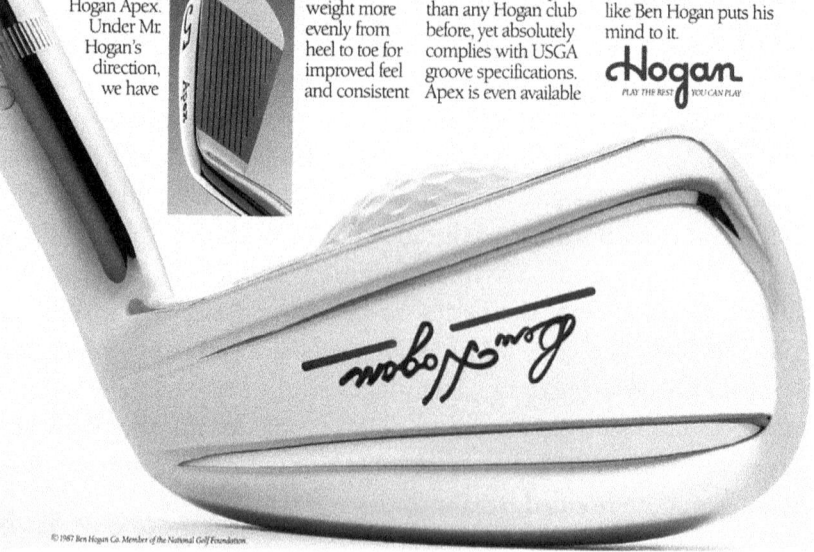

Hogan
PLAY THE BEST YOU CAN PLAY

© 1987 Ben Hogan Co. Member of the National Golf Foundation

100 Years of Golf

The Centennial of Golf Celebration was our next opportunity to share Ben with the golfing world, up close and personal. I felt confident he was ready and very comfortable with heading to New York to see a lot of old friends. We would leave on Sunday midday as the itinerary for the celebration began with a golf tournament Monday morning, a cocktail party Monday evening, followed by dinner, and then the Centennial of Golf Celebration dinner.

On the plane, I asked Ben if he wanted to have dinner that night, and he declined, saying he had plans to see some old friends for dinner but did not mention who. I shared that I was playing in the morning tournament at Saint Andrew's with legendary Johnny Miller as our professional, as well as Doug McGrath, our VP of sales, Dick Lyons, our marketing director of hard goods, and Pete Piotrowski, our VP of research and development. If he needed anything at all, Joe Kelly would be available to assist him until I would pick him up that evening for the cocktail party. There was no plan for Ben to be involved with the golf tournament as it would be a very hot day, and no one wanted to expose Ben to that heat at his age.

The tournament would consist of twenty-eight groups of four players with twelve professionals and other dignitaries acting as the team captains. The Hogan team professional was Johnny Miller, and we felt very grateful to get Johnny as our pro. The tournament would start at 8:00 a.m. with the last tee time at 12:30 p.m. We had an unbelievable time playing golf and celebrating the hundred-year history of the game with many incredible golf legends that had gathered to help celebrate this event. During the round of golf with Johnny Miller, he would ask us about who we were and what we did for a living. When he found out we were with the Hogan Company, he was very interested in knowing more about Ben. He had not had a chance to meet Mr. Hogan and looked forward to the cocktail party, so he could.

While we were all playing golf, Ben decided he wanted to go to the golf course and see what was going on. So he called Joe and asked him if he could set that up. Joe handled his request and picked up Mr. Hogan and headed to the course. I was on the golf course and having the time of my life. Who would have ever thought a poor boy from the south side of Chicago, who did not find golf till late, would be rubbing elbows with some of the greatest names to ever play the game? The *Golf Magazine* would publish in the July issue of 1988 the one hundred names that were honored at the celebration.

As I returned to the hotel after the golf tournament, Joe Kelly informed me about the rare privilege he had of escorting Ben Hogan to the Player of the Century Hero-Am at Saint Andrew's Golf Club in Yonkers, New York. Joe Kelly, along with Ron Reimer, the *Golf Magazine* equipment director, and several security folks for Saint Andrew's, was able to assist Mr. Hogan through the crowd and into the clubhouse. Mr. Hogan, while not playing that day, was clearly the star of that moment, for it was a very rare occasion for him to be seen in public. Hogan performed as an absolute gentleman who was courteous and always patient with each person he talked with. An estimated hundred-plus people stood in line for well over an hour to get his autograph. When asked to stop for a break to rest, Hogan graciously said, "These people have waited a long time to see me, and they deserve to have me sign my name." More amazingly, he agreed to an impromptu television interview with a local TV station, which was staged outside in the sun. Even though he did not wear his signature cap, he labored through a long interview without complaint. That interview would provide even more publicity for the Hogan Company. Ben then took the time to do an interview with Peter Arrichiello for the local paper in regard to how he and Jack Nicklaus differ on golf technology.

When finished, he thanked everyone involved and asked to be escorted out on the course to see a little of the action. At one point, Jack Nicklaus, who, upon seeing Ben Hogan, walked up to say hello. Mr. Hogan asked Jack how it was going. Jack gestured like he was putting and said, "You know how it is, Ben," alluding to what every golfer at some point knows that the putter is usually the first thing to go away. Mr. Hogan laughed and wished Jack good luck.

After a brief time watching the golf, he asked to be escorted back through the crowd to the clubhouse to relax a bit. Ben would end up sitting at a table in the clubhouse with Joe Kelly and Ron Reamer, having a conversation about golf. If you are a golfer and love the game, this would certainly be one of the top items on your bucket list. After a while, Ben decided he was ready to leave and headed for his waiting limousine, and with a final wave to his adoring fans, he left the scene. During a break in the action, Joe pulled out one of the ads we had placed in *Golf Magazine* for the Hogan Apex and asked Ben for an autograph. To my knowledge, this is the only ad Ben ever autographed. Later, Joe briefed me on the day's activities, as we now looked forward to the private cocktail party in the Waldorf Astoria.

Nicklaus and Hogan differ on today's golf technology

By Peter Arrichiello
Staff Writer

Ben Hogan and Jack Nicklaus have always been a little different from everyone else.

Hogan is a conformist. His righteous attitude drove him from the game he loved most into a life of solitude.

Nicklaus is a purist. The way the game was played 30 years ago fits him just fine. Head-to-head competition is what Nicklaus thrives on and what made him one of the most feared players of all time.

But, as different as they may be from everyone else, they are also different from one another when it comes to the game of golf today.

"I enjoy seeing the technology in the game," Nicklaus said. "But, I think it's getting a little out of hand. All this stuff about square grooves and improved golf balls is taking the gamesmanship out of the game. There are too many great courses in this country that are 65 or 60 hundred yards that are left out of major championships because these guys can hit the ball so far.

"I understand that the golfer of today is in a little better shape and the facilities to improve physical performance are better, but I don't think that makes up for the differences in the game. It's time that we either put a stop to all the innovations or at least regulate them a little. You don't have to play a course at twenty-one hundred yards for it to be a great course. The innovation is fine for the amateur because it makes their game more exciting, but it takes the fun out of the pro game."

Hogan sees golf differently.

"I think it's great that these guys hit the ball so far," said Hogan, who made his first public appearance in over ten years last night at the Centennial of Golf celebration. "I watch a guy like Greg Norman smack that ball and I say 'wow.' He adds a new life to this game that it lacked for a while there when Jack (Nicklaus) and Arnold (Palmer) slowed down.

"The lack... player. With all this money out there everybody thinks the players are better. That's not necessarily true. For the most part the players of today are very fine, but there are still those bad apples. No matter what kind of equipment you have, if you don't practice and work hard you won't ever be better than the next guy."

Hogan and Nicklaus, who both own their own golf equipment manufacturing companies, were each better than the next guy in their prime.

There is one thing both agree on and that's competition.

"The thing that junior golf, high school golf and college golf all lack is match play," Nicklaus said. "The kids today grow up and play strictly stroke play through high school and college and that makes them less hungry than the Europeans.

"There is nothing like playing match play against another guy to get that mental toughness. Too many guys come out of college without that toughness and it's tough for them to make it on Tour. It takes the mental toughness of match and skill of stroke play to win on Tour and the kids today don't have that. I go around to colleges and universities talking about that and if there is one thing I can change about this game, it's that."

Hogan agrees.

"There are only two ways to become a great player," said Hogan, the winner of seven major titles including four U.S. Opens. "The first is to practice every chance you get. I still hit balls today at 76 years old and I know I can get better. I may be restricted because of my health, but I can look at any great player and draw something from them. That's one of the great things about this game. You never stop learning.

"The second thing you have to do is play as much golf against another player as you can. You can be in the position to win with skill..."

Golf legend Ben Hogan waves to well-wishers at St. Andrews day after making a rare public appearance.

NICKLAUS' MILESTONES

MAJOR VICTORIES
U.S. Open — 1962, 1967, 1972, 1980.
Masters — 1963, 1965, 1966, 1972, 1975, 1986.
British Open — 1966, 1970, 1978.
PGA Championship — 1963, 1971, 1973, 1975, 1980.

YEAR-BY-YEAR
1959 — Won U.S. Amateur by beating Charles Coe 1-up in the 36-hole final at Broadmoor, Colorado Springs.
1960 — Finished runner-up and set an amateur mark of 282 in the U.S. Open. He finished two strokes behind Arnold Palmer.
1961 — Won the U.S. Amateur championship for the second time, this time 8-and-4 over Dudley Wysong at Pebble Beach.
1962 — First pro tournament was the L.A. Open, where he won $33.33 ... Beat Arnold Palmer in an 18-hole playoff for his first win at the U.S. Open ... Finished as the third leading money winner and was named Rookie of the Year.
1963 — Won the Masters and the PGA Championship for the first time ... Also won three other events and was the Tour's second leading money winner.
1964 — Won the money title with $113,284 ... Also won four Tour events ... Runner-up five times including the Masters, British Open and PGA Championship ... Had lowest stroke average on Tour at 69.9.
1965 — Won money title for the second straight year and also took the Masters for the second time, shattering Ben Hogan's... third time and also was named PGA Pro of the Year ... Won four events including Westchester Classic ... Was the World Cup fourth time with Palmer.
1966 — Won the Australian Open and his events ... Was runner-up at the U.S. and Opens and in money earnings.
1971 — Became first golfer to complete Grand Slam twice with his British Open victory ... Established new money winnings record of $244,490 in earnings.
1972 — Tied the late Bobby Jones by winning his 13th major title with his third U.S. victory ... His fourth Masters title also set a mark.
1973 — Named PGA Player of the Year the third time ... Became the first player to surpass the $2 million mark.
1975 — Won six events, including the Masters for a record fifth time and the PGA Championship for the fourth ... Captured money title for seventh time and PGA Player of the Year for the fourth to tie Ben Hogan.
1978 — Won the British Open for the third time and thus completed the Grand Slam for the third time ... Surpassed the $3 million mark.
1979 — Par the first time since turning pro went winless ... Named Athlete of the Decade Golfer of the Seventies.
1980 — Won the U.S. Open for the fourth and PGA Championship for the fifth — increased championship victories to 19.
1983 — Captained the United States...

192

Now we were all getting ready for the cocktail party. I donned a tuxedo, and my wife looked amazing in her elegant evening dress. Everyone was dressed to the nines, which was helpful because we would be rubbing elbows with the most famous people in the game of golf. I never dreamed I would ever have an opportunity like this. I was attending this party, escorting Ben Hogan, Valerie Hogan, and Valerie's sister to the party. As I opened the door for Ben and his family to enter the room, it took a couple of minutes for the people in the room to notice who was walking in. Then all hell broke loose. Every camera in the room moved toward Ben and started taking pictures. The flashbulbs, so bright we could not see where we were going. I started to panic as I had promised Ben this would not happen. My staff was supposed to protect him from this kind of assault. I quickly looked around the room and was able to spot Dick Lyons, Pete Piotrowski, Doug McGrath, and Doug Hendershot with their wives sitting at a corner table protected from the crowd. I was able to get Mr. Hogan to the table, and we formed a ring around him to allow him to enjoy the party without any harassment. I would act as the gatekeeper and only allow one person at a time that Ben would agree to greet. Johnny Miller would be the first, as we just played golf together. Johnny came over and asked me, "I have not met Mr. Hogan. Would it be possible for you to introduce me to him?"

JEROME AUSTRY

I respectfully leaned to Ben. "Johnny Miller would like to come in and say hello. Would that be okay?"

Ben said, "Yes, of course."

So I moved toward Johnny and told him, "Ben is waiting for you."

This went on most of the party, as one after the other wanted to meet Mr. Hogan and thus came over. As I looked around the room, I could see Jack Niclaus, Greg Norman, Arnold Palmer, Gary Player, Sam Sneed, Ken Venturi, Patty Berg, Jan Stephenson, Tom Watson, Kathy Whitworth, Mickey Wright, Julius Boros, Ray Floyd, Cary Middlecof, Charlie Sifford, Chi Chi Rodriquez, Ben Crenshaw, Byron Nelson, Fuzzy Zeller, Nancy Lopez, and Billy Casper just to name a few. Everyone appeared to be having the time of their life, mingling with the greatest names the sport had to offer and listening to them sharing their stories with each other.

After a while, an announcement was made to head to dinner, where the greats would be on stage, and all the guests would be seated in front of the stage at tables viewing the podium. I was lucky as Pete Bonanni, the event creator, would favor the Hogan Company because Ben was there, so I was seated just in front of the podium about 15 feet from the stage. At our table was Valerie Hogan, her sister, Dick Babbitt, and his guest from Cosmo World, Hilary Watson, who was the wife of an up-and-coming tour professional Tom Watson, myself, and my wife, Sharon. We could see everything that was going on. To the left of the podium were Ben, Byron, Patty, and Sam. To the right of the podium were Arnold, Kathy, and Jack. As we got seated and introduced ourselves to each other, Valerie's sister noticed she was wearing the same exact polka dot, black-and-white dress as Hilary had on. You can notice the matching outfits if you check the photo just in front of the podium.

As everyone was mulling around before the program was to start, I looked up and noticed a line of people in front of Mr. Hogan. Ben had the largest line of autograph seekers at the stage. This went on for a while, as I kept tabs on Ben to see that he was okay. Minutes later, as I looked up at the stage, Ben looked at me and, with his index finger and middle finger, waved at me to come to the stage to get him. I walked to the left of the stage, where I was met by Ben. I asked if he was okay, and he said he needed to go to the bathroom. Okay, and I walked with him off stage to the restroom. Ben was coming off a very serious illness last fall, so his health continued to be a serious concern to all of us. As we got to the bathroom door, Ben said, "Wait here, and do not let anyone in because I want to have a cigarette." Ben had supposedly quit smoking after his illness, so even Valerie did not know he was smoking again. After his secret smoke, I asked him if he was enjoying himself, and he said, "Yes, this has been a very pleasant trip, and seeing a lot of my old friends gathered here today to celebrate the great game of golf was worth the effort." As we went back to the stage, the minute he sat down, the crowds started to form again in front of Ben. They could not get enough of him, and with all the great names of golf there, Ben would stand tall.

Golf Magazine did a fabulous job outlining the accomplishments of each of the heroes they were honoring. They would cover the impact these greats had on the game. The demographics of these legends came from all corners of the globe. The amount of money they had earned, along with the number of tournaments they won, was sensational. There were several famed women at the event, even with the majority of honorees being male. I was surprised no one commented on the fact that Jan Stephenson was the only female golfer on the cover of *Golf Magazine* out of their one hundred sixty-one covers produced. The facts covered the amount of money that the honorees would win, a total of fifty-two million in earnings. The number of wins for the group, men's tour held one thousand twenty-two victories, and ladies tour held five hundred eighty-three victories. They also recognized the players that had become authors, whereas I was amazed that Mr. Hogan's name was omitted from the list, as his *Five Lessons on the Modern Fundamentals of Golf* was one of the best-selling books ever. The public relations effect this would have for the Hogan Company could not be measured, but it kept the company in the news all summer long.

THE HOGAN EDGE

The biggest award for the Centennial Celebration of Golf was the last of the evening. Many figured Ben Hogan would be the recipient. When the announcement came, the Player of the Century honor went to a deserving Jack Nicklaus. Mr. Hogan was gracious and congratulated Jack for the career honor he was still in the process of developing.

I also had ample opportunity to spend some time with Peter, the publisher of *Golf Magazine*, and thanked him for working with us on our Hogan ad campaign and the ad package we negotiated with his magazine. He also got to spend some time with Ben during the celebration. He would feature that time together in their Player of the Century, September edition of *Golf Magazine*, which turned out to be a special commemorative edition with Ben featured in many of the photos they would release inside the front cover of the edition. On the plane ride back to Fort Worth, I felt especially privileged to be a part of this historic celebration and how important it was for Mr. Hogan to be in attendance. Peter would also confirm to me that it would have been a great celebration, but adding Mr. Hogan truly made it the celebration of the century.

THE HOGAN EDGE

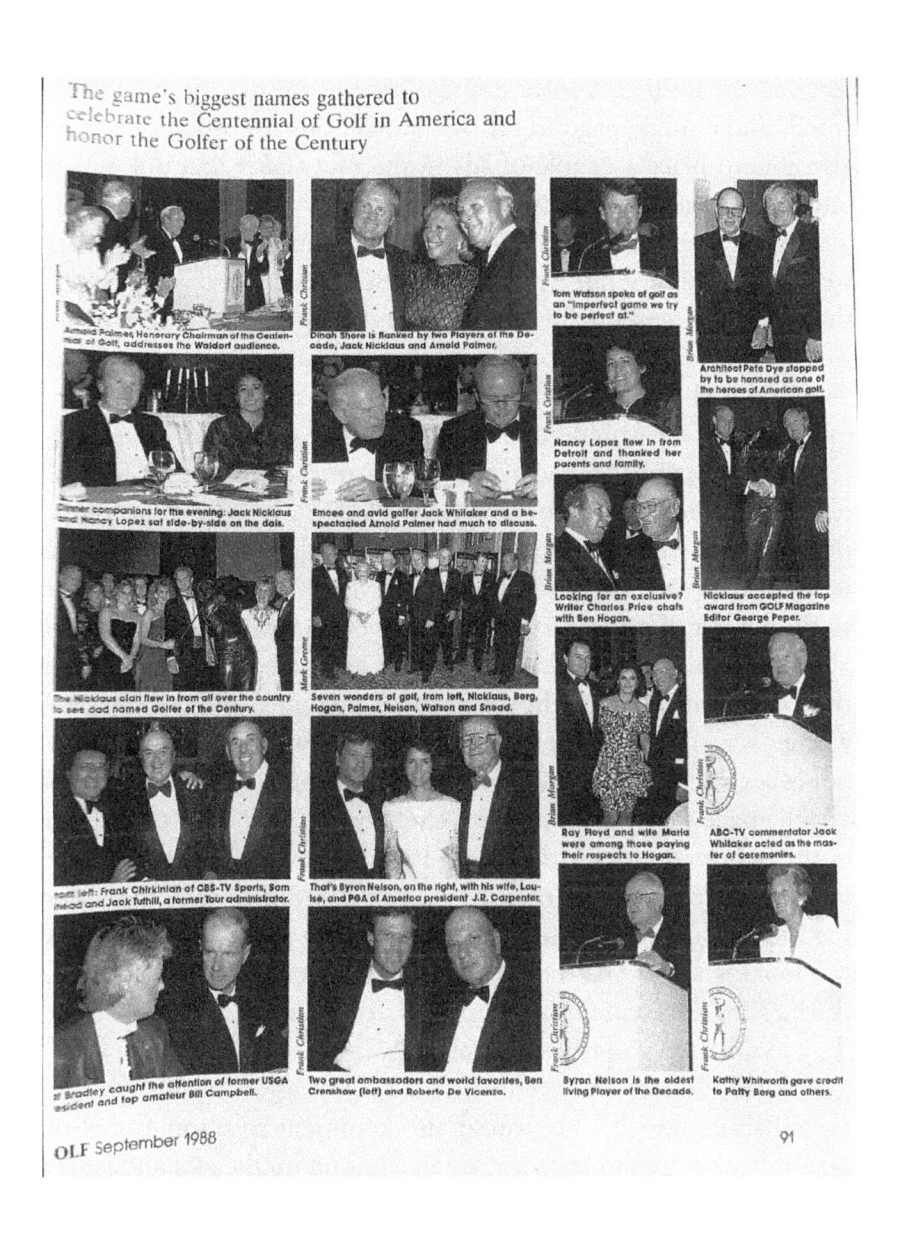

The game's biggest names gathered to celebrate the Centennial of Golf in America and honor the Golfer of the Century

Arnold Palmer, Honorary Chairman of the Centennial of Golf, addresses the Waldorf audience.

Dinah Shore is flanked by two Players of the Decade, Jack Nicklaus and Arnold Palmer.

Tom Watson spoke of golf as an "imperfect game we try to be perfect at."

Architect Pete Dye stopped by to be honored as one of the heroes of American golf.

Dinner companions for the evening: Jack Nicklaus and Nancy Lopez sat side-by-side on the dais.

Emcee and avid golfer Jack Whitaker and a bespectacled Arnold Palmer had much to discuss.

Nancy Lopez flew in from Detroit and thanked her parents and family.

Nicklaus accepted the top award from GOLF Magazine Editor George Peper.

The Nicklaus clan flew in from all over the country to see dad named Golfer of the Century.

Seven wonders of golf, from left, Nicklaus, Berg, Hogan, Palmer, Nelson, Watson and Snead.

Looking for an exclusive? Writer Charles Price chats with Ben Hogan.

From left: Frank Chirkinian of CBS-TV Sports, Sam Snead and Jack Tuthill, a former Tour administrator.

That's Byron Nelson, on the right, with his wife, Louise, and PGA of America president J.R. Carpenter.

Ray Floyd and wife Maria were among those paying their respects to Hogan.

ABC-TV commentator Jack Whitaker acted as the master of ceremonies.

Pat Bradley caught the attention of former USGA president and top amateur Bill Campbell.

Two great ambassadors and world favorites, Ben Crenshaw (left) and Roberto De Vicenzo.

Byron Nelson is the oldest living Player of the Decade.

Kathy Whitworth gave credit to Patty Berg and others.

GOLF September 1988

It was now the end of June, and the national sales meeting would be next month, and the introduction of the Edge would follow. We were able to further advertise in the May issue of *Golf Magazine* and received the inside cover for a single-page ad for the Series 56 metal woods and a single-page ad for the Radial irons and woods. We were also able to place a couple of ads in the *Met Golfer* that did a piece on the Centennial of Golf Celebration. They asked us if we would like to run a few pages, which we normally would not do. But we felt we could maximize our exposure because they featured a single page showing the Centennial celebration and a picture of Ben with Joe Kelly just relaxing at the country club. So we placed a single page for Series 56 and a single page for the new Ayn Young Sportswear line for women. This would be the June/July issue of the magazine.

I was anxious to show Ben the pictures of him and Joe and review the other two ads to see what he thought. He took time to read the copy and study the presentation. He would smile as he read the headline, "What Just May Be the Best Metal Wood of 1988 Began as the Classic Wood of 1956." Then we discussed the Ayn Young Sportswear ad. He smiled and started to compare the Series 56 ad to the sportswear. The way the product was presented and the copy was written was something Ben would approve. I waited for a comment, but other than a smile, that was about all I would get. Then I pulled out the page that was from the Centennial of Golf with the picture of the honorees' stage with Arnold Palmer speaking. Then I pointed to the picture of Ben sitting with Joe and pointing to something that Joe was holding in his hand. I asked Ben if he remembered what he was looking at, and he thought for a minute and then replied, "The pairings for the Centennial Hero Golf Tournament AM."

I said, "Do you regret not playing?"

Again, silence and then he said, "At my age, I would not want to embarrass myself." He would also comment that some of these guys probably should have just ridden around on the cart and let the young men play.

I said, "You look pretty good in that picture, Ben, and certainly a lot younger than some of the honorees that played that day."

THE HOGAN EDGE

Ben and I had spent every weekday morning together, now going on three years when I was in town and felt he was very comfortable. He was aware of how we used his commercials and how each ad was built. He was able to see the quality of the ad and the copy that was created with his image. With everything that was going on and how fast things were moving, I regrettably failed to communicate to Dick Lyons how much Ben liked the ads. Looking back now, I probably should have let the creative folks at the agency know they were spot on with the work they were doing. I prepared Ben for the upcoming sales meeting and outlined the news conference schedule, along with reviewing the new Edge ad, which kept him in the loop for the next couple of months. He would ask me about Cosmo World and what, if anything, they were asking us to do that was different from what Minstar demanded. At this point, other than a few conversations with Dick Babbitt and replacing our financial VP with a Cosmo World auditor, they were going to send an employee from Cosmo World for me to work with and expose him to anything he wanted to review. Other than that, just some conversations with Dick Babbitt about our marketing program and some comments he made that the Hogan brand has been under-marketed for years and our revenue should be double what it is today.

So far, Cosmo World had kept their distance from getting involved with the day-to-day operation of the company. I do expect to see and hear more from them prior to the sales meeting next month, and I would expect we will have a lot of visitors at the meeting.

On the return to the plant, we were still experiencing some employees sabotaging floor operations in order to create problems with production. There was some sympathy for the workers because many of the first-line supervisors were friends and neighbors with them. The majority of the workers were loyal and hardworking people whom we cared for. It was rumored the final closing price from Cosmo World was $58 million. This was a hefty sum for a little over two years of ownership by Minstar. Even with these problems, we were moving forward, and the Edge product was moving through production with the new manufacturing process to control and protect the cavity back design as well as maintain the weights needed to meet swing weights tolerance.

THE HOGAN EDGE

Then one day, I got a surprise call from Babbitt that he would like a meeting with my staff at the Los Colinas Country Club in Irving, Texas, on a Saturday morning. He failed to inform us what the meeting was going to be about, just be there. When we all arrived that Saturday morning, he had some psychologists all set up to give us a presentation about how color-coordinated sportswear would triple our sales. He would spend most of the morning with charts covering how the choice of colors was the most important factor in determining your success. He had brought in an unrecognizable golf professional with him that day. This bizarre meeting left each of us wondering what we had just witnessed and why.

As the next week began, we started to plan our upcoming sales meeting, which would be the most important one of our lives. It was time to introduce the Hogan Edge, and the new owners would be in attendance to hear what the marketing people had to say. This would be the biggest presentation Dick Lyons would ever give in his career. Dick was a very sharp marketing mind, but his public speaking was not one of his best attributes. Often his presentations included some off-color comments which had little place in the business setting. Dick and I discussed getting some help from the Tracy Locke Agency in preparing his speech. The guy we used was Blair Franklin, who was a little younger than Dick, both in their middle to late twenties. Through my research for this book, I made contact with many of the people that were a part of those Hogan years, and one man, in particular, kept all the records in storage. The public relations department of Tracy Locke and the creativity of Blair Franklin provided the speech for Dick which hit the mark on every important objective. Everyone in the room would give Dick more than one standing ovation, which was a first for Hogan.

The next part of the meeting was to go to the range to actually hit the Edge product, which meant to create some additional excitement. As we approached the range, you could see several prominent touring professionals already hitting the Edge product.

THE HOGAN EDGE

JEROME AUSTRY

The Hole in One Speech

The sales meeting was held in Fort Worth over a three-day period, spanning July 22, 23, and 24. Presentations would be made by the department heads to bring the sales force up to date on the current state of the business.

The final day would be a speech by the marketing director to present to the sales representatives, Hogan's top management and the new Japanese owners of the company, a business overview, and a new product preview. There were four main objectives of the speech:

- Instill confidence in sales representatives about operational improvements and incentives.
- Excite the team about new products, primarily the Hogan Edge.
- Win the confidence of the Japanese owners.
- Establish the 1988 sales slogan "Forging the Future."

To meet these objectives, the speech would have to address business problems and successes candidly to win the respect of the audience. A metaphorical theme (relating the Hogan business to a round of golf) and audiovisual support would help the audience identify with the speaker and help Dick feel comfortable with the topic. The Japanese were all sitting at one table without anyone from the Hogan Company sitting with them. For the next few minutes, we'll take a look at the Hogan business from the point of view we're all familiar with, the golfer's point of view. In a typical round of golf, there are a lot of good shots and some bad shots, but when you get done, the overall performance for the round could have been good enough to win the tournament. He went on to outline how we played the front nine holes with some bogeys and some birdies.

- Bookings for our products were up 10 percent.
- Our back orders for the product had grown to $3 million to date from $1 million compared to the prior year.

- We had more than $150,000 of back orders in golf clubs.

Then he would pause and say we also hit some very good shots this year:

- Apex irons shipped 10,000 sets versus 7,000 the prior year.
- Sales increased 33 percent to about $1.6 million.
- Apex putters had a record sales year surpassing $500,000 versus the prior record of $189,000.
- Lady Hogan became the best-selling ladies club ever, selling 4,000 sets which more than doubled the amount the year before.
- The golf ball business exploded, with sales increasing by 34 percent over the prior year.

JEROME AUSTRY

Now we're making the turn to the back nine and have a chance to improve at this point. The lights in the room dimmed, and Dick was looking at a long list of wins so far and how we were going to play the back nine by "Forging the Future" and that we as a company will have to play more aggressively to reach our goal.

Dick then introduced the new products that will help us make a lot more birdies on the back nine. He presented a new persimmon wood as well as the new Series 56 metal wood line. We also added a special seller by including the Hogan book, *The Five Fundamentals of Golf*, with each dozen golf balls purchased. Finally, we introduced that one great shot that would put us on top of the leader board—the first cavity back forged club ever produced by the Ben Hogan Company. When we announced the Edge, the room erupted to a standing ovation. I have been to many sales meetings, and that never happened. Dick would also let them know that early in the next month, we would be having a new conference to generate more publicity for the Edge.

Dick completed his speech by adjourning to a conference room to see the product and then to the range where Bob Tway would be hitting this new Edge iron. The crowd would stand and give Dick another standing ovation.

Step one of the introductions was complete as we had presented the Edge to the sales force. It took us three years to get to this point, starting way back in 1986 with the changes to our advertising strategy, a strike, and the sale to new owners. I was so proud of my group as they kept moving ahead through all the changes and strived to put the Hogan Company at the head of the class in the golfing world.

The last event was a dinner meeting with Ben Hogan at Shady Oaks Country Club that ended with Mr. Hogan giving his final remarks to send the salesmen off for the fall-booking season.

You never know what Ben was going to say, but I was hoping he would reinforce the Edge introduction. As he spoke, the room became silent as everyone hung on his every word. He hit all the right points to totally support the Edge product. He had everyone eating out of his hand. Then out of nowhere, in front of the room, which included the Cosmo World owners and Dick Babbitt, he stated, "We have worked very hard this last year to bring you the Edge. You know, I never had a son, but if I had one, I would have wanted him to be like Jerry." I felt every eyeball turn in my direction. My face warmed with color. Everybody went crazy. As the room calmed, Ben concluded by saying, "You all know my feelings about golf clubs. A golf club should look like a piece of art, like a piece of fine jewelry." Ben sure knew how to close the deal, and his support for me was obvious to everyone in the room. The sales force was now prepared to run through walls to make this product launch a success.

After the sales meeting, I would meet with Ben in our morning meeting, where I thanked him for those wonderful comments. I also briefed him about the comments that Babbitt made, so he was aware that Babbitt was not on board with the direction we were heading. He, as always, would smile suggestively but not comment about Babbitt. I also let him know that Hogan was planning a special news conference just before the PGA Championship in Oklahoma, where the details of the Hogan Edge series would be released. I truly believed we would rise to the top of the mountain after this introduction. The news conference was scheduled for August 8, 1988, at the Hyatt Regency at the DFW airport, which coincided with all the sportswriters coming through DFW on their way to the PGA Championship in Oklahoma. The news conference was set up, and the timing was perfect. The young man we would be working with would be Bair Franklin of the Tracy Locke Agency.

The media kit was entitled "The Hogan Edge," with the famous Hy Peskin one iron shot from Ben Hogan at Merion image on the cover. The media kit would showcase a biography of "Ben Hogan—Golf Legend by Will," a business profile "Sharing the Legend: The Ben Hogan Company," and it would also include biographies on three individuals, myself, Jerry M. Austry, president and chief executive officer, Peter J. Piotrowski, vice president of research and development, and Dick Lyons, director of club and ball marketing. Most importantly, though, it introduced the first and only forged cavity-backed irons with perimeter weighting "The Edge." It included

"Forging the 'Impossible' Club" that had a detailed background, features, and benefits of the club. In addition to the media material, which was about twenty-five to thirty pages long, the writers provided enough material to use with any editorial they wanted to write. We also provided pictures of the club and a sample of the Edge with an engraved stamp of August 8, 1988, for the day of the conference. We would be the pioneering company to combine a forging with the cavity back perimeter weighting features that the golfing public would devour once given a chance.

I had never been involved in a public relations campaign, so I really had nothing to compare this one to. The photos provided of the Edge jumped off the page. The headline of the Impossible Club would fit the effort. The features and benefits were simple to understand—forged carbon, perimeter weighting with no substitute, straight leading edge, and one of the most identifying features of a Hogan product. It looked like a fine piece of jewelry. It is now up to the media to take the ball and run with it.

The Hogan Edge

Forging the "Impossible" Club

The buzz from the conference gave us all a positive feeling that the media was impressed and would write gleaming reviews in the weeks to come. We had one more surprise for our sales force with the July issue of *Golf Magazine*. It would be a special collector's edition of the Centennial of Golf in America, 1888–1988. The publisher of *Golf Magazine*, Peter Bonanni, rewarded the Hogan Company for Ben's appearance at the celebration by helping us in this addition. We seemed to own the magazine. There were multiple pictures of Ben Hogan at the celebration as well as single-page ads for the Radial, the Series 56, the Apex, and they also featured Ben's book, *Five Lessons on the Modern Fundamentals of Golf*. As usual, I would review these ads with Ben and point out the features that reflected his character and design features he believed every golf club should contain. All I was expecting was another "Okay." But this time, he took a little extra time and studied each ad and reviewed the copy. When he finished his review, he looked up at me and unloaded, "These are really good. I like what you boys have done."

I could not believe what I had just heard. I said, "Thank you, Ben," and left his office. Holy shit, did that just happen? Ben told me he really liked what you boys have done. No greater compliment could be given to my team.

Now we waited to see what kind of articles would be written about our Edge and us. The *Dallas Morning News* was one of the first with the headlines "Hogan Company Introduces New Irons," and the article covered all the key selling points we made in the news conference. Then another three editorials were published in *The Port Arthur News*, *Fort Worth Star-Telegram*, and *Ennis Daily News* with the headline we were looking for "Hogan Edge: Forging the Impossible Club." Then came the headline we were all waiting for from *Golf Magazine*, "Hogan Edge Irons, First-Ever Forged Cavity Back Perimeter Weighted Club Ever Produced." In all, there were over forty-five different editorials written about the Hogan Edge, but one of my favorites was by *Golf Digest*, "Hogan Got the Edge on the Competition with Its Early Introduction of the Edge." Everybody was using the material that was distributed in our media kit provided by Blair Franklin from the Tracy Locke agency. That would be the only time the Hogan Company would ever call a news conference. I was pretty much on an island at work as I had no contact with anybody from Cosmo World and very little contact with Babbitt other than a random call to talk about marketing and his concerns about using Ben as the main feature in our print ads. He would never ask about sales or production or profits on any of his calls. Every once in a while, my executive assistant Fannie Meyers would come in and let me know Babbitt requested another fifty sets of Edge clubs to be sent to Hawaii, free of charge, to our head pro there, Gary Planos. He never explained why he needed so many sets, and no one ever asked. It was becoming apparent to me our relationship needed to change if I was going to survive. But there was very little if anything I could do to change it; Babbitt held all the cards. All I could do was continue down this path to see where I would end up.

The good news was that the Edge program was an outstanding success, and every day, things were getting better both in sales and delivery, which ultimately would mean increased profits. The orders for the Edge were rolling in at a record pace, and the September kick-off ads had not been seen yet by the public. We were a few short weeks away from the September issue of *Golf Magazine* and *Golf Digest*. There would be two different ads for the Edge coming out. The one in *Golf Digest* would compare the Edge to all cavity back clubs on the market, and the Edge would blow them away. The *Golf Magazine* ad would feature the Edge with a focus on the craftsmanship it takes to produce a forged iron. We used two different headlines for the ads, "The Impossible Golf Club Has Just Been Made Possible" and "Cast Irons Will Never Give You a Proper Feel for the Game."

The copy would highlight the feel of forged steel, the playability of perimeter weighting, the feel of forged versus casting that most golfers believed to be true. I could not wait to share these ads with Ben. I could imagine Ben himself using words to describe the perfect club.

The *Golf Magazine* issue would be a *special commemorative edition* again but this time featuring a forty-page tribute to Jack Nicklaus. It would have pictures of the Centennial celebration and just one club ad in the entire magazine, the two-paged Edge spread. Just before you started to read about Jack, you would see photos of the celebration with Ben clearly present in more than one photo. Just as you were in the middle of the article about Jack, our two-page spread for the *impossible club ad* would jump at you. How good was that placement in the magazine? Once the magazine came out, I was eager to review them in detail with Ben. I was so excited as I walked into his office, where I couldn't help myself, and began talking a mile a minute.

Ben would calm me down by saying, "Jerry, Jerry, Jerry, calm down."

I finally capitulated, but I still wanted to show you the Edge ads. I exclaimed, "We did it. We did it. The Edge is now a reality, and from the looks of the response at the sales meeting and the news conference, this could be the most successful club we have ever had." I said I loved the look of the Edge ad. I think we nailed the headline, and the copy reflected the craftsmanship and quality expected from the Hogan Company. The second spread was in *Golf Digest*, and the ad separated Hogan from every cavity back club in the marketplace. "Ben, there is no comparison! Ben, I wanted to thank you for your help because, without you, this would never have happened."

I was not expecting any response, but Ben replied, "Jerry, we made a good team." I let Ben know my phone had been ringing off the hook with positive comments about the ads and the product. Everyone is saying the same thing; only the Hogan Company would attempt to make a product like the Edge.

As we headed into the fall, the orders for the Edge continued to increase to a level no one had anticipated. For over thirty years, Hogan has been introducing quality irons to the golf market, and the most sets ever sold in any one introduction was about thirty thousand sets. By the end of September, we were barely out of the gate and had booked over fifty thousand sets of Edge. No one had to tell us we were gaining market share. The results of the daily orders received proved that. I remember thinking how these results would surely help convince Babbitt of what we were doing. By the time we got to October of 1988, we were approaching one hundred thousand sets of Edge, which helped to eliminate most other worries.

The year 1988 was heading to be the best year Hogan ever had for sales and profits. I had been president of the Hogan Company for nearly three years, and so much had transpired in this short time. I felt grateful that somehow the powers that were decided to take a chance on me. After three years, we owned the hottest selling iron in the industry, and the revenue that would be generated by Edge would make Hogan one of the top manufacturers in the business. We were planning another celebration at the 1989 PGA Show in Orlando, Florida. The buzz about the product was also being felt internationally. This international exposure would also increase our orders for Edge. With so much positive news, what could go wrong?

I was not getting any feedback from Babbitt regarding the 1989 Hogan budget, which was strange because we needed to finalize the numbers and compensation for the management team for next year. Rumors were also starting to surface that Babbitt was interviewing candidates for the new president of the Hogan Company. I called him several times to inquire about what else he needed to wrap these items up, and he replied smugly that he needed nothing, but he would be down in Fort Worth near the end of the year to review the budget. I was starting to feel uneasy about my situation. I had one of the greatest jobs in the world, which afforded me the opportunity to work with one of the greatest icons in the golf industry. With the silence from the top, I started to review what we had done to see how precarious of a position I was in. I was planning a vacation with my family to Hawaii in December, and that would give me time to relax and review what, if anything, I needed to change. I would have one last morning session with Ben before I went on vacation. I brought him up to date on the orders we have received for the Edge, and we looked like we would hit one hundred twenty thousand sets. I shared with Ben that I was not sure what was going on with Babbitt because I have been hearing rumors that he is interviewing my replacement as we speak. I told him that I might need your help with Babbitt when I get back. He said he was in my corner. Now I am not sure what I thought Ben could do one way or another as he had absolutely no contact with anybody from Cosmo after that first meeting at Shady Oaks. There wasn't much Ben could do, but it made me feel good that he said he would do anything he could to help me.

Off to Hawaii, I went for our family vacation. We had a wonderful vacation where I was able to reflect on the amazing success we were sitting on. Even though we were vacationing, I was still looking forward to the upcoming 1989 PGA show to celebrate the amazing success of the Edge. The time off was good for my family and me. When we arrived home, I felt rested and invigorated for the new year at Hogan.

On my first day back at the office, I got a call from Babbitt to meet for dinner a few days before New Year's Eve. It was a Sunday night about a month prior to the 1989 PGA Show. When I arrived at the restaurant, Babbitt was sitting there, awaiting my arrival. Next to him sat the consultant from the accounting firm that was assigned to review the Hogan books for Cosmo World. There was tension from the onset of the dinner. We exchanged a few pleasantries, but quickly, things got serious. Babbitt wasted little time before he told me that Cosmo World has decided to go in a different direction with the Hogan Company.

I replied, "Okay, what do you want me to change to follow that new direction?"

Dick replied, "No, you don't understand. This new direction does not include you."

My jaw hit the floor. I took a second to collect my thoughts. Anger seeped up into me. "This company is exploding, sales are up, profits are up, and you do not want me to be involved? It is not about that."

Babbitt stated, "The Hogan Company has been undervalued for years, and I intend to fix that."

I fired back, "I thought that is just what I did, as revenue is going to go above seventy million, and again, this will be the best year the Hogan Company has ever had." I looked over to the consultant and asked, "Did you inform Babbitt of those numbers?" He did not respond.

Then Babbitt said, "I do not want you to go back to the plant tomorrow, so if you want, you can go to the plant tonight to clean out your office."

I stood there frozen in shock. The rumors were indeed true that he had hired someone else to replace me, and my journey at the Hogan Company was now over. I would not be given the opportunity to say goodbye to all the great people that helped me turn the company around.

The last time the president of the Hogan Company was fired, Roger Corbett was given an office by Minstar at the Montgomery Street plant so he could conduct a new job search. I would not be provided that luxury. I immediately left the dinner and went to the plant to clean out my personal items from my office. When I got home, my wife could see the look on my face and knew something was wrong. I informed her that I was just fired. Instead of going eagerly to the PGA Show to celebrate the great year we had, I was not allowed to visit the Hogan booth at the show. The new Hogan president would be taking the bows for the advertising campaign and the Edge introduction he had little to do with. The firing ripped my guts out, and trying to figure out why was even harder.

The direction the company was going had increased sales by 60 percent and as much increased profitability. We were enjoying a historic climb to the top through industry-changing innovation and award-winning marketing. This is the direction Cosmo World wanted to change to improve the Hogan brand. I could help but remember the first meetings Ben had with the Cosmo owners at Shady Oaks when he pointed his finger at Babbitt and Mr. Isutani and told them how they had just brought the family jewels, now don't fuck it up. I guess they were not listening because they were about to take the first steps to fuck it up.

Babbitt's first move was to fire me. Then he removed Ben from the advertising program. He then changed advertising agencies. The next move was to sign PGA star Tom Kite because Babbitt felt Mr. Kite's words would carry more weight with the golfing community than Mr. Hogan's. Who in their right mind would think Tom Kite or any other touring player would have more of an impact on the Hogan brand other than Ben himself? Babbitt chose to ignore the University of Minnesota focus group data about the Hogan product line being stale and the perception the public had for Mr. Hogan. He also ignored the Golf Shop Operation Market Survey that pointed out the need for metal woods and a forged cavity back iron. The first ad Cosmo World would place in 1989 lacked any images of Mr. Hogan. They merely showed only the Hogan products in all their respective glory. Babbitt continued his destruction of all we had built. He made it clear that all the top management positions of the Hogan Company would be changed. A little more than a year after the Hogan company was featured in Golf Shop Operation in their 1987 PGA show special "The Golf Business and the Ben Hogan Company" detailing how successful the company was in 1986, everyone would soon be gone, and a new team with very little experience would take their place. By the time the Edge reached its first-year anniversary, the product had sold one hundred and fifty thousand sets.

Babbitt believed present-day tour players would have a greater impact on the Hogan product line than Mr. Hogan himself. That is why Cosmo World increased the number of players on the payroll carrying the Hogan bag and clubs. They also created the Ben Hogan

Tour, as they felt this was the best tool to grow the revenue of the company. Once the tour was created, you could see the advertising main emphasis change to showcase the tour and not the products Hogan was making. The last change Babbitt made was to modify the Edge and go back to more of a player's blade with a small cavity which they would later learn was instrumental in killing the Hogan Edge.

Looking back on his decision, Babbitt was right. I would not have supported their position, and thus, he had to get me out of the way. Babbitt's ego was bigger than King Kong's, and if he believed something, no amount of factual evidence would change his mind. The new strategy for the Hogan Company that Babbitt would pursue killed the original Edge by 1990, and the replacement products never reached that level of acceptance in the marketplace. With all the money Cosmo World was spending on tour player sponsorship coupled with the new Ben Hogan Tour, no one could argue this strategy destroyed the company.

I officially left the company on January 1, 1989, and instead of going to take a victory lap, I was looking for a new job. I did attend the PGA Tour Show in January, but not without some difficulty. I was not able to get a hotel room anywhere, but my friend Joe Kelly allowed me to stay with him. Without his help, I am not sure I would have been able to find a hotel as every room in town is normally sold out. I spent three days at the show and visited with everyone I knew. I let them know I was looking for a new position. It was quite gratifying to hear everyone's comments about what we had done at Hogan and how much everyone knew it was a smashing success and could not believe they had asked me to leave. I had a couple of offers that would require me to relocate. I did not want to leave Fort Worth as my youngest son Mark was just entering high school. It didn't take long, but I found and accepted the position as president of Head Golf. The Head Company wanted me to develop a golf product line for them to enter into the golf market. This position would keep me close to the Hogan Company, where I could utilize my contacts and see if they foundered under Cosmo World. The start-up Head golf plant was only about 10 miles from the Hogan Golf facility, so I would see many of the Hogan employees going to lunch a couple of times per week. They all seemed to keep their distance as no one wanted to be seen with me and face being reported to Babbitt.

Then in early January, I would hear who the new president of the Hogan Company was. It was the former chief executive of the National Golf Foundation, David Hueber. I thought to myself, *How is he going to assist in this new direction? What qualifications did he have that I did not?* His previous job was to research and provide information to the golf manufacturers about the industry and game. He also spent some time working for Deane Beamon, the commissioner of the PGA Tour. Many people felt that he was being groomed to replace Deane as the commissioner one day. David's background did not include any hard goods manufacturing or marketing of golf products. He was very visible in the industry and spent a lot of time with the most influential people in the business. I was told that one of the first moves he made as the president of the Hogan Company was to decorate his new office. My office had been in the center of the operation between the marketing, sales, customer service departments, and close to the manufacturing operation. The office David picked was next to the front lobby of the company, where the president before me had worked. David hired an interior decorator to refurbish this office. They had decided to move a wall one foot to be able to get in the new furniture. This created apparently created conflict as the maintenance group would not want to spend that kind of money to move a wall one foot. I was told this got back to Hueber, and he was going to fire the manager if he did not apologize for creating this problem.

As the year progressed, I would get calls from my friends at the Hogan Company, who would share the changes being made at the company. All the executive team that was responsible for the Edge's success were fired or resigned. As the sales of the Edge were still exploding, the new group at Hogan was inundated with production problems. I also heard that Deane Beamon had recommended David Hueber to Babbitt and which was one of the main reasons he got the job. Hueber was figured to be the guy to get the new Ben Hogan Tour off the ground. I learned that this new direction of signing more PGA Tour players and starting the Ben Hogan Tour would cost the Hogan Company $6.7 million a year to fund. When I took over the company in 1986, Hogan had just lost $2.5 million the previous year. In 1986, we made $2.5 million in profit. In 1987, the new Hogan campaign enhanced our profit to $5 million. The year 1988 was, without doubt, a significant increase from the previous year. The first year of ownership by Cosmo World, the Hogan company was well on its way to reaching double digits in profitability. Sales of $80 to $90 million a year were possible with the new Edge introduction. The Hogan Tour, though, would consume most, if not all, the profit generated by the company. This is not a decision an experienced marketing executive would ever make. Babbitt knew I would never have supported that decision, and so he had me fired.

Knowing Ben as I did, I couldn't imagine having to present the Hogan Tour idea to him. I could picture him saying that is a wonderful idea, but shouldn't that be something the PGA Tour bankrolls? Why were you going to give that much of your profit away before it was ever made? None of this was ever made known to Mr. Hogan. This is what Babbitt meant when he said they were going in a different direction. Revenue was growing because of the success of the Edge introduction and would continue for the next couple of years after I left. At the same time, they were replacing Ben Hogan from the ad campaign in lieu of sponsored tour players as they once had plentiful. They added additional staff to manage their tour obligations. The unsubstantiated and shocking change was they were modifying the original Edge product. Our focus groups told us in no uncertain terms, the Edge had to look like the Ping club, and once it did, consumers would choose the Edge over Ping because of the forging feel. Rumors had reached my ears that the reason that Cosmo World bought the Hogan Company was to be able to create a real estate company using the Ben Hogan name in which to purchase Pebble Beach Golf Course. The story circulated that they wanted to turn Pebble Beach into a private country club and sell membership to Japanese businessmen for $475,000. They would allow up to two thousand members, who created nearly a billion dollars of revenue for Cosmo World. That sure made more sense to me because the people they had put in charge of the Hogan golf plant did not have a background in manufacturing, and the main corporation was not providing much guidance that would help with production problems.

It did not take long for the deal for Pebble Beach to go south as Cosmo wasn't allowed to take the famed course private. Cosmo World was forced into getting rid of the property after only owning it for one year. The interest alone cost them $1 million dollars a week. Cosmo World took a $300 million loss when they sold Pebble Beach for $500 million, so it cost them about $350 million for one year of ownership.

I was sent a copy of the 1991 Hogan catalog in which the cover had a bunch of Hogan's golf trophies and a picture of Ben at the Riviera Country Club. As you opened the first page, Ben disappeared, and Hogan was showcasing its nine new tour players that they had assembled to endorse the product. The catalog's emphasis was the Ben Hogan Tour and what a great idea it was and how successful it was in providing a training ground for young professionals seeking a PGA Tour career. The Apex iron was still the featured brand, and they also were promoting the Apex persimmon wood instead of a metal version even as the golf market was moving away from wood woods. The new Hogan management team managed to put the company back in the red by 1991.

While the Ben Hogan Tour success or failure was yet to be realized, the talented pool of sponsored players was certainly a fantastic group of golf superstars. My experience with the Hogan Company was certainly not the same as these players. Many of them began their careers through meager beginnings only to capture some of golf's brightest moments.

Tom Kite

Cosmo World had a defined strategy in place, especially when it came to its marketing department. This strategy entailed hiring many of the best players in the game to use and play with their equipment. This wasn't a difficult sell as Hogan's image and quality were considered tops among most PGA professionals. One of the early moves for Cosmo World was aimed at Tom Kite. The Dallas native grew up playing at River Lake Country Club under the tutelage of club pro Harry Todd. The club's proximity to the Dallas Open events garnered him access to some of the major PGA professionals, whom he was able to follow around. Kite's parents fostered his love for golf and moved to Austin at the age of twelve. Tom's collegiate career at the University of Texas has become the stuff of legends alongside his competitive rivalry with Ben Crenshaw, set the two up for a historic career. While at college, Kite applied himself in the classroom as well as on the golf course. His finance degree complemented his golf career perfectly.

Kite's first sponsor was Wilson Sporting Goods, who signed him to three consecutive five years contracts. The Wilson years afforded him ample opportunities to play with legendary Sam Sneed, who also found a home with Wilson Sporting Goods. After Wilson underwent some internal changes and a downturn in the company's business, the Hogan company stepped in. Kite had known a few of the Cosmo World owners from his visits to California, and the Hogan Company's new marketing strategy made Kite a perfect fit. The subsequent talks and negotiations ended with Kite signing at the time an unheard-of-ten-year sponsorship contract in 1988. The contract with Hogan would rock the industry as these large and lengthy contracts were not the norm. Most tour players would sign one-, two-, or three-year deals and just renew year to year after that. Kite's Hogan contract was one of the richest on the tour at the time. It opened everyone's eyes to the big-money contracts that golf companies needed to capture the top players. Kite's contract went into effect in 1989 and would carry Kite until he reached the age of forty-nine years old. Kite became a regular visitor to the Hogan factory in Fort Worth. Tom and his father would drop by to pick out some new clubs, say hello to certain people, and always get some face time with Mr. Hogan.

Gene Sheely always found time for the visits, as did Ronnie McGraw, the tour representative. Kite's success had been built around his wedge play, and thus the club grinders were an integral part of his progress. Kite's initiation of the sixty-degree wedge onto the tour became a major sticking point for Sheeley and McGraw at the factory. As soon as Kite joined the Hogan team, the company incorporated a sixty-degree wedge into their line. They would create a three-wedge package which included a pitching wedge, a sand wedge, and a grind wedge. One particular visit to the Hogan factory happened shortly after Kite's contract was inked. Kite made a visit to have a new set of clubs created to his specifications. Kite, along with Hogan's president, went to Hogan's office for a visit. After the initial pleasantries, the discussion moved toward the large glass-surfaced coffee table around which they sat. The beautifully crafted table had inlaid in it the entire collection of iron heads created by the Hogan Company from the years 1954 to then.

The inquisitive Kite asked Mr. Hogan which of these irons would he consider the best of the bunch. After several seconds, Hogan responded, "Well, the best club we ever made here never got produced."

Kite quickly responded with "Really? Well, which one would that be?"

Hogan stood up, stepped to the back corner of his office, and retrieved a club leaning against the wall. "The marketing guys didn't like this club as much as I did," Hogan suggested.

Kite looked toward the Hogan president as if to share the sentiment and then back at Hogan. The president blurted out, "Well, this ought to be the next club we make."

That moment marked the day when Hogan Company initiated the idea of the club called The Grind. The Grind was a significant player to the Hogan Company, especially after Kite would use this club famously to chip in on the seventeenth green at Pebble Beach and ultimately win the 1992 US Open. Kite considers his Hogan years to be his best on tour with a player's championship, a US Open, along with a majority of his tournament victories.

It was the lack of innovation from Hogan that mattered as much as their extreme dedication to quality. The innovation seemed to be coming out of the Southern California golf companies—things like cast clubs, heel-toe perimeter-weighted clubs, the metal woods, etc. Kite believed the products coming out of Fort Worth came from the directive of Mr. Hogan himself and reeked of the highest quality conceivable.

As Kite's time with Hogan was beginning, the Cosmo World people retained tremendous regard for the founder of the company, but he was no longer making any decisions for the company. Ben Hogan was relegated to figurehead status, but this wasn't anything new. Hogan's age and Kite's career never allowed the two to play together in any capacity. Kite felt fortunate to have the time with Hogan that he did. Years later, Hogan began showing early signs of ALS and dementia, which made his visits all more important to Kite.

It was around this time that Kite's close friend, a pilot for American Airlines, called him. This friend had traveled the world throughout his career and acquired quite a collection of rare books and magazines from bookstores he would discover. Kite's friend had stumbled across a copy of the April issue of *Life Magazine* 1954 as well as the May issue in 1955 issues that had become a sought-after collector's item. Both issues featured Ben Hogan and a cover story regarding Hogan's secret to the game. The friend delivered these found copies to Kite. Kite decided to bring them with him on a trip to the Hogan plant to get them signed. When Kite had his chance to see Hogan, he showed him the *Life Magazine* issues he had for him to sign. Hogan was seated when the magazines were laid in front of him. He stared at the article and associated picture for probably five or six minutes of measured dead silence.

Kite just stood there, not quite knowing what to do, when suddenly, the silence was interrupted with Hogan saying, "You know, that looks like a pretty good golf swing to me, don't you think?"

Kite nodded in agreement to Mr. Hogan, and he picked up the pen and gave his autograph. Kite still has these rarities prominently displayed in his collection.

Ben Crenshaw

Kite's iconic rival and fellow Austin, Texas, born and raised professional golfer Ben Crenshaw was a longtime admirer of Mr. Hogan for his play on the golf course, and despite the fact he was never a sponsored player, he appreciated the precision and high standard that preceded the Ben Hogan name. He used the Hogan clubs prior to becoming a sponsored player by Yonex. Crenshaw would meet Mr. Hogan through mutual friends at Shady Oaks Country Club. That friend was a guy named John Griffith, who was married to Fort Worth legendary businessman Marvin Leonard's daughter. Her name was Marty, and she would become one of Fort Worth's biggest advocates. Griffith would strike up a friendship, and each time Crenshaw played the colonial tournament, he would find time after to go fishing at the Leonard's Star Hollow ranch in Tolar. Crenshaw loved that place. Crenshaw made it a point to ask Mr. Hogan each time they saw one another about two guys, Jimmy Demaret and Jackie Burke, and his eyes would just light up. He was great friends with them and, of course, Byron Nelson as well. Crenshaw was able on occasion to spend some private moments with Mr. Hogan at Shady Oaks. He loved just watching Mr. Hogan swing the club. The two would visit the practice range, where more often than not, Crenshaw would watch in fascination as Mr. Hogan almost effortlessly swung the club.

Crenshaw knew Hogan loved hitting his four wood. Hogan was like a machine. The ball was hit with such force, and it was just on a line. It was a driving shot, and it would just streak right out there toward the target. Crenshaw also made it a point never to ask Mr.

Hogan about his golf swing. He knew not to go there as so many others did not. I actually watched him hit balls on two occasions, where he hit some three irons and some four woods. Crenshaw went to the Hogan plant a few times early because he was between contracts from McGregor, but he wanted to have some clubs made from Gene Sheeley. If there was a finer club maker than Shelley, then Crenshaw had never met him.

On this visit, Crenshaw asked for a set of Hogan Apex irons. Hogan showed up and asked Crenshaw, "Let me see what driver you're playing."

So he pulled out his Tommy Armor McGregor driver that he had played with for a good while with some success attached to it. Mr. Hogan picked it up, and he looked at it up and down, and then he turned it like a rifle. He looked down the shaft upside down, and then he handed it back to me with the words Crenshaw will never forget. "This looks like a goddamn doorknob." The comments jolted Crenshaw quite a bit. Hogan followed that with "Look in that corner right there. Look at those two drivers there." Crenshaw picked one up, and Hogan offered, "Isn't that beautiful?"

Curious, Crenshaw replied, "Mr. Hogan, this doesn't have much loft, and it doesn't have any bulge and roll," meaning the radius from heel to toe.

Hogan just stared at Crenshaw and then countered, "An iron doesn't have any radius, does it?" Crenshaw remembered thinking how perfect a point Hogan had just made to him. Mr. Hogan would add to the experience by giving Crenshaw one of these personal drivers, which he cherishes to this day. Gene Sheeley would fashion both a three and a four wood for the former Masters champion. Even though he was unaffiliated with the Hogan Company, he was still treated like he was. He played with those handcrafted Hogan clubs for about six or seven months and loved them. Unfortunately, Crenshaw got another offer from another golf company to play with their clubs and moved on, but he never wavered in his love nor admiration for Mr. Hogan and the quality craftsmanship his company put out. Crenshaw moved to Yonex and then the Walter Hagen Company.

Ben Crenshaw was also privy to one of the most talked-about moments in Ben Hogan's history in 1971. Crenshaw played as an amateur at Champions Club in Houston at the Champions International Tournament. He was headed down number seventeen when he noticed Mr. Hogan teeing up on number three. Everyone just stopped playing and stood there and watched him tee off. He was playing with Charlie Coody that day.

As the story goes, the fourth hole at Champions was a really long par three, and Mr. Hogan hit his tee shot just down the bank of the green. As he went down to retrieve it, he wrenched his knee as he bent over. He picked up his ball and walked to his golf cart. He announced to Coody and the others in his entourage, "I'm done. That's it." Ben Hogan climbed into the cart and was driven to the clubhouse. That would be the last time and the last hole that Ben Hogan ever played in the competition.

The conversation with Charlie Coody was overheard by Mr. Hogan telling Charles Coody, "I'm sorry, but I've got to go in."

Hogan looked at him and said, "Never get old, Charlie."

Crenshaw's admiration for Hogan's swing was shared by many. Numerous books were written about just this. Ask any pro from that era, and they likely tried in some form to emulate the smooth swing of Ben Hogan.

"You just couldn't replicate it, but you never got out of your mind the way that he hit the ball," Crenshaw explained. "You would have a conception of what he was doing, but no one could ever duplicate that. Many people tried. He, meaning Hogan, played with a pretty weak grip. His clubs had very stiff shafts and were fairly light which made them even stiffer. I had to have a little more head weight to bend the shaft a little bit more, but Mr. Hogan was just so strong. His hands and forearms were really strong. The way that he went into the ball was just unbelievable. It was a blur, really quick and powerful. You had a concept of what it was, but you couldn't duplicate it." Crenshaw also made a mental note of Ben Hogan's attire. Whenever he was with Hogan, he dressed like no one he had ever seen before. "His clothes were just neat as a pin, and they were very different and all custom-made. He was very particular about his clothing, and many times he wore a suit to work, and then he'd change back there in the locker room at Shady Oaks, but he was just immaculately dressed." Crenshaw shared that "Hogan showed the pride that he had in being a professional golfer. He was a very proud man."

Gentle Ben Crenshaw remembered the Centennial of Golf Celebration fondly. He was one of the many players honored that night, but when Mr. Hogan got up to speak, you could hear a pin drop. "I don't think there's any individual who had a hold on the public as he had. He was just altogether a different person. He was just a voice of authority. Whenever he spoke, his voice, I'll never forget his voice, it was deep and resonant, and he meant every word he said and very authoritative and commanding tones really. He was just no BS at all. He spoke with so much conviction, and after all, I've loved everything about what has ever been written about him." Crenshaw even helped coauthor a book called *The Hogan Mystique,* where he wrote an essay. The book was turned into a television documentary special in 2019 called *Hogan,* which aired on the Golf Channel and was narrated by Kyle Chandler.

Crenshaw had always respected Ben Hogan and very much wished to play for him. Youth and naivety prevailed early on as Crenshaw accepted a better offer from Yonex then the Walter Hagen Company to play and endorse their clubs. Crenshaw had met Mr. Hogan through a mutual friend named John Griffith at Shady Oaks in Fort Worth. John was married at the time to Marvin Leonard's daughter Marty. Crenshaw had occasion to chat with Hogan and would discuss old mutual friends Jimmy Demaret and Jackie Burke, who Hogan knew quite well. This made the conversation easy for both. Byron Nelson also connected the two. Crenshaw had originally stopped by the Hogan factory while he was between contracts to see Gene Sheeley as per an offer by Hogan himself. Crenshaw found himself mesmerized by the skill and craftsmanship of Sheeley. It would be a tremendous selling point as well. Crenshaw knew without a doubt that Hogan's clubs stood for quality. That first meeting with Sheeley left Crenshaw with a new set of Hogan irons, along with one of Hogan's own drivers, which he cherishes to this day.

Crenshaw's favorite Hogan memory took place in 1971 as he was playing as an amateur at Champion's International Tournament in Houston. As Crenshaw was completing #17, he bore witness to the fifty-eight-year-old Hogan teeing off on #3. Everyone in view, players included, stopped playing and just watched Mr. Hogan hit. Hogan that day was playing with Charles Coody, who would, one month later, win the Masters Tournament at Augusta. This day at the Champions tournament, Hogan, who was competing as a favor for two buddies who founded the club, struggled off the 221-yard par-three tee box, putting three balls into the canyon fronting the hole. As he went to retrieve his balls on the steep slope, he re-aggravated an old knee injury sustained in his near-fatal car wreck with a Greyhound bus some twenty-two years prior. He asked his caddy to pick up his ball, and he shook hands with his playing partners, Dick Lotz and Coody, offering his apologies for having to leave. He smiled at Coody and told him, "Charlie, never get old." Hogan then climbed into his golf cart, drove back to the clubhouse, and officially withdrew from the tournament. He was seen playing gin rummy later that evening in the locker room with several friends. None of them would have known that Ben Hogan would never play competitively again, including the unknown individual who famously approached Hogan during the gin game, saying, "You might not remember me, but we played golf together back in 1958."

Hogan, upon first glance, replied, "You're right. I don't remember you." Upon which, he turned around and went back to his game.

Crenshaw, whose career went on in legendary form in his own right, would pay homage to Ben Hogan as one of his icons. At the Centennial of Golf Celebration in New York, golf's greats all converged for the event. Everyone received their appropriate time of recognition, but Hogan stole the show. As he took the stage, the lively crowd became hushed as every set of eyeballs yearned to hear Hogan's every word. His hold over the audience was without equal. He was the undeniable voice of golf authority. The deep and resonant voice commanded each and every word that he spoke. This night remains deeply powerful for those who adorn golf's Mount Olympus. Hogan represented everything good and significant about the sport of golf. Crenshaw would go on to author a book called *The Hogan Mystique*, outlining the immense influence Hogan held over the sport.

Crenshaw was one of many golf greats to attend the funeral of Ben Hogan.

The gate to Mr. Hogan was guarded tightly against the outside world. His personal secretary, Clarabelle, indeed held the keys. If you were not a close friend or a Hogan professional, you needed to go through Clarabelle, and she always knew whose ticket to punch. Once through her office, Hogan was known for his immense kindness extended at every level.

Crenshaw had many occasions to watch Hogan practice during his tenure as a Hogan touring pro. His swing made those around him study him harder than other greats around him. Hogan's swing left an impression on Crenshaw that he admittedly never could forget. Crenshaw tried mightily to replicate, but he knew as all others knew. It was nearly impossible to replicate. Hogan utilized a weak grip coupled with a very stiff shaft on fairly light heads, which only emphasized the stiffness of the club. His strength and grace in his swing always mesmerized Crenshaw, among others. Hogan's hand strength and forearm strength were noticeable in his handshake. His swing was a blur, really quick and powerful. We all seemed to have a concept of what he was doing, but none of us ever fully copied it. Many, and I mean many people, attempted to break it down and explain it, but its execution was perhaps its mystique.

Lanny Wadkins

Lanny Wadkins first met Ben Hogan in December 1970 at the Gold Tee Awards in New York. Wadkins was there as the reigning US Amateur Champion. The dinner and presentation were a sensory overload for the young Wadkins. Somehow, after dinner was over, Wadkins found himself amidst a group of his heroes posing for some photos. At one point, Wadkins was asked to smile for the photographer and did so, but when he glanced to his right at the others in the photo, he couldn't help but be amused at the gentlemen he was coupled with. Ben Hogan, Byron Nelson, Arnold Palmer, and Jack Nicklaus filled out the shot—a memory and photo still cherished by Wadkins. It wasn't till years later that Wadkins joined the Hogan tour family in 1981 that a closer friendship was forged with Mr. Hogan.

Wadkins, who took up the game at the age of seven with help from his father, would break eighty for the first time as a ten-year-old and break par for the first time at the age of thirteen. He was well on his way to a legendary career. Wadkins's time in Fort Worth became very common in those days. He frequently visited the Hogan factory to see Mr. Hogan or Gene Sheeley for a new club. Mr. Hogan loved to take Wadkins to Shady Oaks for lunch and a few rounds. Often, they were joined by Chip Bridges, the Hogan tour representative, who fit in nicely with the group. The fourth, on many occasions, became local man John Miles, who worked for Eddie Childs at the local western company.

Miles had been a very good amateur player and even held the course record at Riviera in 1963. Miles was talented enough to play

Mr. Hogan's heads up. The joy Mr. Hogan felt being able to play with some really good players was palpable. The money games between this group were something to be imagined but always led to that final drink together in Mr. Hogan's reserved spot.

Wadkins had been coached during his first Ryder Cup team in 1977 by Dow Finsterwald, who served as the head pro at the Broadmoor Hotel in Colorado Springs. Dow and Lanny would develop a longtime friendship as a result, and Wadkins would befriend Dow's son, Dow Finstrewald Jr., who served as a head pro for Fort Worth's Colonial Country Club.

Once upon a time, Hogan was playing with Lanny Wadkins and Chip Bridges at Shady Oaks. John Miles had taken ill that day, leaving just the three of them. As they made the turn, an unknown man, along with his golf cart, showed up with an announcement that he would be joining us. The three stood there for a few seconds, absorbing the news. Then Hogan simply turned to Wadkins and asked if he was ready to go. Wadkins replied, "Yes, sir." Indeed, he was ready. They climbed into their respective golf carts and drove off, leaving the stranger standing there wondering what could have been.

A few days later, Wadkins received a personalized note in the mail from Hogan outlining his condolences for the unorthodox manner in which their round ended. Included in the note was a check made out to Wadkins in the amount of $4 for the skins he had lost to Watkins. This check now lives at the World Golf Hall of Fame in St. Augustine, Florida.

Mark O'Meara

The Cosmo World push toward Hogan-sponsored players linked up with PGA star Mark O'Meara. O'Meara had known Ben Hogan for years through mutual friends, Gary Lofland, who was close with Mr. Hogan and Rayburn Tucker, who was close to Gary. O'Meara didn't start playing golf until the age of thirteen. His first set of clubs had been his mother's. It was a Christmas morning when Santa left a set of used Top Flite irons under the tree that gold turned serious. Those Top Flite got him off the ground, but O'Meara was a Hogan guy from early on. When he won the US Amateur Championship in 1979 at Canterbury in Cleveland, Ohio, he beat John Cook, who was the defending amateur champion and considered the best player in the country with a set of Hogans. When the *Golf Week* came out, the cover was a photo of me during a rainstorm under my Hogan umbrella. This must have exposed my secret that he loved the craftsmanship and feel of the Hogan equipment. O'Meara would take his Hogan clubs to college with him, where his career took off. His idea was to stay an amateur as it offered him an invitation to play in the Masters Tournament. He would then play in the US Open, where he went to defend his title in 1980, but as soon as he lost to Willie Woodin the second round in North Carolina, he knew his time as an amateur was up.

O'Meara was on a plane the very next day to Dallas. His friends, Rayburn Tucker and Gary Lofland, had set up a meeting for him to meet Mr. Hogan for the first time with the idea to turn pro in his office. O'Meara wasn't concerned about the money but rather more about the fact of meeting the great Mr. Hogan. Ben Hogan hadn't officially subscribed to paying players to use his products at the time. He felt in his mind that the reason we were with the Hogan Company was that he made the best stuff. O'Meara arrived at the Fort Worth plant of the Hogan Company with a new haircut, donning a sports coat and tie, where he was escorted into Hogan's office. A reporter was on the scene as well, which wasn't well received by Mr. Hogan. Mr. Hogan was behind his desk, and O'Meara walked in nervously.

Hogan announced, "Mark, take a seat." Mr. Hogan started asking questions about where he grew up, how old he was when he started playing golf. Hogan seemed genuinely interested in O'Meara and quickly eased the tension in the room. The *Star-Telegram* reporter sat quietly in the corner, listening to their discussion and taking notes on a small notebook.

O'Meara asked Mr. Hogan, "Sir, do you mind if I ask you some questions?"

To which he replied, "No, please go right ahead."

O'Meara was well aware of Hogan's life but couldn't resist the opportunity to ask him questions. "When did you start playing?"

Hogan then opened up to O'Meara and shared his story firsthand. "When I turned pro, I didn't have any money, and to be fair, I got out there, and I was terrible. I hooked the ball really badly, and I had to figure out one of two things. One, I needed to get off the tour and learn how to swing the club properly, to where I could come back out and maybe make a living out of this game, or I had to go get a job, like delivering milk."

The intimate conversation lasted an hour in his office, and the door was shut. So it was basically just the two of them and that reporter. Hogan shared the terms of O'Meara's contract as a ten-thousand-dollar sponsorship deal for his yearly service to the company. Toward the end of our meeting, Hogan wanted to show him around the factory and introduce him to Gene Sheeley. As the pair rose from their chairs, Mr. Hogan looked over at the reporter and said, "Bill, I'll look forward to seeing this in the *Fort Worth Star-Telegram* tomorrow and the fact that Mark is going to represent my company."

The reporter looked back at Mr. Hogan for a few seconds blankly and then said, "Mr. Hogan, I retired ten years ago."

Mr. Hogan's face contorted to one with a puzzled expression. "Then what the hell are you doing in my office? Get the hell out of here. What have you been doing sitting here?" The moment left a lasting impression on the young O'Meara, one he won't ever forget. A photographer was on hand for the tour of the plant. O'Meara still treasures the picture of the two of them standing in front of some Hogan woods. Hogan seems to be pointing out some Hogan woods to him in the photo. O'Meara would continue to play as a Hogan-sponsored player for six years. The relationship grew over that time. They shared a multitude of dinners together as well as time hitting balls together. Mr. Hogan would personally involve himself in the clubs O'Meara played and often asked him to bring in his golf bag for closer inspection. O'Meara would describe Hogan's treatment of him as one of a grandfatherly sort. O'Meara credits much of his early success due to his time in and around Ben Hogan and his company.

Each time O'Meara played the colonial tournament, Hogan would invite him to dinner at Shady Oaks or visit him in his office. One visit to Hogan's office, he arrived carrying his Hogan golf bag. O'Meara placed his bag next to him as the two sat down to talk. Hogan wasted no time and rose from his chair to inspect the golf clubs. Hogan pulled the headcover off of O'Meara's five wood and discovered inside a Cobra Baffler. Hogan pulled it out of the bag, and he set it down on the ground without uttering a word. O'Meara recalls sitting there in fear, thinking, *Oh my god! Here we go.*

Hogan turned his glance to Mark and said, "Mark."

"Yes, sir."

"What the hell is this thing?"

Mark nervously replied, "Sir, that would be a Cobra Baffler."

Hogan piped back, "Well, I can read that. What the hell is it?"

O'Meara answered, "Well, sir, it's like a five-wood head with four wood loft, and it got these rails on the bottom, so if you hit it in a bad lie or you're in the rough, it's a little easier to get it in the air." O'Meara was attempting to explain the logic he had garnered from

Tom Crow, who owned Cobra and who designed this club. Hogan listened to O'Meara finish, and then he returned the headcover to the club and placed it back in O'Meara's bag.

Hogan turned and walked back to his chair behind his desk, where he turned and spoke, "Son, let me give you a little piece of advice."

"Yes, sir" came the reply.

"First of all, let me explain something to you. When you're playing in a tournament and you're trying to win and you're coming down the stretch, you do not need to be setting the ball straight up in the air, son. Are you listening to me?"

O'Meara confirmed he was. "Yes, sir, I'm listening."

"You need to keep that ball along the ground. You get what I'm saying?"

"Yes, sir, I totally get what you're saying."

Hogan continued, "Then do yourself a favor. You get that piece of shit out of your bag, and you get your Hogan iron back in the bag. Are you perfectly clear with me?"

O'Meara, with little options, replied, "One hundred percent, sir. I'm one hundred percent clear with you, sir." That was the last day for that baffler. It was typical Hogan for those who got close to him. That's the way he was.

After six years of sponsorship with Hogan, Taylor Made came after O'Meara with an offer that substantially bested the Hogan money, and O'Meara moved to the fledgling company, where financially he could not say no. This wise business decision would never change O'Meara's love for the man whose career and dedication to create the highest quality golf clubs would be second to none. O'Meara would, though, find his way to Hogan eventually. He considered the Hogan Company revolutionary back in those times, and the equipment that was produced stood as the best, so it was a no-brainer to represent him and his company in early 1980. O'Meara was named Rookie of the Year, with earnings for the year of $76,000, which ranked him fifty-sixth on the PGA money list. O'Meara, though, was struggling with consistency in his swing, losing a playoff in

Tallahassee. He incredibly had made it this far in his career without the benefit of a teacher or coach. He knew he could play but felt lost at times and admitted to heavily relying on his wood.

There was a time in 1982 or 1983, O'Meara was struggling pretty badly on the course and was getting ready to go over to the British Open. His bank account was suffering mightily, so he penned a handwritten letter to Mr. Hogan, asking him for help. O'Meara flew to England, hoping to find a dose of magic to help him capture his first British Open in his second year on the tour. One evening, after he completed an unextraordinary round at the tournament, he called home to his wife at the time, Alicia. She informed him that Mr. Hogan had called the house and was looking for him. When he asked her what she said to him, she said, "I told him you were over at the British Open." Mr. Hogan said to have Mark call him when he gets back in the States.

So Mark returned to the US with a subpar performance at the British Open in hand. His flight landed in Virginia for the Anheuser Busch Golf Classic at the Kingsmill Resort, and he went straight to the course. There he went into the clubhouse to a pay phone and called the Hogan Company. Hogan's secretary answered the phone, and O'Meara told her that Mr. Hogan asked him to call him when he got back stateside, and that is what he was doing.

She said, "Hold the line, please, Mr. O'Meara."

Then Mr. Hogan got on the phone. He said, "Mark, where are you?"

O'Meara replied, "I'm at Kingsville in the Anheuser Busch, getting ready to play in the tournament."

Hogan answered, "Oh, okay, good. I got your letter. It was very nice, but I got to tell you something, Mark."

O'Meara said, "Yes, sir, what is it?"

Hogan snapped back, "I don't teach."

O'Meara said, "Well, sir, I am literally in a pay phone in the clubhouse, and you know, sir, I represent you. I turned pro in your office. I've never had a teacher. I don't know. I felt like I needed to turn to somebody, and so that's why I wrote the letter, thinking maybe you could point me in the right direction or where I could get some advice."

Hogan listened intently and countered, "Well, first of all, you know I don't teach."

O'Meara said, "Yes, sir, I understand that."

Hogan inquired, "Well, what are you doing wrong?"

"Well, sir, I'm hooking the ball really bad."

Hogan replied, "Well, let me tell you why I don't teach, Mark. I don't teach because I wouldn't want to screw anybody up." Hogan then embarked on a long conversation about how he wouldn't want to ever destroy somebody or hurt somebody's golf swing. O'Meara would throw a few "yes, sirs" and "I understand" along the way as Hogan continued on. Then Hogan paused, and the line was quiet.

O'Meara, fearing Hogan may have hung up, said, "Mr. Hogan, are you still there?"

"I am" came the reply. He continued on, "Mark, let me just say this. When do you think you could come here? I might want you to hit some balls. I might not, or I might want you to hit some balls, and I might not say anything."

O'Meara replied, "Sir, I can appreciate that, but I don't know when I can get there. Right now, I'm just staying on tour, trying to make the top twenty-five, so I have to play every single week, but hopefully, someday, I can come, and maybe you could give me some guidance or watch me hit balls."

Hogan said, "Yeah, I think we can probably make that happen."

That concluded the phone conversation. The two wouldn't connect until later that year, but by the time, O'Meara had met golf instructor icon Hank Haney on the range at Pinehurst, and the rest is history. O'Meara swing underwent its major change during 1983 as he struggled to reinvent himself. It was the following year, he won his first tournament and finished second on the money list. In 1985, O'Meara sunk a thirty-foot birdie on the seventeenth green to defeat Craig Stadler in the Hawaii Open and its ninety-thousand-dollar purse. The next week was the Colonial Open. O'Meara received a phone call from Mr. Hogan asking him to come and hit balls with him at Shady Oaks. When O'Meara arrived at Shady Oaks, Hogan was having lunch with Irwin Jacobs, the owner of Minstar, who had recently purchased the Hogan Company from AMF. When Mr. Hogan saw O'Meara, he told him to go down and grab a cart and head to the range. Kris Tschetter, an LPGA pro, was with me, and Kris was very close to Mr. Hogan. O'Meara, in view of Mr. Hogan, pulled out his five iron and began hitting at the yellow flag at one hundred eighty yards. O'Meara remembered hitting really well that day and thought to himself, *This shit is going to be awesome, and he's going to be so impressed with my new swing.*

Hogan, after ten minutes or so, stepped out of the cart and reached for one of O'Meara's clubs and stood behind me. O'Meara asked him what he thought, to which Hogan didn't say anything except, "Keep on hitting." Hogan came around to the side, leaning on his club, watching him address the ball. O'Meara kept swinging as Hogan tugged on his cigarette behind his dark sunglasses that concealed the answer that O'Meara wished to know.

"Mr. Hogan, what do you think?"

Hogan leaned heavily on the club with his head down, he took a long drag on his cigarette, and he let it out, "Awful!"

O'Meara, not knowing what to do or say, chuckled and said, "Thank you, sir."

Hogan gave O'Meara a stern look and asked, "Mark, what are you doing?"

"Sir?"

Hogan said, "Where are you going?"

Confused, O'Meara answered, "Uhm, sir, I went to Long Beach State and got my degree, so I'm not sure I understand the question."

Hogan replied, "It's really easy. Where are you going?" and then he pointed out the yellow flag and said, "You're going that way, aren't you?"

O'Meara confirmed he was. O'Meara knew he had been nearly hitting the flag almost with his five irons, so what could he be doing so wrong?

Hogan was ready. "Why you got to go backward to go forward?"

"Sir?"

"I guess you don't have to go backward to go forward." Further confused, O'Meara didn't quite understand, but what he figured was that he had a little hitch or slid vertical slide backward off the ball. Hogan knew what he needed to do. He walked over and set O'Meara what could only be described as a hunched over sprinter's stance like if you were a hundred-yard dash guy.

Hogan told him, "Don't move your lower body at all and go and hit this one." On his next attempt, O'Meara, following his instruction, tried not to move his lower body and do exactly as he was told. The first one went way right and wasn't very good. Hogan said, "Okay, hit another one." O'Meara addressed another ball. His lower body didn't move. "Just try to turn behind it, semi hosel to the right again. Do it again," commanded Hogan. Three in a row went terribly. Hogan then looked right at me and said, "Okay, now that's way better. Just do that." Hogan then turned and climbed into the golf cart with Irwin Jacobs and drove off. O'Meara looked at Kris Tschetter with a look of complete confusion. That would be his only private lesson from Ben Hogan.

One of O'Meara's Hogan memories took place at one of the Hogan dinners. O'Meara was placed between Mr. Hogan and his wife, Valerie. Mr. Hogan said, "Mark, I want to show you something, but you can't tell anybody else."

Intrigued, he said, "Okay."

Hogan asked the waiter for a paper napkin. Hogan began, "I'm going to show you something to write down, but you cannot tell anybody what I'm going to show you." Hogan's tone and expression expressed to O'Meara how serious he was.

"Yes, sir. I won't say a thing."

"All right."

Hogan pulled a pen from his jacket pocket, and he drew these two lines. He said, "Do you see these two lines here?"

"Yes, sir."

He continued, "This is the fairway on number five at Colonial."

"Yes, sir."

Hogan drew two tee markers on the front side of the napkin, and on the back side, he drew a green with two bunkers. "Obviously, it's one of the toughest holes in golf and blah, blah, blah, and water to the right, just a slight dogleg, and I know I drew a straight line, but it's okay, you know that."

"Yes, sir, I do."

"All right, when you're playing your practice rounds, Mark, are you hitting it at the pin because you know they're not going to put the pins there?"

O'Meara replied, "Uhm, yes, sir, I understand that."

Hogan repeated, "All right, I'm going to show you this, but you can't tell anyone."

Confirming again, he said, "Okay, yes, sir."

Hogan continued, "Now one day, they're going to put the pin on the back right." He kind of drew a dot on the green where the pin would be on the back right on the fifth hole of Colonial, and he said, "When the pin is going to be back there, here's what I want you to do. I want you to go way over here on the left side of the tee marker, right here by the left. You can stand outside the tee marker, but I want you to tee your ball up here. Do you understand?"

"Yes, sir, I'm listening."

Hogan said, "I want you to start it down the tree line and hit a draw so you get over to the left side of the fairway because that'll give you your best angle of attack against the back right pin." Hogan continued drawing more lines over the left side of the paper fairway. "Now you swing more aggressively with your second shot into the right-side pin."

"Okay," replied O'Meara.

"Now vice versa, the next day, they may have the pin in the back left or the front left, so now what I want you to do. You're listening to me, right, son?"

"Yes, sir, I'm listening."

"Now I want you to tee it up over here on the right-hand side of the tee, and I want you to hit down to the left side of the tree line fading and try to get it as tight as you can over to the right side of the fairway, so you have the best angle of attack to the pin."

Now these lines were kind of going all over the place as O'Meara sat, just watching and listening and being respectful.

"Are you following me?"

"Yes, sir. I'm following you, sir."

"Do you understand what I showed you?"

O'Meara confirmed, "Totally."

Hogan asked, "Do you have any questions?"

"Yes, sir, I do."

Hogan replied, "What is it?"

O'Meara asked, "Well, what happens if I tee off over here on the right side and the pin is going to be on the back left and I'm trying to hit a fade and I snap hook it over here on the left tree, and it's over against the fence?"

Hogan looked at him, and without pause, he answered, "Son, I can't help you with that. You do that, that's your problem." Hogan then picked up the paper napkin, and he crumbled it up so O'Meara couldn't take it away, and he put it inside his jacket, and that was it. While O'Meara sat there perplexed, he knew that Hogan was trying to share a hefty secret with him. Hogan was so different, and yet this was so him. That napkin represented to Hogan something special he wished to share with someone he trusted. The moment wasn't lost or forgotten by O'Meara.

Another memorable private moment from O'Meara took place at the Hogan plant as the two were walking toward the back of the factory. They were headed to pick up a set of irons that Sheeley was making for O'Meara. During the walk, O'Meara asked him, "Mr. Hogan, do you mind if I ask you a question?"

"Sure, what is it, Mark?"

They stopped the walk in the hallway, and there was no one there. O'Meara said, "Sir, in an imaginary world, if you put a ball down right here right now and you took out a six iron and forget about pin placement or whatever and if you took that club back with your six iron and you hit that golf ball, if you looked up, what would the ball be doing?"

Hogan replied, "There's no question. If I looked up, there'd be a slight little draw. That's a perfectly struck golf ball." Hogan continued, "You know the balls to the side of you. You got to swing at a mark. The ball should be a slight little draw. Mark, I've told you this story before. I went from an uncontrollable hooker to a controllable drawer that could fade it at any time."

O'Meara knew the rarity of this story he had just been offered.

"Business-wise, my take is that I'm a real loyal guy and am fortunate like even at this stage, at age sixty-three getting ready to turn sixty-four. I represent five really good companies. In my relationship, I don't bounce around. I never wanted to bounce around. I represented Toyota and Lexus for thirty-eight years, the same company, so I'm just a fortunate guy that got lucky. I was hoping to just make a living, get out there, and make a living playing professional golf, and I'm getting ready to start my forty-one year, and I still compete and still try to play well. I am fortunate that I love people, so in golf, there is no greater sport than our game that connects with individuals and people. I have more fun personally playing in my pro ams with my amateurs. It doesn't matter if I'm playing with a thirty-eight handicapper or a scratch player. I want to get to know them, know about their families, what they do for a living, and I want them to know me. So to be fair, my relationships on that end of the spectrum and my business relationships are ones that I'm very appreciative of, and I want them to know that any relationship works when it's beneficial for both sides. It can't be a one-sided relationship, or it's never going to work. That's the way I've always viewed it, and I take a lot of pride in when I get done playing in a pro-am, that my guys will walk away and think—you know what, we had the greatest time. To me, that means more than winning the tournament or making money or this or that, but you know, just to leave that type of mark, that I'm very appreciative of the people that play this game—not at the professional level but at the amateur level."

When O'Meara turned pro in 1980, his hope was to make a living out of this game. He tells new players about how he had to pay for range balls for a third of the tournaments that I played in my rookie year on the PGA Tour. Corporate hospitality didn't exist just yet. No courtesy cars or red carpets were being rolled out for us. O'Meara played tournaments with a total purse equaled $300,000, so unless you found the top ten, you may not be able to pay for your trip. Things started to graduate quickly, and when Tiger Woods came on the scene, it went through the roof.

"There are so many different stories, and a lot of us in our lives don't take time to once in a while sit down and maybe realize what's transpired, but the opportunities I've had to finally break through at forty-one years of age to win two majors in a year. Maybe I'd felt like I'd come and gone and that my time may be making that happen wasn't going to come to fruition, but let you know, I have so many other good memories. I played with my father at the Pebble Beach Pro Am a couple of different times. We made the cut both times, and the second time, I went on to win the tournament, and then I was playing in the final group on Sunday at Pebble Beach with my father right alongside me and won. So there's just not another sport where that can happen. It comes, and it goes, and some people will remember, and some people don't, but those are moments that I cherish like immensely. Like the opportunity a couple of weeks ago [2021] to play in the father-son tournament, for me to be able to play with my son Sean over the sixteen years that we've played that event, every year, it's special. For him to have the opportunity to play with Mr. Palmer, Mr. Nicholas, Floyd, Johnny Miller, Seve Ballesteros, and you name it, my son played with all those players. He's played, which I would have never dreamed that I could have had that opportunity, so that's where I felt blessed that I had those opportunities to share those moments."

Ed Sneed

Ed Sneed joined the Hogan family officially at the end of 1977. Sneed's introduction into golf happened as an eleven-year-old boy caddying for my grandmother in Roanoke, Virginia. She didn't start playing golf until she was fifty years old. She never broke a hundred, but she made her future golf hall of famer and read the *Golf Book of Etiquette*. He would play golf for the Buckeyes at Ohio State. Sneed then worked at the Scioto Country Club as an assistant teaching professional in the late 1960s, right out of college. This was the same place where Jack Nicklaus learned to play golf. McGregor grabbed his attention early on as they owned that market. He would become a loyal subject of the Hogan brand soon enough and continued to play Hogan golf clubs through his first couple of years on the Senior Tour, which comprised eighteen years. Sneed played in the Colonial for the first time in 1971, but it was the following year out at Shady Oaks on an invitation by a Hogan tour representative.

Sneed was on the McGregor staff at the time and had been since he started the tour. Sneed and Hogan spoke briefly. Sneed didn't switch to Hogan clubs for a few more years, but he had toyed around with the Hogan clubs and actually did play with a Hogan two iron and sand wedge while with McGregor. He'd visited the Hogan factory a couple of times over the years.

In 1976, Sneed decided to play just Hogan golf clubs while he was still under contract with McGregor. He negotiated his agreement with McGregor that allowed him to play exclusively Hogan clubs but officially remain with McGregor. The following year, he joined as a

Hogan staff member. His reasoning was simple. He felt strongly that Hogan was the best equipment in the market and what he played the best with. For him, the clubs just appealed to him and felt superior.

One of the incidents that led him to Hogan happened in 1976. Sneed was changing the shafts on his McGregor irons. As he pulled the shafts out of the clubs, he discovered a bunch of lead had been dropped down into the shaft to balance the club—in other words, to make it the correct swing weight. The clubs were too light, obviously after they put them together, so they dropped some lead down the shaft and different amounts of lead in each one. He ended up drilling all his clubs out just to see, and the similar results rubbed Sneed the wrong way. The Hogan people never did that. They grounded the clubs accurately to weight, and the quality of the club was better. Sneed felt the finishing of their clubs seemed better, and the Hogan grind was more consistent through the set. This opened his eyes to Hogan and would endear them to his game for the rest of his life.

Sneed, as did the lucky few, had access to the preeminent golf club maker in the world of golf, Gene Sheeley. Each time he visited the Hogan factory in Fort Worth, he would go during the colonial tournament and then during the Byron Nelson tournament. He enjoyed the visits with Ben Hogan as well. He would always come away from his meetings with Sheeley with new clubs to play or try. Sneed learned much about the science of golf clubs from watching Sheeley, as he was always the patient teacher with us players. Gene Sheeley would always check the lie and the loft every time Sneed visited.

Over a period of time, forged clubs, which are softer, will bend, especially if you hit balls on hard ground. Gene was such an expert, and he used an old block of lead along with a lead hammer to bend the clubs like most of the club makers did in those days rather than put them in a machine and bend the hosel. He would show those he crafted clubs for how to do it themselves. Gene just knew everything about the clubs. There was a time when Sneed had lunch with Ben Hogan at Shady Oaks. The Hogan player rep, Chip Bridges, invited Sneed to lunch and some practice with Mr. Hogan, an opportunity no one turns down. Sneed arrived at the par-three practice tee with his Hogan clubs, and he had been a staff member for about a year. Sneed, though, spent the first hour just watching the Hawk hitting balls. Hogan never conversed much as he practiced, but Sneed got to watch him go through his routines and everything else. Then Sneed's turn came. Hogan would watch for a while without hardly a comment, but he did comment on his equipment. He began peering into my bag, even taking a few practice swings with them. He seemed to be testing the shafts of the club, seeing how thick it was. Hogan would then quiz Sneed me about the shafts and related matters of his equipment. He told Sneed he thought his iron shafts were good and stiff enough, but he thought Sneed ought to maybe go to a stiffer shaft in your driver. He offered to call Gene Sheeley and have him pull a couple of shafts to show him. Hogan had a bin of shafts in the back there as his personal stash. Hogan pulled two shafts, and Sheeley put them in two drivers for me. These were the Hogan Apex shafts, but he had tipped the shaft a little bit, a Hogan five shaft.

Sneed relied on one of the stiffest drivers on the tour. Sneed's drives improved dramatically after that. Sneed would never actually play a round of golf with Hogan, but watching him practice up close a number of times left a lasting impression on him. Sneed's time in Fort Worth led him to develop a deep friendship with sportswriting legend Dan Jenkins, another of Fort Worth's finest. Jenkins would write countless articles on golf's finest players, including his friends, Ben Hogan and Ed Sneed.

Sneed regrettably took a break from competitive golf for eight years as his body seemed to be breaking down. A chronic back ailment led him from the course and to work at an investment firm. He still played a few tournaments a year but was a far cry from his former life. He still bled Hogan and visited Mr. Hogan when he could. I got to meet Sneed around this time, even though he wasn't playing at the same level as before. Sneed considers this eight-year stint away from the game as the biggest mistake of his life. As his back returned to normal and his desire to return to the game flared up, Sneed joined the Senior Tour. Luckily, Sneed had kept his bag full of his Hogan clubs. The new innovative Hogan Edge found a prominent spot in his days on the Senior Tour. For Sneed, it had the profile and appearance of a bladed club.

One day, Sneed had gone back over to the factory so Sheeley could put in some new shafts that Hogan had him pull. Sneed went back to Hogan's office afterward, wanting to know if Gene had taken care of everything and if there was anything else that he could do. Inside Hogan's office, I noticed some of Hogan's clubs that caught my attention. The Hogan, older wooden clubs, used to have quite a bit of curvature on the face from the heel to the toe and from top to bottom. These clubs weren't flat across the face. No club is today, but they were more so in those days. But Ben Hogan's fairway woods had virtually no heel-to-toe radius, and nothing from top to bottom appeared to Sneed. He believed that the clubmaker would need to put a straight edge on the face. Also, the weight underneath his sole plate was in a different place, when most of the time, the soleplate of a wooden club had a cavity in the center where the makers would place the weight in that cavity. They would swing a wood that way to make sure it was the proper swing weight. Sometimes, the cavity, the weight, was at the very back of the club or on the back end of the driver, but there was a cavity in the middle. Well, Ben Hogan had the cavity up close to the insert in his fairway woods. That makes the club play a little differently than a normal club. Sneed noticed that he had no radius on his clubs to speak of. One could put a straight edge on it and see hardly any radius.

So Sneed asked him about that. He just casually said, "I was looking at a three and a four wood of yours, and I noticed something. It appeared to me, there was no roll from top to bottom on the face and no roll heel to toe, and I wanted to know why." Sneed thought for a second because there was a long pause, and it was one of those times where you're thinking, *Have I said the wrong thing?*

Hogan finally looked at Sneed and said, "Well, Ed, I never thought I was good enough to hit the ball with the doorknob." Meaning the curvature on the face.

Sneed chuckled and said, "Well, seriously, why would you want to roll the club from top to bottom?"

Hogan paused then steadily replied, "If you hit the ball on the bottom of the face, why would you want the loft decreased, and if you hit the ball high on the clubface, why would you want the ball to go even higher?"

Sneed grinned widely back at Hogan as the logic made perfect sense. Hogan felt he could control the flight of the ball better, and it was more consistent.

Sneed's career found much success, which was highlighted by seven professional wins and coupled with eight years as a broadcaster for ABC television. He garnered the most fame from his 1979 Master's Tournament performance. He began the final day with a five-stroke lead and visions of a green jacket. With three holes to play, he held a three-stroke lead but would bogey them all, leading to the first time the Masters was settled by a sudden-death playoff. On the second hole playoff at Augusta, Sneed would lose the hole to that year's champion, Fuzzy Zoeller. Sneed's career admittedly suffered because of that Masters debacle, but his experiences have been quite noteworthy. He advocated for Hogan's equipment as he knew it was the best. He knew most of golf's greats personally and was especially fond of Ben Hogan. Hogan was larger than life, even to men that had been to the top of the golfing world. "Hogan was something to watch, I'll tell you." Everyone has Hogan stories, but Sneed remembered watching him practice several times at Shady Oaks over the years. He'd always leave the range with Hogan thinking that there was no player that could have dumped those balls on the ground and hit the ball all the way to his caddie with the precision that he did. Often, these stories get exaggerated where the caddie just stands there down range and never moves. Hogan's caddie would never move more than a few feet at distances of one hundred and eighty feet. The one thing that impressed Sneed more than anything else was once the caddie would set the practice bag down on the ground, he would walk to a distance he knew Hogan would be hitting depending on the club. He would stand almost motionless as Hogan hit balls at him. Ben Hogan never hit a shot that flew past the caddie. The ball would always land in front of the caddie, and if he was off, it wasn't more than five or ten feet at the most.

"I can recall a few shots that he would hit a little thin, but I never saw him hit a real fat shot, never saw him hit the ball more than twenty feet offline with an iron. It was spectacular to watch him just practice."

The Move

In the year 1990, the Hogan Company would reach ninety million in sales with a substantial profit. Golf Shop Operations published an article detailing the tremendous number of orders for the Edge product. The article explained how the success of the club was overwhelming the production line, and thus delivery of the clubs was way behind. The article failed to explain how Hogan was fixing the production problems and when the customers could expect to see some relief in shipments of Edge. News leaked later that the Hogan Company was under a direct order from Cosmo World to ship most of the Edge products made to Japan. They were shorting shipments to the American market as their sales reached record levels. No one knows how many more Edge clubs could have been shipped to waiting for customers in the United States to help alleviate back orders and satisfy Hogan accounts if they had kept the United States' first policy instead of shipping larger quantities of Edge to Japan. In addition, the margins on the clubs sold in America were double what the margin was when shipping overseas, and the impact on profitability was devastating. That decision to short the American market would weaken their business in America and also impact profits as the clubs sold to the Japanese were at a lower margin than the clubs sold in the United States. No one paid attention to that detail.

Things looked great on the outside as sales were through the roof. The Hogan Company was considered the number one forged-iron club maker in the world at this time, with the largest roster of sponsored tour players. On the inside, production problems piled up. Decisions were being made that would eventually kill all that momentum that was created with the Ben Hogan advertising campaign and the successful introduction of the number one forged cavity club in the market. Cosmo World's inability to run the Hogan Company quickly became insurmountable. Once the Pebble Beach deal crashed and the Hogan Company started to lose money again, Cosmo World wanted to dump this sinking ship. They would look to sell them as quickly as they could.

Enter the Virginia millionaire, Bill Goodwin. Goodwin, a novice in the golf business and despite the Hogan company now losing money, still badly wanted to own the Hogan Company. Godwin had made his fortune in real estate and, more notably, his acquisition of the AMF bowling chain in 1986 for two hundred twenty-three million then selling to Goldman Sachs ten years later for north of a billion dollars. Could Mr. Goodwin use his wealth to rescue the suffering brand and put it back on its feet? What would be his plan to restore the Hogan Company to greatness it once had? The future turned out to be as hectic as its most recent past. No one knew what Mr. Goodwin would bring to the table, but the rumors were very strong that he would move the Hogan Company to Virginia, where he lived.

The first thing Mr. Goodwin did when the sale was complete was to rid the company of the Ben Hogan Tour. The next thing Mr. Goodwin did involve more cuts. He believed the Hogan sales force was overpaid and underworked, so he directed the new Hogan president to cut a third of the sales force and expand their territories. This would save money for the company, he hoped. Walter Hagen and Wilson had tried the same move back in the late seventies when I was still growing in this business. This same strategic move by Godwin would cut into the ability of the Hogan Company to sell its product by one-third. By cutting the number of salesmen, you effectively cut the number of calls that could be made trying to sell your product. The loss of sales would eventually offset any reduction in cost that the company would realize. Additionally, Mr. Goodwin was not a fan of unions and was planning to move the factory to Virginia. He would separate the golf ball factory to Ohio to get it away from the union and be able to reduce wages as Ohio was reeling with layoffs from the automotive industry and had a skilled workforce trying to find employment. Mr. Goodwin seemed to ignore the history of the success the Hogan Company had enjoyed prior, instead deciding to eliminate the most important feature of the Edge product, the forging.

Mr. Goodwin's plan was to eliminate all the skilled labor that built the products and the reputation that helped create the Hogan Company and farm out all that work to the vendors to bring in a finished club head for assembly. The heavy manufacturing operation would be done outside of the plant, such as grinding, polishing, plating, which require a more skilled labor force to operate. He would create an assembly plant, which is appropriately referred to as a stick and ship its operation. The farm, out of all skilled workers, left the relocation to Virginia of just twenty-two Hogan employees.

Once completed, he would have set up the cheapest facility possible to minimize the cost of labor to build a golf club. He would be able to get rid of the heavy costs for benefits, unemployment, social security that are added to each employee in the plant if you bring the parts in incomplete. It is simply a material cost and nothing else. Mr. Goodwin replaced the majority of the skilled labor with a casting product and its associative minimum labor cost. I was told his plan was to copy the Ping model, as their margins with their cast product were much higher than the forged Edge. The plan was set in place, and the Hogan Company moved to Virginia, leaving several large empty buildings with nothing but a mostly proud history to speak of.

Once Goodwin's plan started to fail as we expected it to, he started to lose a lot of money. When he purchased the company, revenues were hanging at the sixty-million-dollar mark, but during his five-year ownership stint, revenues fell to ten million, and the dream for Goodwin was over. His decision would not take long. Mr. Goodwin finally decided to unload the Hogan Company. The days of Ben Hogan being a major player in club manufacturing seemed over. Spaulding bought the company with ideas of their own. These ideas would never translate into a rebirth of the once-great company, and

Spaulding was already in financial trouble from the onset. Callaway took the Hogan Company off their hands in 2003 where they would discontinue the product line five years later. Finally, Callaway sold the brand to Perry Ellis, where they started to license the Hogan name for hard goods to a group in Fort Worth that started assembling Hogan clubs in 2017. Today, the Hogan brand is in a small twenty-thousand-square-foot facility with ten to twenty employees with a direct-to-consumer-only golf equipment company strategy.

Ben's business career manufacturing golf clubs was on par with his storied playing career. My exposure to Ben was only one of many chapters in my life and career, but his influence on me has been prevalent throughout my life and will last for the rest of my days. No player has been able to obtain the success Ben achieved in golf and in business, and his company record from 1953 through 1992 reflects that success. I am sure it would still be going today if the ownership understood the principles that he used to operate the Ben Hogan Company. His main goal was not chasing profit; it was to make the best golf clubs you could produce. How many of our manufacturing companies have faced the same fate chasing profit? The Hogan brand, even today, is still remembered and held in high regard as one of the greatest brands in golf at the time. Many of the pro golfers who played on tour in the 1980s reflected back on the quality of the clubs, the high standard that Mr. Hogan required of his clubs. Mark O'Meara, a Hogan-sponsored player in the 1980s, stated, "I always felt like the Hogan clubs were so good. The Apex shaft was of the highest quality and easily my choice for its time. Mr. Hogan was a revolutionary back in those times and the equipment that he made was."

After all the time I had to reflect on my time at the Hogan Company, I struggled to make sense of my being fired. The company was making more money than ever before, and the products that we were selling were in high demand in the marketplace. The answer was quite simple. Dick Babbitt wanted my job. Who wouldn't have wanted my job? Working with Ben every day, going to premier golf events around the world, and playing golf on the best courses in the world is hard to beat.

Goodbye to Mr. Hogan

In 1997, as Bill Goodwin was preparing to sell the Hogan Company to Spaulding, I received the phone call that I had long expected. Two years prior, Ben had undergone emergency surgery for colon cancer, which he would never fully recover from. Shortly after, he had been diagnosed with the onset of Alzheimer's. On July 25, 1997, at the age of eighty-four years old, Ben suffered a major stroke stopping his heart. The great Ben Hogan passed quietly away into history. Sadly, I had not seen nor talked to Ben since December of 1988, when I was fired. The citywide funeral was held at The University Christian Church in Fort Worth. I was feeling a little apprehensive about who I might run into that would bring back a lot of emotions. I was able to muster the courage to attend as Ben deserved to be honored. Little did I know how going to the funeral would overwhelm me.

My time ended with Ben upon my dismissal, and I quickly jumped to the Head Golf Company, a few miles from where the Hogan factory was located. The people that hired me were the presidents of Head Tennis, Head Skis and Tyrolia Ski binding companies. They were all formerly owned by AMF before Minstar had raided the corporation. When Minstar sold Hogan to Cosmo World, it was the first time these two companies, Hogan and Head, were not owned by the same corporation. Head was interested in expanding its name into the golf market, but no one in their company had any experience in the golf business. They asked me to develop a product line for them and operate this new golf operation. After four years of successfully building the Head Golf Company, their corporate group wanted to combine Head Golf with their Head distribution center and relocate the golf operation to Boulder, Colorado, which would require me to move, and that is something that I did not want to do. The year was 1994. We had developed a great group of supportive friends since moving here. My youngest son was in the middle of his high school years and was very active in athletics. My oldest and middle sons were both in college, and I really wanted to keep my family in Fort Worth, so I decided to buy a small retirement planning firm. For the first time in twenty-some years, I was no longer involved in the golf business.

At the funeral, I was overwhelmed by the enormous crowd in attendance to pay their respects and celebrate the life of Ben Hogan. This brought memories flooding back. As soon as I laid eyes on some of the Hogan employees, I was suddenly filled with all kinds of emotions—anger, grief, guilt, and regrets. I was still holding onto some anger toward Ben that I had been carrying with me since my departure nine years earlier. I had asked Ben to help me when I felt I was going to be fired, and he said he would do all he could to help. He had pledged his support, and then he didn't or couldn't save me from getting fired by the new owners. I felt somewhat betrayed. My wife even had written a letter to Ben criticizing him for going back on his word and not standing up for me. She and I both felt our relationship with Ben was much more than simply a business association.

The more time I thought about the circumstances, I started to feel regret. I began to realize I did not give him the chance to help me as I never contacted him after I was fired. I had been holding this grudge for this long, and sitting in the church made me realize I did not reach out to him after they had informed me that my services were no longer needed. The new company owned his lifetime contract, and nobody would expect him to jeopardize his financial security over replacing the president, which they had the right to do. I also made a big mistake when I accepted the president's position from Minstar by not requiring an employment contract of any kind to protect me, which is a common practice for most C-suite and president-level positions. I had never been a president, and I felt fortunate to be given the opportunity of becoming president, so I was not going to do anything that might jeopardize the offer. Without this protection, the new owners had no legal obligation to retain me after the sale, regardless of how successful the operation was and the profit the company was now producing.

I knew deep down that Ben had nothing to do with my termination. As I was sitting there, continuing to run through a range of emotions, I regretted deeply that I did not contact Ben after my termination. I should have at least called to say goodbye and to thank him for helping me turn around the company. He was now gone, and all I could do was pray that he knew that I was wrong to take my anger out on him. As I turned my mind back to the eulogy, it was obvious the minister knew who Ben was and what kind of life he lived. The church was packed. Every seat was taken, both on the main floor and the second floor. You could not find a seat, and you could have heard a pin drop as the minister spoke. As I looked around, I could see celebrities, politicians, local Fort Worth dignitaries, and many of the golfing greats all in attendance, wanting to pay their respects to Ben Hogan. It spoke volumes on the life Ben led.

The church was packed! There was not a seat available. Ben's funeral commanded the executives from the largest organizations governing professional and amateur golf in the United States, Tim Finchem, commissioner of the PGA, Jim Autrey, chief executive officer of PGA of America, and Judy Bell, president of the US Golf Association. In addition, also attending were Sam Snead, Ken Venturi, Tommy Bolt, Bryon Nelson, Ben Crenshaw, Lanny Wadkins, and Kris Tschetter. Ben had twenty honorary pallbearers, Mr. Jim Awtrey, Mr. George Beggs, Mr. Tommy Bolt, Mr. Tim Finchen, Mr. William Goodwin, Mr. David Hueber, Mr. Dan Jenkins, Mr. Herman Keiser, Mr. Dee J. Kelly, Mr. Shelley Mayfield, Mr. William Miller, Mr. W. A. (Tex) Moncrief Jr., Dr. James D. Murphy, Mr. Jim Murry, Mr. Fred Parks, Dr. Ken Pearce, Mr. Gene Sheeley, Mr. Leonard S. Slater, Mr. Gene Smyers, Mr. Sam Snead, Mr. Rayburn Tucker, Mr. Ken Venturi, and Mr. Mike Wright. There had to be a couple of thousand people in attendance.

Try as I may, I could not hold back the tremendous regret that welled up inside me—the things I did not do during my time at the Hogan Company. Would I have been able to stop the ultimate destruction of his company? I wondered why I did not do more when I was first informed that Minstar was going to sell the Hogan Company to the highest bidder. I wondered if I could have pulled a group together to buy the company to continue the path we were on. I should have gotten on a plane and flown to Japan to meet with our Japanese distributor, J. Osawa, and ask them if they were interested in purchasing the Hogan rights for the Asian market. The price that Minstar was asking was well above the valuation that anybody in the United States would be willing to finance a deal. Cosmo World was paying much more than anyone in America was willing to offer. I pondered, if the deal was split in half, the American portion would have been about $25 million. That could have worked! But I did not try. Who knows what would have happened if I had made that trip to Japan to see? I also regretted not discussing this option with Ben. After all, he and I would speak every day, and this was one of the most critical times for the Hogan Company.

I regret not discussing this approach with Ben. Ben knew a lot of "money" people in Fort Worth, and he was not supportive of the new Japanese ownership. This combination might have opened the door to the possibility of matching the Cosmo World offer. I did not take the initiative to have that discussion. I sat on the sidelines and let it happen instead of becoming a player and maybe controlling the direction. I was beating myself up. Nobody knew more about what we had done than me at that time. I did not realize the strength we might have presented with the right buyer until I was sitting in that church pew, mourning the loss of my real boss.

As the service continued, I thought of the times Ben and I spent together, and I truly did miss this gentleman. What a fortunate privilege of having known him and worked with him. The eulogies reminded us of his work ethic, which was his attribute, I most admired and hopefully emulated. Ben worked hard for everything that he ever had. Nothing was given to Ben. He fought for what he wanted in his life from an early age, and that drive stayed with him throughout his life. As we were leaving the church, some of the Hogan employees I had known came up to me to say hello. We had just lost the patriarch of the Hogan family. Every paper in the country would carry the news of Ben Hogan. Every day, someone would write an article about Ben Hogan. Headlines covered every aspect of his passing. *Golf World* has an empty place. "Remembering a Champion." To Keiser, Hogan was a friendly foe. Tributes came pouring in from the most famous players of our time. They all highlighted the characteristics of Mr. Hogan. They would describe him as someone with obsessive drive, a fierce competitor, determined to succeed, and demanding perfection in everything he did.

The service was completed, and every one of the Hogan employees started gathering around and sharing memories of the great years we all had shared. One story in particular shared with me by Randy Kelch stood out for a couple of reasons. One, I was very close to Ben during those years and never heard that story, and two, it presented a wonderful image of Ben and the life he shared with others.

Randy started, "Ben Hogan always had a soft spot for organizations that aided suffering children. He often gave his time freely when he could add value to someone's life. The United Way, as well as the Make a Wish Foundation, and Randy was his liaison and had several opportunities to spend time in Hogan's company. I found these moments extremely telling of the now reclusive man. Mr. Hogan was a very focused and determined man and knew how he wanted things to be done, products to be produced, and was sometimes quite confrontational when it didn't go the way he envisioned. He could be blunt, rude, and almost mean to those who he perceived had let him down. However, these qualities of Mr. Hogan are not new to those who knew him and his history. I was very fortunate to see him in a very different light. I had the privilege of being with him when he welcomed these young kids and their families into his office, plant, and his country club. He displayed the kindness of a doting grandfather with not only the kids but also the parents and siblings who were in awe of this legend of a man. He spent as much time with them as they wanted and was clearly enjoying the time he had with these families. I will always treasure my time with him not only in the professional setting but also these very personal times many never witnessed."

Once everybody shared their experience, we dispersed and went on our separate ways.

As I combed through the articles, I could not find one that was written about his business career, the establishment of his company, the leadership he would provide through the years just to keep advancing his club-making trade. What kind of manager was Ben? How was he to work with? No article would be written about that part of his life. No one would write a story about the evolution of his company.

Ben had removed himself from the limelight for a good twenty years, and AMF and the Hogan Company failed to involve him in the company's market presence. Reading all those articles brought back all those great abbreviated conversations now relegated to my memory.

In my years working in corporate America, I have never met anyone like him. He never played politics with anybody and never cared to make an impression. Any statement he would make, you would understand what he was talking about. There was no hidden meaning in his words. He was the same person whether he was a celebrity golfer, dignitary, or a Hogan employee. It was always very clear; his only goal was he wanted to make the best golf clubs anybody could ever buy. The by-product of this effort would be to become a successful company. Ben would manage his company from the beginning just like he played the game of golf, with a single goal and a plan to complete the task. When he played golf, he would decide how he would attack the course and thus create a plan for himself to play each hole and what shot to make. His ultimate goal was to play the course to the plan, and if the plan was followed, his score would reflect the effort. Ben never made excuses or made anything personal. It was always about the result. If you ran into a problem, his concern was not excuses but rather how do we get back on plan to accomplish our goal.

In the days following the funeral, I spent a lot of time just thinking about Ben and was able to make peace for not keeping in contact with him after my termination. I also was able to find resolve for my anger, guilt, and regrets that I had carried with me for the last nine years after I left the company. I had the extreme fortune to have many great memories of the man. The development of the Edge product with Ben was one of my fondest memories that I will take to my grave. My emotions were raw, and seeing all these people brought back a lot of sad memories, in particular, just as I viewed the casket passing, I could not stop myself from thinking if you looked close enough, you could find the fingerprints of Minstar and Irwin Jacobs and Cosmo World and Dick Babbit and David Hueber and AMF and Mr. Bill Goodwin all over the dead body of this iconic company.

As I was doing my research for this book, I came across many references to Ben's employment contract. One executive from Cosmo World, David Hueber, was so embarrassed about the money Hogan was making compared to the company's tour players that he decided to quadruple his contract which put him on par with Hogan Company's top tour player's contract. In his internal memo, he stated, "It seems crazy to him that this eminent figure who had founded the company and established its principles and commitment to excellence would be paid at the salary level provided in the 1960 sales agreement with AMF." This statement intrigued me. What a benevolent gesture on the part of that executive, so I decided to research what Hogan's compensation looked like. I started digging around to see if I could find the original sales contract and the employment contract covering the details of the 1960 sale of the Hogan Company to AMF. I finally got a hold of the original sales agreement and Ben's first employment contract as well as the extensions to the original, and finally, the new contract with the stated reported a quadrupling of his royalty payments.

Ben Sells His Company

The original sale of the Hogan Company was concluded in 1960 to AMF. At that time, sales had reached $1,870,000 and were showing a profit of about $193,656 per year. AMF paid about two times revenue and roughly twenty times earnings to buy the Hogan Company. Ben started the company seven years prior with his idea and about eight of his friends that helped him bankroll the operation. The early years many littered with well-documented stories about Ben throwing out clubs that did not meet his quality standards which aided in losing some of his investors.

By 1960, he had a thriving business and was considered a premier golf club manufacturer in this country. The Hogan balance sheet would show that about 75 percent of the revenue was through woods, irons, and putters. The future looked so bright for Hogan that AMF called. They wanted to add these quality products to their corporate family. AMF negotiated to buy Hogan for $3,707,718.90. The deal involved cash and a trade of Hogan stock for AMF stock. The Hogan stockholders received about $2.7 million in common and preferred stock in AMF in exchange for the Hogan common stock. Ben received about $1 million in stock and cash for his creation and development of the company. In addition, Ben negotiated an employment contract as he wanted to stay on and continue to contribute to the future success of the company. Each employment contract would originally have a term of five years.

The AMF Corporation really wanted the Hogan Company to add to its portfolio of products to enhance the overall value of its stock. AMF owned the Hogan company for almost twenty-five years before they were raided by Minstar. AMF operated the company to maintain and grow its revenue and products. The revenue under the AMF leadership would grow into the millions, and at the time of the sale to Minstar, the revenue for the Hogan Company was about fifty million a year. Surprisingly, Ben would receive an annual salary of $35,000 per year as well as a 1 percent royalty on all goods sold, but not to exceed $65,000 per year. So Ben would max out his income royalty when the company would reach six and a half million in sales. So Ben was making about $150,000 per year when I was running the company. His wife, Valerie, was provided a severance package in case he died "not to exceed" $32,500. Ben also had a $50,000 life insurance policy provided for by AMF upon his death. He also was allowed to retain the royalty agreement that was in place with Biltwell Sportswear that paid an annual payment of $50,000 from a sportswear and men's slack line they were selling with his name on them. So every five years, AMF would draft a new employment agreement with Ben. Then in 1978, AMF added the words after December 31, 1978, to read and thereafter continue indefinitely (subject to the provisions of section 5 of the agreement). So to my surprise, Ben was not making anywhere near what I thought, and as revenue would grow, the inequity would get bigger.

Then in 1991, a new contract was negotiated with Ben by Cosmo World, the new owner of the Hogan Company. The following changes were included. Ben's compensation would be increased to $200,000 per year. All royalty payments of any kind were eliminated. For the use of the Ben Hogan name to directly name a golf course, Ben would receive a payment of $100,000 upon the opening of the course. Also, the course owners would pay Ben for any and all input in design work regarding the layout or construction of the course $50,000 additional and allow for two visits to the said golf course at $50,000 each. The new Cosmo World contract provided a new death benefit for Ben's wife of $60,000 annually until her death that apparently replaced the $ 50,000 life insurance policy on Ben's life.

The End

As I concluded my book, I started to think about the commitment I made to Matt Adams of the Golf Channel. I was on his show several months ago, and he asked me if I would come and discuss my book with him once published, and I agreed. So I started to panic. What if he asked me what irons I am playing with today? How could I say Callaway X22 castings? The book is about the greatest club ever introduced in golf, even today, so if that is true, why am I not playing with the Edge irons today? How credible would my book be if I am playing with a casting and not a forging? So up to my attic above my garage, I went and pulled out a box of brand-new 1987 Edge from the original production of that club. As I opened the box, I could see the grips had emulsified from being stored in my attic in Texas with hundred-degree days during the summer for thirty-three years. So off to Edwin Watts I went to buy some new grips and re-grip the Equalizer, nine iron, eight iron, and seven iron to replace the Callaway irons in my bag. If this truly was the greatest introduction of all time, then they should still stand up in today's market. I was surprised by how easy it was to change the grips.

Once finished, out to the driving range I would go. Now I am seventy-nine years old, and I typically play golf three days a week as well as hit balls three days a week. My scores, on average, are low to middle seventies from the senior tees. As I got to the range and took the Equalizer out of my bag and laid it behind the ball, it brought back memories of the first time I did that with Ben in his office, thirty-three years ago. In the address position, the club was perfect. The top line and leading Edge gave you the confidence you were going to kill the ball. After a couple of hits, the soft feel of the forging came back to me, and I could not believe the difference between the cast clubs I had been playing. After about twenty minutes, I was ready to go the next day as I would unveil my new clubs to my golfing group.

I was feeling great now. If Matt would ask about what clubs I was playing, I could respond, "The 1987 Edge." So we started the round, and I noticed I was not hitting the Edge clubs as far as the Callaway irons. The harder I tried, the worse it got. This happened over the next three weeks, and it was obvious the Callaway clubs were hitting the ball farther than the Edge. Frustrated with the results, I took the clubs out of my bag and put them back in the garage. So now I was playing with the Callaway irons once again, and what kind of credibility would that give my book if I was not playing with this breakthrough product? I was agonizing over my predicament. So I called my old buddy, Steve Dryer, who was still working for the new Hogan Company in Fort Worth. I explained the problem, and Steve immediately responded, "Jerry, you have been out of the business too long and forgotten that back in 1987, the lofts on the Edge would have been four to six degrees weaker than your current Callaway irons." I was embarrassed to admit it, but I did forget that.

So I set up an appointment with Steve to re-loft the irons to today's standards, and that should fix the problem. As I was loading the clubs into my car, I could not find the pitching wedge. I looked in the attic and called the course to see if I had left the club there, but no one found the wedge. I pulled out the set box from the attic to see if I put it back in the box, but the club was not there. Five clubs were missing from the box, and I only had four that I found. I was bummed as I knew I could not replace the pitching wedge, so what am I to do now?

After a few days with no other options, I decided to go back to the 1987 catalog for that product to check out the set makeup. When I opened the page for the Edge, I was embarrassed to see the original set makeup was three through E. There was no pitching wedge in the set, and the Equalizer was the wedge. What a senior moment that was. I forgot when I re-gripped the clubs, there wasn't a pitching wedge. The Equalizer replaced the pitching wedge with the Edge product. So off to Dryers I went with the four clubs in hand and my Callaway for comparison. When we put the Equalizer on the loft machine, sure enough, it was four degrees weaker than the Callaway pitching wedge. This was true for the nine irons—eight iron and the seven iron as well. Once the lofts were adjusted, off to the range I went to see if that made the difference. This time I would hit the Callaway club and then hit the Edge counterpart. Every club reacted the same, and the Edge club felt so much better due to its comfort as a forging.

So I have been playing with my "new" Edges for a while now, and my scores are still in the low to middle seventies. After thirty-three years, the design of this product is still the leader in the class of cavity back perimeter-weighted clubs. I can honestly say that the Edge was a breakthrough in 1987, and it is still the one and only forged cavity back club even today. All the features that were provided to the average golfer in 1987 would still be provided in 2020.

I am relieved because when Matt Adams from the Golf Channel asked me that one question, "What clubs are you playing today?" you know what the answer will be. Of course, the 1987 Edge.

When I was fired back in 1988, I never would see Ben again, and other than a few people that I kept in touch with, I never got to say goodbye and thank everyone that helped me find the Hogan Edge. Unfortunately, they lost it again.

To everyone that I had the pleasure of working with at the Hogan Company, I would like to say thank you for helping me share the greatest time of my life. Looking back at those years, it brought back so many wonderful memories. It felt like I was watching the movie classic *It's a Wonderful Life*, starring Jimmy Stewart, where he relives his life and the impact he had on others. This movie comes on each Christmas and always reminds me what really is important in our lives—people and relationships, not money.

About the Author

Jerry Austry was hired in 1984 as the VP of manufacturing by the Ben Hogan Company in order to solve their production problems. At that time, the company was considered to be the premier brand in the golf marketplace and in the eyes of golf consumers. The AMF Corporation had owned the Hogan Company for the past twenty-five years and was considered a pillar in terms of profit and stability. Unfortunately, just a year and a half later, AMF was taken over by a corporate raider, and the Hogan Company lost money for the first time since Ben Hogan started the company in 1953. The new owner's only goal was to sell the company to the highest bidder. Jerry was given the task of turning the company around and was promoted to president. Jerry then formed a partnership with Ben Hogan, returned the company to profitability, revamped the company image, modernized the company product line, and took them back and above the leadership position that they'd held for the last twenty-five years.

Lightning Source UK Ltd.
Milton Keynes UK
UKHW020651170822
407432UK00010B/1236